MAX WEBER'S THEORY OF MODERNITY

Classical and Contemporary Social Theory

Series Editor: Stjepan G. Mestrovic, Texas A&M University, USA

Classical and Contemporary Social Theory publishes rigorous scholarly work that re-discovers the relevance of social theory for contemporary times, demonstrating the enduring importance of theory for modern social issues. The series covers social theory in a broad sense, inviting contributions on both 'classical' and modern theory, thus encompassing sociology, without being confined to a single discipline. As such, work from across the social sciences is welcome, provided that volumes address the social context of particular issues, subjects, or figures and offer new understandings of social reality and the contribution of a theorist or school to our understanding of it. The series considers significant new appraisals of established thinkers or schools, comparative works or contributions that discuss a particular social issue or phenomenon in relation to the work of specific theorists or theoretical approaches. Contributions are welcome that assess broad strands of thought within certain schools or across the work of a number of thinkers, but always with an eye toward contributing to contemporary understandings of social issues and contexts.

Also in the series

Sociological Amnesia
Cross-currents in Disciplinary History
Edited by Alex Law and Eric Royal Lybeck
ISBN 978-1-4724-4234-5

A Sociology of the Total Organization
Atomistic Unity in the French Foreign Legion
Mikaela Sundberg
ISBN 978-1-4724-5560-4

Arendt Contra Sociology
Theory, Society and its Science
Philip Walsh
ISBN 978-1-4094-3863-2

Being Human in a Consumer Society
Edited by Alejandro Néstor García Martínez
ISBN 978-1-4724-4317-5

Max Weber's Theory of Modernity
The Endless Pursuit of Meaning

MICHAEL SYMONDS
University of Western Sydney, Australia

LONDON AND NEW YORK

First published 2015 by Ashgate Publishing

2 Park Square, Milton Park, Abingdon, Oxfordshire OX14 4RN
52 Vanderbilt Avenue, New York, NY 10017

Routledge is an imprint of the Taylor & Francis Group, an informa business

First issued in paperback 2020

Copyright © Michael Symonds 2015

Michael Symonds has asserted his right under the Copyright, Designs and Patents Act, 1988, to be identified as the author of this work.

All rights reserved. No part of this book may be reprinted or reproduced or utilised in any form or by any electronic, mechanical, or other means, now known or hereafter invented, including photocopying and recording, or in any information storage or retrieval system, without permission in writing from the publishers.

Notice:
Product or corporate names may be trademarks or registered trademarks, and are used only for identification and explanation without intent to infringe.

British Library Cataloguing in Publication Data
A catalogue record for this book is available from the British Library

The Library of Congress has cataloged the printed edition as follows:
Symonds, Michael John.
  Max Weber's theory of modernity : the endless pursuit of meaning / by Michael Symonds.
    pages cm.—(Classical and contemporary social theory)
  Includes bibliographical references and index.
  ISBN 978-1-4724-6286-2 (hardback)
  1. Weber, Max, 1864–1920. 2. Civilization, Modern.
  3. Sociology—Philosophy. I. Title.
  HM479.W42S96 2015
  301.092—dc23
                                                           2015004242

ISBN: 978-1-4724-6286-2 (hbk)
ISBN: 978-0-367-59851-8 (pbk)

Contents

Acknowledgements   *vii*
List of Abbreviations   *ix*

1   Preparatory Remarks   1

PART I   THE PARADOX OF MEANING

2   Western Religion and Science   15

3   The Economic Value-Sphere   35

4   The Scientific and Political Value-Spheres   55

5   The Aesthetic and Erotic Value-Spheres   77

PART II   MEANING, MODERNITY AND BROTHERLINESS

6   The Concept of Brotherliness   95

7   Brotherliness and Modernity   119

PART III   IMPLICATIONS

8   Prescriptions   147

9   Applications   173

Bibliography   *183*
Index   *189*

To Cathy

Acknowledgements

The following people helped make this book possible: Cathy Symonds for her patience and encouragement over many years, and for her editorial skill in the closing stages; Paul Jones for his unwavering faith in the project; Hal Ginges for his checking of the German; and the Dean, Peter Hutchings, and the School of Humanities and Communication Arts at UWS for their uncritical toleration of the slow progress of this work. But the biggest thank you must go to Jason Pudsey who, as my student and then collaborator, was pivotal in the formation of the ideas and arguments to come. The long days of discussion with him at Byron Bay allowed Weber's most difficult concepts to become clear and now those times provide an idyllic memory of what the intellectual task at its best can aspire to be.

List of Abbreviations

When specific page numbers from Weber's works are referenced, the following abbreviations will be used:

AI	'Author's Introduction' to *GARS* – the common acronym for the 1920/21 publication of *Gesammelte Aufsätze zur Religionssoziologie* (Collected Essays on the Sociology of Religion) – but this 'Author's Introduction' is usually found as the introduction to *The Protestant Ethic and the Spirit of Capitalism* in English
AJ	*Ancient Judaism*
AS	*The Agrarian Sociology of Ancient Civilisations*
China	*The Religion of China*
ES	*Economy and Society*
GEH	*General Economic History*
IEEWR	*Introduction to the Economic Ethic of the World Religions* (entitled the 'Social Psychology of the World Religions' in *From Max Weber: Essays in Sociology* (FMW), the collection edited and translated by H.H. Gerth and C. Wright Mills)
India	*The Religion of India*
IR	*Intermediary Reflection* ('Religious Rejections of the World and their Directions' in FMW)
Method	*The Methodology of the Social Sciences*
PE	*The Protestant Ethic and the Spirit of Capitalism*
PS	'The Protestant Sects and the Spirit of Capitalism' (in FMW)
PV	'Politics as a Vocation' (in FMW)
SV	'Science as a Vocation' (in FMW)

For page references to the original German texts the following abbreviations will be used:

Einleitung	'Einleitung' in *GARS* (*Introduction to the Economic Ethic of the World Religions*)
Hinduismus	*Die Wirtschaftsethik der Weltreligionen: Hinduismus und Buddhismus*
PB	'Politik als Beruf'
PE	'Die protestantische Ethik und der Geist des Kapitalismus' in *GARS*
WB	'Wissenschaft als Beruf'

WG	*Wirtschaft und Gesellschaft: Religiöse Gemeinschaften*
Zw	'Zwischenbetrachtung' in *GARS* (*Intermediary Reflection*)

See the Bibliography for more detail.

Chapter 1
Preparatory Remarks

Introduction

In his 1917 lecture, 'Science as a Vocation', Max Weber tells his audience of university students how the great questions of meaning, that have been central to the intellectual projects of humanity in religion and philosophy, can no longer be answered within the academy, the place of institutionalised, legitimate reason in the modern world.

> ... what is the meaning of science as a vocation, now after all these former illusions, the 'way to true being', the 'way to true art', the 'way to true nature', the 'way to true God', the 'way to true happiness', have been dispelled? Tolstoi has given the simplest answer, with the words: 'Science is meaningless because it gives no answer to our question, the only question important for us: "What shall we do and how shall we live?"' That science does not give an answer to this is indisputable. (SV[1]: 143)

Earlier in this lecture, he had also used Tolstoy to answer this question of the relation between science and meaning, from a different angle.

> You will find this question raised in the most principled form in the works of Leo Tolstoi. He came to raise the question in a peculiar way. All his broodings increasingly revolved around the problem of whether or not death is a meaningful phenomenon. And his answer was: for civilised man death has no meaning. (SV: 141)

Even if intellectual reason can no longer engage in answering the questions of meaning – the ultimate questions of life and death – Weber himself continues to

---

1 Following most of the secondary literature, the now standard English translations are used, e.g., by Gerth and Mills in their *From Max Weber* collection, and by Parsons for *The Protestant Ethic and the Spirit of Capitalism*. A few challenges to these standard English translations will, however, be needed. Parallel quotations from the German are given when the argument benefits from such inclusions. Also in keeping with current practice, the idiosyncratic names that Gerth and Mills gave to their translations of 'Zwischenbetrachtung' and 'Einleitung' (both from *GARS*) have not been retained and here these texts have been designated as *Intermediary Reflection* and *Introduction to the Economic Ethic of the World Religions*.

be concerned with meaning as part of his intellectual task. The argument to follow will try to demonstrate how, through this focus on meaning, Weber in fact provides us with a complex, precise theory of modernity.

Interpretations

Before beginning this argument in detail, the vast interpretative literature on Weber – some of which directly engages with meaning and modernity – will have to be confronted.[2] In their magnitude and breadth of topic the primary writings of Weber himself are daunting enough, but the secondary literature is so extensive that it might now well lie beyond the reach of any one human life of devoted study.[3] Weber's own stress on the fate of specialisation in modernity (PE: 182), and especially in academic work (SV: 134–5), proves eerily apt when reflexively applied to his own legacy.

Some sense of the scope of the secondary literature might be made by means of three broad points.

Firstly, the great bulk of work that uses and/or interprets Weber pays scant attention to modernity and its relation to meaning. It is often the case that sections of Weber are employed as foundational in a range of studies of social life – from the sociology of bureaucracy to theories of universal social action – and, in such limited use, questions of meaning and modernity can simply be ignored. It is also the case that, when his work is given a more overall depiction or interpretation, from Weber's usual place at the start of introductory sociology textbooks to the array of more advanced academic accounts of his extensive writings, meaning (in terms of the Protestant Ethic thesis, the sociology of religion and disenchantment) might rate a mention but only as a small part of such general accounts. The present argument is not overly concerned with these standard utilisations and interpretations of Weber, where meaning is absent or notional, although there will be some intersection of ideas at times.

Secondly, when the extent of the secondary accounts is taken into consideration, and in opposition to the claims of some of the most important interpretations of Weber, it now seems futile to try to maintain the position that some essence or golden thread can be discovered which somehow provides the means of thematically unifying all of Weber's writings.[4] It follows that all that can be offered

---

2 After this brief survey of the secondary tradition, for the rest of the following argument detailed accounts of the interpretive literature are only given when the relatively new concepts of 'paradox' and 'brotherliness' are discussed, although some further references will also be made as aids to the understanding of specific points.

3 Sica (2004) lists 4,600 entries in his bibliography of works in English on Weber.

4 Following Gane (2002), who rejects the search for the unitary theme. Exponents of the essential theme approach include: Tenbruck (1980) with the theme of rationalisation; Hennis (1988) with life-conduct (*Lebensführung*); Schroeder (1992) with culture (meaning);

here, with the present argument, is one more interpretation which, it is hoped, will provide a fresh understanding of just part of Weber's overall oeuvre.

To give some sense of this interpretative tradition, which has conjured up a series of 'Webers' as well as many, highly varied appropriations of his work and which leads to the conclusion that there is no one essential Weber to be discovered, an image might be invoked where Weber's works are imagined as a mountain rich in ore and minerals. This mountain has been mined many times, with shafts and tunnels crisscrossing the rock, and various valuable materials have been extracted in great quantities. These tunnels might meet up at times, and some areas might be mined out, but no one mine can succeed in extracting all the wealth that is available in the whole mountain. This process has now been going on for a very long time, but, as it will be shown, there is still more wealth to be found when we pass into the mine-shaft of meaning and begin to follow some seams of ore that have not yet been thoroughly explored.

So, thirdly, let us enter this tunnel of interpretation and consider the work that does explicitly deal with meaning and modernity in Weber. There are two groups that might be roughly identified here. The first group includes those who seek to understand how meaning functions in the modern world, and while Weber plays a significant role in providing the theory of how modernity arrives at its current meaningless state, his role is lessened when it comes to what happens to meaning thereafter, i.e., in modernity itself. In this camp we might position: the American Durkheimians like Robert Bellah[5] (e.g., Bellah, 1970, 1975); the philosopher

---

Goldman (1992) with self and power. It might be added that this basically essentialist, reductionist approach to Weber's thought would itself seem to be highly 'un-Weberian'. Weber is at pains to caution against using a one-sided explanation of the social reality. So, for example, an empirical, historical example of religion has to be explained through a huge number of causes. Also, Weber's understanding of the intellectual task as one of devising 'ideal-types' is directly pitched against essentialist claims to truth. If Weber's work itself is regarded as the reality to be understood then the attempt to find thematic unity smacks of a methodological view that is in opposition to the methodological outlook of that which is being investigated. This is not contradictory – the investigators might well be opposed to Weber's position or refuse the connection between Weber's writings and social reality – but it is a tension that is worth noting. For an argument in favour of regarding the myriad interpretations of Weber as examples of 'ideal-types', i.e., applying Weber's own theory and method back onto the very tradition that has sought to interpret Weber, see Pudsey (1996).

5 Seidman has provided a neat summary of the relation between the Weberian and Durkheimian legacies: 'The Durkheimians take issue with the Weberian claim of the dissolution of sociocultural unity and the thesis of the secularisation, segmentation, and privatisation of moral and existential meanings. The Durkheimians argue that every society rests upon a religiously based set of shared moral understandings which by virtue of integrating the personal and social system provide a basis for identity and societal community as well as a transcendent standard of judgment ... Thus, Durkheimians insist that the Weberian notion of a great transformation from a "religious" to a "secular", or

Charles Taylor (e.g., Taylor, 2007, 2011); and Jurgen Habermas (e.g., Habermas 1984, 2008).[6] In all these cases Weber is, on the whole, regarded as the theorist of disenchantment, secularisation and meaninglessness, and the answers to questions of the continued place of meaning in the modern world lie in testing, beyond and against Weber, the tense relation between reason and religion itself.[7] Beyond this approach to meaning it will be argued that Weber's theory of the development of Western meaninglessness lays the foundation for an additional theory on the working of meaning in modernity, but that this theory, although based on the history of religion in the West, precludes the strategy of seeking answers through some sort of return to religion.

The second group of scholarly interpreters of Weber is composed of those who have taken up his theory of meaning, including its place in modernity, as their pivotal theme.[8] Indebted as this present study is to this particular tradition of Weberian interpretation, a fundamental difference needs to be noted before the argument is engaged in detail. The disagreement here is one of method. The strong tendency in this scholarly tradition is to try to complete or make sense of Weber's theory through employing three strategies, either separately or in some sort of combination:[9] firstly, the use of external intellectual debates or other theorists,[10] particularly from Weber's time; secondly, the attempt to explain difficulties in Weber's theory through reference to Weber's biographical circumstances; and thirdly, the introduction of modern values and concepts that are largely extraneous

---

communitarian to utilitarian individualist, society is mistaken' (Seidman, 1985: 111). The assumption Seidman shares with the Durkheimians, i.e., that Weber just provides a secularisation thesis on the development of modernity, will be disputed in the coming argument.

6   For other variations of this outlook, see: Luckmann, 1967; Berger, 1967; Wilson, 1976.

7   As examples of this tendency see: Bellah's ambivalent relationship to his notion of 'civil religion' (e.g., Bellah, 1967, 1975); Taylor's attempt to overcome Weber's distinction between science and the irrational realm of religion in modernity (Taylor, 2007: 550 esp.); and Habermas' dialogues with Catholic theologians in what he calls a 'post-secular age' (Habermas, 2007, 2010).

8   Examples here include: Seidman (1983); Scaff (1991, 2000); Schroeder (1992, 1995); and Gane (2002).

9   Some of these strategies apply to recent scholarship on Weber more widely, especially the use of biography and other thinkers of the time (see Chalcraft, 2008: 23ff esp. for an overview of past and present Weber scholarship). This approach to Weber within the academic community will have to be confronted on several occasions during the course of the following argument.

10   Let it be noted from the start that if there is one theorist who has come to dominate the Weberian scholarly method and which will be opposed here, it is Nietzsche. Of course, much of value has been gained by linking Weber and Nietzsche, but it has been at the expense of allowing access to Weber's full viewpoint on meaning.

to the Weber texts in question (like freedom and subjectivity).[11] Now, illuminating as these interpretations can be – and they often display an extraordinary level of intellectual virtuosity – it will be argued that they are flawed, at least in terms of the ability to develop Weber's viewpoint on meaning. In contrast then, this study will adopt the approach of explaining Weber's theory of meaning and modernity by piecing together what Weber himself has said on the topic, and will not introduce other theorists, the biographical background, or values external to those Weber himself has used in his understanding of meaning. There is no doubt the adoption of this method throws up some very large obstacles: Weber's ideas and the relevant terms are scattered throughout his writings; arguments are densely interwoven and need to be teased out,[12] often through the use of a number of different texts; and Weber's position is incomplete at times and will need to be joined together with some measure of speculation. Yet, despite these very real problems, a surprisingly comprehensive, consistent theory of meaning and modernity can be constructed from what Weber himself has written.

So, to pursue the earlier metaphor, this current work will try to open up a new section in the Weber mountain, that goes a bit deeper and at a different angle to the mine that has already been dug in the search for meaning. The seam that will be followed contains those terms from religion that Weber has employed to make sense of the workings of both meaning and meaninglessness in modernity.

Elements of the Argument

To start, a brief account needs to be given of the texts that will be used. Weber's theory of meaning is exhibited primarily in a series of works that might loosely be said to fall under the umbrella of his sociology of religion. This obviously includes his empirical studies of various religions and the intervening commentary that is collected in *GARS*, the sections on religion in *Economy and Society*, but also the two Vocation lectures. What becomes apparent is that Weber preserves the perspective of meaning throughout these texts, which is obviously not hard to discern in the direct accounts of religion, but it also applies when Weber directs his discussion, within this sociology of religion, to modernity. This occurs particularly with his theory of the value-sphere structure of modern society[13] that is most

---

11 Although Schroeder is less able to be categorised in this way.

12 Weber's arguments are, at times, so densely knotted together we will need to revisit certain key quotations as the different strands of his argument are examined in turn.

13 The value-sphere model necessarily plays an important role with those interpreters listed above who have meaning as their guiding theme, but it has also been understood with meaning absent or notional. See, especially, Habermas (1984) and Brubaker (1984). Such interpretations, where this theory of modernity is cleanly extracted from its context of religion, is not in any way surprising of course, given the multifarious approaches and utilisations which constitute the secondary tradition. A note should be made here on the

explicit in the *Intermediary Reflection*, described to a lesser extent in *Economy and Society*,[14] assumed in the Vocation lectures, and is emerging in the first, 1905, publication of *The Protestant Ethic and the Spirit of Capitalism*.

In the period from 1904/05 to 1920, from the first publication of *The Protestant Ethic and the Spirit of Capitalism* to *GARS*, it will therefore be assumed that there is an overall unity in Weber's theories stemming from his constant concern with meaning and the maintenance of the perspective of the sociology of religion. It is, however, commonly recognised (e.g., Whimster, 2007: 5) that Weber will tend to focus on capitalism in the earlier works and then will tend to broaden this outlook to something we can term 'modernity'. But even if this point is acknowledged, it will be shown that this whole period is of sufficient theoretical coherence in terms of meaning to allow it to be regarded as a unified whole. The different terms[15] employed by Weber to indicate the object of his studies will be taken as basically pointing to this common theory of meaning.

Let us now try to make sense of Weber's arguments on meaning and modernity by looking at their elemental features. Two basic factors might be initially glimpsed, and both suggest that they are part of a greater theory that demands articulation.

Firstly, what are the terms and ideas that Weber employs throughout these texts, which are indicative of this perspective of religion and meaning? Remarkably, when modernity in its most secular aspects is described by Weber, he employs concepts taken from his accounts of religion, especially Western religion. So, discussion of sectors of the modern social order such as the economy, politics and art utilises expressions like 'spirit', 'vocation', 'salvation', 'redemption', 'fate', 'brotherliness', 'cosmos', 'gods', 'daemon' and, indeed, 'meaning', as well as images of death. The value-sphere model of our social order is constructed within this set of ideas. The task that this terminology therefore sets, is to follow these

---

work of Charles Turner (1992). In common with the argument being presented here, Turner puts great stress on the *Intermediary Reflection* and the value-sphere structure; and he strenuously opposes interpreters like Habermas and Schluchter who have emphasised the theme of rationalisation leading to a modernity that has broken from its medieval religious origins. In contrast, Turner wants to preserve the religious perspective on modernity used in the *Intermediary Reflection* and must, therefore, explicitly cite the ethic of brotherliness as the basic orientation at work for Weber (Turner, 1992: 99–100). But, in contrast with the argument to follow here, Turner's argument takes a tack that leads away from the perspective of religion and the ideal of brotherly love, and he will fill out his account with reference to a range of theorists which includes Simmel, Kierkegaard and Nietzsche.

14 Initial formulations of the value-sphere structure were present in *Economy and Society* in 1913; then developed in the *Intermediary Reflection* when it was first published in 1915, with some additions made in the 1920 version (Turner, 1992: 120–21).

15 So Weber states that he is explicitly dealing with 'economic ethics' (e.g., in PE and IEEWR), 'life-conducts', e.g., in his comparison of Protestant asceticism with the East (China, India), and then onto the 'values-spheres' and vocations of the modern world which will be the last depository of the questions of salvation and theodicy (IR, SV, PV).

terms through the texts and see how, and indeed if, they can be fitted together into a coherent theory without any external additions.

The second elemental aspect that might make us feel compelled to explore Weber on meaning and modernity, beyond the current interpretations on offer, comes with consideration of what has been termed Weber's philosophical anthropology, where meaning is part of the universal human condition itself.

As many commentators have remarked, it seems clear Weber assumes that there is a universal human need for meaning, which will come to be articulated in the varieties of religious belief. In the *Introduction to the Economic Ethic of the World Religions* Weber makes the statement:

> Many more varieties of belief have, of course, existed. Behind them always lies a stand towards something in the actual world which is experienced as specifically 'senseless'. Thus, the demand has been implied: that the world order in its totality is, could, and should somehow be a meaningful 'cosmos'. This quest, the core of genuine religious rationalism, has been borne precisely by strata of intellectuals. The avenues, the results, and the efficacy of this metaphysical need for a meaningful cosmos have varied widely. (IEEWR: 281)

In the *Intermediary Reflection* he states that:

> At all times and in all places, the need for salvation – consciously cultivated as the substance of religiosity – has resulted from the endeavour of a systematic and practical rationalisation of life's realities. To be sure, this connection has been maintained with varying degrees of transparency: on this level, all religions have demanded as a specific presupposition that the course of the world be somehow *meaningful*, at least in so far as it touches upon the interests of men. (IR: 353, Weber's emphasis)

In addition, from his methodological writings ('Objectivity in the Social Sciences and Social Policy'), comes the notion that as 'cultural beings' (*Kulturmensch*) humankind gives meaning to the world:

> 'Culture' is a finite segment of the meaningless infinity of the world process, a segment on which *human beings* confer meaning and significance. (Method: 81, Weber's emphasis)

The questions of meaning are, most basically, just what Weber voices through the words of Tolstoy: 'What shall we do and how shall we live?'; but the ordering of 'life's realities' to provide such meaning will tend to consider, in various ways and with different degrees of emphasis, the questions of death and unjust suffering in the world (the problem of theodicy) (see, especially, IEEWR: 275).[16] Moreover, it befalls 'the strata of intellectuals' to develop this 'metaphysical need' rationally into the 'meaningful cosmos' exhibited in religion.

Two qualifications should be made at this point. Firstly, it needs to be noted that the following argument will place great emphasis on these dual dilemmas of death and suffering as they are manifested in the Christian, Western worldview, since this will be the content that will inform Weber's views on meaning and modernity. However, the theological balance of these issues in the Christian West is of course far from universal and such a stress on, e.g., salvation from death, will not be found, for example, in the cases of Confucianism[17] and Ancient Greek religion (e.g., China: 228, where Hellenic and Chinese beliefs are compared precisely on this point).

Secondly, it should also be noted that most meaningful belief does not involve an 'other-worldly' salvation but is more concerned with the ordering of life in the 'here and now' with an emphasis on 'health, a long life, and wealth' (IEEWR: 277). Further, in all religious belief it is the here and now of the psychological state that is crucial – from Puritan certainty of grace to the ecstasy of Dionysian orgies (IEEWR: 278).[18] In other words, religious meaning for Weber should not just be

---

16 This slight ambiguity in the way Weber speaks of death and suffering throughout his writing can be detailed as follows. Very often death and suffering are both mentioned, and might be taken up as two separate, but somehow interlinked, issues for religion (IEEWR: 275, 280; IR: 330). Sometimes, however, each is discussed without reference to the other (IEEWR: 270ff on suffering; SV: 139 on death, as quoted above). Consequently, the meaning of death alone is often interpreted as the great anthropological problem for Weber (e.g., Brubaker 1984: 92). For Weber, there are sociological reasons, in terms of class/strata interests, why each might be distinguished. The privileged classes will usually seek legitimation for their success rather than an explanation of suffering, which will be more the concern of the underprivileged (ES: 492). Making sense of death will thus be more likely to be the major concern of the upper classes. The intellectual strata will also, on the whole, be more interested in this meaning rather than 'salvation from external distress' (ES: 506). The different uses of these two great issues can, therefore, sometimes be understood through the context of Weber's class/strata discussion; however, for the privileged in some religions, such as Hinduism (India: 132–3) and Ancient Buddhism (India: 220–21), finally escaping death is also a release from suffering. Death, in a sense, is subsumed into the problem of suffering here, and the previous class interests are rendered almost redundant by the rationalisation of religion. In 'Science as a Vocation' he concentrates on the meaning of death, and in the *Introduction to the Economic Ethic of the World Religions* and the *Intermediary Reflection* there is more of a stress on theodicy.

17 Confucianism will provide imperatives for right conduct in a highly rationalised cosmos (see China), but since it does not develop a theology concerned with death and suffering Weber therefore expresses some doubt as to whether Confucianism does count as a religion (IEEWR: 293).

18 Although, the rational aspect of theology, as opposed to the emotive, can also be decisive (IEEWR: 286).

associated with exceptional escapes from the world, but with a more everyday sense of meaning.

The philosophical anthropology – this human need for meaning – is given a different, crucial conceptualisation by Weber in terms of 'ideal interests' (See IEEWR: 270, 271, 277, 288; IR: 353; India: 34; China: 19).[19] As opposed to material interests (e.g., food, shelter), the notion of ideal interests captures the common human concern with how to live in the world, and usually such interests will, in varying measures, be directed to the facts of human death and suffering. All humans, for Weber, will be engaged in following ideal as well as material interests – with religion the obvious fulfilment of this 'ideal' relation to the world.[20] To understand meaning in terms of ideal interests is to give emphasis to the way the pursuit of meaning, like the pursuit of material needs/interests, is an ongoing, constant factor for human life – even, it would seem to follow, in the most secular places of modern meaninglessness.

These two basic features of Weber's understanding – the unswerving use of religious terminology, and the assumption of the human pursuit of meaning or following ideal interests – mutually reinforce each other and promote the idea that a theory of meaning and modernity is present. It should be added here that, of course, this theory has nothing to do with the meaning that can so obviously be found by going back to the church or by following one of the abundant 'spiritual' alternatives that have always been on offer in modern times. In fact, Weber sees ideal interests and meaning at work in the meaningless structures themselves, which he still puts under his lens of the sociology of religion. To put it bluntly: there is meaning within meaninglessness.

The key idea, as others have tried to develop, is Weber's understanding of modernity as structured into the separate value-spheres. But how do we find a way into an understanding of Weber's theory here that will not need the addition of external theorists and values, or personal biography, as others have found necessary? There are two tactics to be followed. Firstly, as already suggested, a difficult theoretical posture has to be adopted which tries to follow what Weber was doing. Namely, the perspective of religion and meaning adopted by Weber has to be scrupulously sustained and the temptation to use values and concepts that would

---

19 Sometimes termed 'religious' interests, 'cultural' interests (Method: 81), or 'religious needs' (IEEWR: 270).

20 However, Weber is at pains to stress that the intellectual theorisation of religion cannot be restricted to explanations based only on ideal and/or material, interests (IEEWR: 268). Many factors have to be included, as his empirical studies exhibit (see AJ and China, in particular). The qualification should also be made that he will extend his use of the term 'interest' to include, for example, military, status, and political interests. But the material/ideal conjunction does have a claim to some theoretical privilege in Weber's work, particularly when the empirical studies are given some sense of an overview in the *Introduction to the Economic Ethic of the World Religions* and in the *Intermediary Reflection*.

normally engage us as secular, intellectualised modernists has to be rigorously resisted. So, amidst modern meaninglessness, we will have to see society, as Weber has done, in terms and values that are redolent with a religious meaning of life and death, e.g., vocation and salvation. Secondly, two concepts from this sociology of religion perspective will be taken up for particular attention: 'paradox' and 'brotherliness'. These concepts have been ones that the commentators have had to use, so common are they in Weber's writings, but their further understanding has almost always been neglected. Concentration on these ideas will provide us with a way into Weber's labyrinthine theory of meaning, and also allow us to sustain the perspective of his sociology of religion. Some brief discussion of 'paradox' and 'brotherliness' needs to be given at this introductory stage.

Paradox might appear an odd idea upon which to focus, and would perhaps seem to be a fairly loose, generalised notion that has widespread application, as indeed it has, and so it has been theorised. However, for Weber, paradox serves as a defining characteristic of Western meaning – in the history of the West and in modernity. To understand meaning as paradox is to grasp how meaning has been fatefully lost, to varying degrees, in its very pursuit, and it is in this way that meaning can be understood to exist within modern meaninglessness. Weber will announce this logic in terms of Western religion in *The Protestant Ethic and the Spirit of Capitalism*; will reapply it within the history of Western science/ intellectual reason in 'Science as a Vocation'; and, in the *Intermediary Reflection*, he will show how it is constantly reproduced in the value-spheres of modernity, i.e., in the spheres of the economy, politics, science/intellectual knowledge, art and the erotic.

The second concept that will need to be articulated is 'brotherliness'. Brotherliness, or brotherly love, is a religious ethic that arises from the problem of theodicy: the fact of suffering in the world. Although it is not just a Christian moral imperative, for Weber the West is fatefully marked by this ethical ideal. As with all the elements of meaning, brotherliness has been, and is, subject to the logic of paradox, both though its history in Western religion and through its place in modernity.

The hope is that, through the development of these two concepts of paradox and brotherliness, Weber's theory of meaning, as it applies in the history of the West and in modernity, will be able to be coherently reconstructed.

A final note on the coming argument is needed in order to provide some indication of how a number of these ideas are tied together. As paradox and brotherliness are examined an overall pattern of ideal interests in the West will start to emerge: the ideal interest with how to live in the world in the face of death and the ideal interest with how to live in the world in the face of suffering will form a differentiated relationship of great tension. The concern with life/death will come to dominate religion as it paradoxically develops in Protestantism, and the concern with suffering that prescribes a life that follows the ethic of brotherliness will be, at the same time, lost or excluded. Also, the value-spheres of meaningless modernity, which have been partly determined by the religious history of the West, will continue to have their inner meaning orientated around the ideal interest in life/death through the heritage of Protestant vocational meaning and the creation of new ways of understanding the meaning of death; while suffering/brotherliness will be systematically excluded from these same value-spheres, although, despite this rejection, brotherly love will be sustained as the moral ideal for modernity.[21]

Applications and Developments

If the major undertaking being attempted here is the explication of Weber's argument concerning meaning and modernity, the following question must be considered: what worth, however slight, does this new interpretation of Weber have? Weber's considerable reputation is based on various understandings of his work with which this argument must, to some extent, disagree. Moreover, it cannot be assumed that just because this relatively novel theory might be part of Weber's overall understanding that it therefore should be accorded the stature of his other well established theories, especially when the difficulties of constructing this theory are remembered.

As the argument unfolds the value of Weber's theory might be revealed, but the two final chapters will explicitly try to meet this query. The penultimate chapter will reconsider the prescriptions that Weber offers in the Vocation lectures; and the last chapter will briefly consider some implications for further research.

A final qualification should be made before the argument is engaged in earnest. Weber's works have been the subject of a huge, highly *critical* commentary. On the whole, the argument to follow will have to ignore these attacks and be largely uncritical of Weber; although, on occasions, certain critical positions will have to be fended off in order to clarify Weber's position. So, all that is being attempted here is a clear articulation of Weber's theory, and some implications that might be drawn from it. Nothing more.

---

21 Another reminder should be made here that, of course, this Western pattern of ideal interests is by no means universal and, for example, is not only opposed to Confucianism, where death and suffering are not the guiding interests of a meaningful life, but, also, to Hinduism, where death and suffering *are* dominant but do not exist in this relation of paradoxical tension. Since Weber's chief concern is with the West and modernity, a large part of the task ahead is to come to some sort of understanding of his argument concerning the paradoxical poles of Western meaning – life/death and suffering/brotherliness.

PART I
The Paradox of Meaning

Chapter 2
Western Religion and Science

Introduction

In order to understand Weber's sociology of meaning in modernity two key concepts from his work – paradox and brotherliness – will be explored and elaborated. In this chapter and the next three we will examine the first of these – paradox.

Weber himself deploys the term 'paradox' as a description for many of the most important changes in cultural history, but he does not provide a specific definition of what he means by this concept. There are substantial problems in providing this precise understanding which arise not only from the complexity of Weber's ideas but also from the very notion of 'paradox' itself. On the most general level, 'paradox' in Weber conforms to the standard view based on the Ancient Greek: '*para*' – 'beyond'; and '*doxa*' – 'belief/opinion/expectations'. 'Paradox', then, implies an outcome contrary to expected results and there are numerous, quite different paradoxes that can be identified under this broad version of the term. But for Weber it is the content and effect of historically specific paradoxes of *meaning* (notably those that developed Western modernity and the ones that now characterise it) that are most indicative of his overall position. Within this particular theoretical practice the general understanding of paradox has been effectively narrowed down to a much more precise definition of meaning as paradox, namely: meaning will be fatefully lost, in varying degrees, as it is pursued and/or develops. This is the definition that will guide us as we try to reconstruct Weber's overall theory of meaning. Moreover, to anticipate some of the conclusions to follow, the meaninglessness of modernity will be understood by Weber as arising, in part, from the way meaning in fact develops in the West – meaninglessness, paradoxically, is the fateful outcome of the very pursuit of meaning itself.

Before we move on to examine how this concept works in Weber's writings, the manner in which the notion of paradox has been taken up in the commentary on Weber needs to be mentioned. Some detail needs to be given here in order to explain how paradox in Weber has been both recognised and overlooked.

Previous Commentaries on Weber's Use of 'Paradox'

Reference to 'paradox' is extraordinarily common in the literature on Weber. However, despite this frequency of use in the secondary accounts, the attempts by scholarly commentators to catalogue the numerous occasions in which the term appears in Weber's body of work, or to try to capture what paradox actually means to Weber, have been underdeveloped at best. The strong tendency in the vast commentaries on the works of Max Weber is to use 'paradox' in an unexplained, self-evident manner, and/or it is used to refer to just one facet of Weber's theoretical landscape. For example: Wolfgang Schluchter employs 'paradox' as the prime term in the title of two of his major studies of Weber (Schluchter, 1979a, 1996) and cites it as a major theme for Weber (Schluchter, 1981: 154; Schluchter, 1979a: 46); Lassman and Velody, in their account of 'Science as a Vocation' and its immediate German reception, use the term repeatedly (1989: 172, 176, 186, 187, 189, 196, 201); as does Scaff (1991: 50, 63, 110, 112, 221, 222, 224); and Habermas, in his final summarising account of the limits of Weber's analyses of moral progress, states that 'Weber speaks of *paradoxes* and not of the partial character of social rationalisation' (Habermas, 1984: 241, emphasis added).[1] Notable exceptions to this general trend are the analyses of Bryan Turner, Robert Merton, Friedhelm Guttandin and Mohamed Cherkaoui. Each of these interpretations will now need to be examined briefly in turn, and the insights and limitations they each offer towards an understanding of Weber's use of the concept of paradox highlighted.

In *For Weber*, Turner outlines a relatively explicit account of paradox in Weber's work:

> ... the actual content of his arguments relates to the question of historical paradox, namely the fatefulness of human intentionality. Weber concerns himself constantly with the theme that in history, social movements are transformed by various processes of institutionalisation into social structures which deny or contradict pristine motives and intentions of the founders of these movements. (Turner, 1996: 178)

The great example of this for Turner is the Protestant ethic and the creation of capitalism (Turner, 1996: 178–9).

Turner is correct, it can be said, in three ways: the stress on the sheer extent of Weber's use of paradox; the fateful, unresolvable character of paradox; and the basic model being the Protestant ethic/capitalism relation. However, Turner's general depiction of intentions being institutionalised into social structures does not quite capture all of Weber's paradoxes, and his description here is very brief and still begs the question of how this constant concern of Weber's is actually manifested in his works.

Robert Merton also adds to our understanding of Weber's use of the concept. In his 1936 article on unintended consequences, Merton links 'basic' or 'fundamental values', with 'paradox' and Weber:

---

1 See also: Bendix, 1977: 280; Brubaker, 1984: 98; Schroeder, 1992: 125; Gane, 2002: 20ff, 35, 61; Kontos, 1994: 224; Baehr and Wells, 2002: ix; McIntosh, 1983: 74ff, among many others. Some more examples will be given in relation to specific points of the following argument.

The classical analysis of the influence of this factor is Weber's study of the Protestant Ethic and the spirit of capitalism. He has properly generalised this case, saying that active asceticism *paradoxically* leads to its own decline through the accumulation of wealth and possessions entailed by decreased consumption and intense productive activity. (Merton, 1936: 903, emphasis added)

He states further: 'Here is the essential *paradox* of social action – the "realisation" of values may lead to their renunciation' (Merton, 1936: 903, emphasis added). Merton mentions other authors here as well, including Hegel, Marx and Wundt, but only as an aside to the 'classical' Weberian study. Crucially, the Weber example is deliberately contrasted by Merton to at least three other categories of unintended consequences – ignorance, error, further non-immediate consequences/interests (Merton, 1936: 898–902). Only where the attainment of basic values leads also to their abandonment does Merton label such an example of unintended consequences 'paradoxical'. So, in this seminal article, Merton begins to distinguish Weber's analysis from other types of unintended consequence in terms of the Protestant Ethic thesis, and he marks this difference by the term 'paradox'.[2]

Although Weber's use of paradox is not yet clearly developed in this article, and, from the perspective of the argument being presented here, is still too loosely linked to other theorists, Merton makes some brief but highly astute remarks on the presentation of paradox in Weber's works. Especially useful is his emphasis on fundamental values (even though this is not yet clearly understood as based on the search for meaning). However, he places these comments in an overview of unintended consequences and social understanding. This placement unfortunately locks Weber's usage into a general abstract debate on unintended consequences and the social sciences, which leads us away from the uniqueness of Weber's understanding. In fact the ensuing academic discussion would never recover the original Mertonian understanding of paradox; indeed, paradox is rarely mentioned again in this debate.[3]

---

2   And in Merton's own explicitly Weberian research on Puritanism and science, he holds that the emerging connections of religion and science were unintended, but that the 'religious ethic formulated by the great Reformist leaders ... progressively developed into a system of values favourable to the pursuit of science' (Merton, 1968: 653, 659). The rising conflict between science and Puritan theology was yet another case where 'the Reformers did not anticipate the full consequences of their teachings' (Merton, 1970: 79).

3   See Dietz (2004), Vernon (1979) and Baert (1991) for examples of this generalised debate, all of which contain scant mention of Weber and no mention of the Mertonian notion of the paradoxical. Boudon's work on unintended consequences does mention both Weber and Merton, but provides a vague and weakly formulated model called 'paradigms of the Weberian type' (Boudon, 1982: 188), which does not include the standard example of the Protestant Ethic thesis. This fundamental absence is, presumably, due to Boudon's vigorous rejection of Weber's primary thesis (Boudon, 1990: 120–23). From such a critical starting point, Boudon is of little help in actually explaining the paradoxes extant in Weber's work.

Such an outcome points to a fundamental problem for the understanding of paradox (and meaning more generally) in Weber's work. The secondary literature will try to make sense of these very difficult areas of Weber's theory by reference to other, external theorists and debates, rather than adopting the strategy advocated here of pursuing these ideas within Weber's own writings. The path of using external sources as explanation can be witnessed in the two authors who do take up the concept of paradox seriously: Guttandin and Cherkaoui.

Friedhelm Guttandin (1998) specifically discusses the role of paradox in Weber's work. Guttandin stresses the paradoxical nature of the Protestant Ethic/capitalism thesis, including the way Protestantism will paradoxically extinguish itself as a kind of religion, and he also examines the paradoxes of politics (Guttandin, 1998: 183–99). Part of the following analysis below will do something very similar. However, Guttandin (never citing Merton) then tries to link this account of paradox in Weber's writings back into the unintended consequences debate (Guttandin, 1998: 1V, 2). He uses the notion of paradox, which he had unearthed in Weber, as a category into which many of the significant theorists standardly mentioned in the unintended consequences debate can be brought together. Here, it can be argued, most of the good work achieved by Guttandin in beginning to identify the role of paradox in Weber's sociology is undone. In associating Weber with a host of other thinkers whose theories can indeed be classified as examples of paradoxical unintended consequence, Guttandin loses the specificity of the Weberian paradox. So, in his comparison of Weber with Smith and Mandeville (the paradox of individual self-interest producing social virtue/bounty), and with the conservative paradox (that radical social action will necessarily produce unknown results far worse than intended) (Guttandin, 1998: 203–5), Guttandin does not note the difference between these theories and Weber's: namely that, for Weber, the final paradoxes are not avoidable. For Smith and Mandeville, the benefits of their paradox are threatened by state action. For the conservatives, the undesirable consequences of radical action can be bypassed simply by maintaining a conservative political agenda (as, most famously, articulated by Burke). For Weber, however, the universal paradoxes and those specific to Western modernity, as we will see, are marked by 'fate'. Paradox is the outcome which cannot be altered.

Guttandin associates Weberian paradox most closely, however, with Marx, Gehlen and Luhmann (Guttandin, 1998: 207–13). Part of the alleged commonality between these theories of unintended consequence is they can each have their respective paradoxes resolved: most famously, for example, by the historical mission of the proletariat in the case of Marx; and, claims Guttandin, by the intervention of the charismatic leader within Weber's position (Guttandin, 1998: 212). Again the distinctiveness of Weber's position is overlooked.

There are a number of points here. Firstly, the charismatic solution is doubtful for Weber. Perhaps the dilemma of bureaucratic/party politics might be alleviated by a strong charismatic leader, but this is not the same as a Marxist resolution. Secondly, Guttandin ignores the in-built paradox of charisma itself: it cannot last and will end up being overcome by routinisation (see below). Third, the very paradoxes Guttandin had just stressed as arising from the Protestant Ethic thesis are not, in any way, resolvable through charismatic measures. Again, paradox is the final result and is not, in fact, open to any overcoming by an historical agent.

It might be said that in trying to slot the Weberian concept of paradox back into the general debate on unintended consequences, Guttandin undermines the crucial distinctive qualities of Weber's position; and, indeed, Guttandin has to distort Weber's conception in order to align Weber with other social theories whose work might be classified under the label of paradoxical unintended consequences. Two areas need developing from Guttandin's work: firstly, the extent of paradox in Weber is more substantial and more specified than Guttandin allows; and secondly, the nature of this paradox is in need of greater definition, in contrast to other social theorists, and in contrast to the general debate on unintended consequences.

The other commentator who has more recently taken up the concept of paradox, and who has done so in perhaps the most thorough way yet, is Mohamed Cherkaoui (2007). This work is useful in confirming the arguments to be presented here on the variety of paradoxes in Weber, but, like Guttandin (who is not referred to by Cherkaoui), it suffers by trying to place Weber in the unintended consequences debate and by explaining Weber's paradoxes through comparison with the other theorists who are commonly listed as dealing in paradox.

After summarising, as Guttandin has done, previous theorists of paradox (Cherkaoui, 2007: Ch. 1), the general approach seeks to categorise Weber's paradoxes in a methodological intellectual setting outside Weber's theory (Cherkaoui, 2007: 7ff, Ch. 9) and so continually leads away from understanding how paradox works within Weber's overarching theoretical structure, especially in terms of the sociology of meaning. Because of this use of an external intellectual debate to make sense of Weber, there are some notable limitations to this work: some of the paradoxes of Weber are overlooked; there is scant reference to brotherliness (Cherkaoui, 2007: 163); how modernity is regarded is largely ignored; and, most significantly, it is again assumed, in keeping with all the other theorists of paradox that are called upon, that Weber's paradoxes are able to be resolved (or, at least, the distinctive quality of Weberian paradox in this regard is not stressed). One of the fundamental points of the importance of paradox in Weber – that paradox is in fact the fate of modernity – is again lost.

At this point, against this trend of going to outside theory to explain Weber's understanding of paradox, let us now turn to Weber's own writings and see how he deploys this concept in religious examples and in the determination of modernity.

Paradox in Religion and the West

An examination of Weber's writings, especially the sociology of religion texts, reveals two crucial dimensions to his use of the term. Firstly, as the Weberian scholars mentioned above have shown, he does demonstrate a 'universal' dimension in the sense that paradox might be found in all cultures at all times. This will be fairly briefly illustrated below in terms of religious examples. Second, and the dimension which tends to be lost in the 'unintended consequences' debate when it operates at the level of abstract categorisation, is how Weber is primarily concerned with the specificities of the unresolvable paradox of Western meaning. The two most important parts to this particular empirical example of paradox are: firstly, the paradoxes that flow from the development of Western religion and science – the discussion of which will form the bulk of this chapter; and, secondly, there are the paradoxes which constitute the value-spheres of modernity, which will be taken up in the following three chapters.

So let us first examine the 'universal' scope of paradox.

'Paradox' as a General Characteristic of Social Life: The Example of Religion

In Weber's extensive works on the world religions the concern with 'paradox' becomes clear. His use of the term throughout these works seems to refer to the way intentions are betrayed by actual events; or, to put it slightly differently, where the means to achieve a particular end undermines that intended end, often by becoming an end in itself. These works contain numerous references to means undermining intended ends. Most importantly, however, these examples refer most often to the paradoxical outcomes that occur in the search for a meaningful way to live in a meaningful cosmos. For example, in his discussion of the religious intentions of monks, Weber notes that:

> The *paradox* of *all* rational asceticism, which in an identical manner has made monks in *all* ages stumble, is that rational asceticism itself has created the very wealth it rejected. (IR: 332; also ES: 586, emphasis added)

Here is a first example of the way the pursuit of meaning results in meaning being diminished and, perhaps, even almost wholly lost. For monks, whether Christian, Buddhist or Hindu, the immediate end or goal, in their religious understanding of how one should live in the world in order to achieve salvation, is the rejection of the things of this world – this is what is valued and brings the believer closer to the divine. Yet this end or goal is in fact undermined by the means necessarily employed by monks – rational asceticism itself – which, through frugal hard work in the monasteries, will create the very wealth and worldly goods that lead away from this religious meaning.

A further example of this paradox, faced by all rational asceticism, comes with the Reformation. Here, John Wesley is nominated by Weber as a Puritan acutely aware of 'the seemingly paradoxical relations' (PE: 175) of Puritan asceticism:

> For the Puritan, however, possessions were as great a temptation as they were for the monk. Like the income of monasteries, his income was a secondary result and symptom of successful asceticism. John Wesley said: 'We have no

choice but to recommend that men be pious and that means', as an unavoidable effect, 'getting rich'. But obviously the dangerous nature of riches for the pious individual was the same as it had been for the monasteries. Wesley expressly focussed upon the observed and apparent *paradox* between the rejection of the world and acquisitive virtuosity. (China: 245, emphasis added)

Weber demonstrates in *The Protestant Ethic and the Spirit of Capitalism* the manner in which Wesley develops the fuller implications of this paradox. Wesley is quoted:

> 'I fear, wherever riches have increased, the essence of religion has decreased in the same proportion. Therefore I do not see how it is possible, in the nature of things, for any revival of true religion to continue long. For religion must produce both industry and frugality, and these cannot but produce riches. But as riches increase, swell pride, anger, and love of the world in all its branches. How then is it possible for Methodism, that is, a religion at heart, though it flourishes now as a green bay tree, should continue in this state? For the Methodists in every place grow diligent and frugal; consequently they increase in goods. Hence they proportionately increase in pride, in anger, in the desire of the flesh, the desire of the eyes, and the pride of life. So although the form of religion remains, the spirit is swiftly vanishing away. Is there no way to prevent this – this continual decay of the pure religion? We ought not to prevent people from being diligent and frugal; *we must exhort all Christians to gain all they can, and to save all they can; that is, in effect, to grow rich*'. (PE: 175, Weber's emphasis)

Wesley would then advise that Christians should give all they could as well as gaining and saving all they could (PE: 176). Here the paradox and its implications were clearly understood – the pursuit of this religious way of life would lead to the, at least, partial loss of the religious ethic itself. There was nothing that could be done, besides giving contradictory advice. Again, results betray intentions: the means to achieve the religious end results in the undermining of that end – the pursuit of wealth leads to the sins of pride, anger, desire, etc.

Many of the examples of the paradox of means and ends, intention and outcome, found in Weber's writing on religion relate to the much-analysed dialectic between charisma and routinisation.[4] Charismatic attempts, most notably by religious leaders, to destroy mundane structures of this world are inevitably overtaken by the need to organise and 'protect' the original charismatic message. An organisation based on routine and predictable structures results: 'The process of routinisation, and thus traditionalisation, has set in' (IEEWR: 297). Weber provides an example of just such a process in his analysis of Ancient Buddhism's attempt to avoid an organised hierarchy:

---

4 Gerth and Mills stress this aspect of Weber and label it 'an attempt to answer the paradox of unintended consequences' (Gerth and Mills, 1948: 54).

> All in all, in consequence of this intentional and consistent minimisation of ties and regulation, Buddhism persisted in an unstructured state which from the beginning was dangerous to the uniformity of the community and which actually soon led to heresies and sect formation ... hence the establishment of an order and likewise the fixing of the teaching, occurred only after the death of the founder and against his own *intentions*. (India: 223, emphasis added)

In order to preserve the teachings of the charismatic founder, a fixed order was formed which in itself stood against the very doctrines of that leader. Such stable structures and doctrines must at least lessen the meaning of the founding message in so far as the original ideas depended on the charismatic qualities of the founding figure and the rejection of institutionalised, traditionalist routines – but, paradoxically, it is precisely that original meaning that is being pursued and, inevitably, lessened through the establishment of such routinisation.

This Buddhist example is put more generally by Weber in his view that all the major religions have their origins in charismatic, communistic communities (ES: 1187, 1120; and specifically on the Essenes, AJ: 407). However, these communities were inherently unstable, not just because of the difficulty of keeping economic/political reality at bay, but because 'once the eschatological expectations fade, charismatic communism in all forms declines and retreats into monastic circles' (ES: 1187).[5] That is, these communities were formed around an indifference to economic/political life based on charismatic religious expectations, but such an existence must be overtaken by the eventual routinisation of charisma (ES: Part 1, Ch. 111, v; also ES: 1121). As Weber states:

> It is only in the initial stages and so long as the charismatic leader acts in a way which is completely outside everyday social organisation, that it is possible for his followers to live communistically in a community of faith and enthusiasm. (ES: 249)

The basic Weberian paradox is plainly evident in these cases. In trying to maintain the values of the community and the charismatic leader after his death, the community and its essential communist values have to be diminished or abandoned in 'everyday social organisation' or routinisation.[6] Again, the original meaning, to some extent, is inevitably lost in the very attempt at trying to maintain it.

---

5   Note that a new form of paradox – that of the 'monks in all ages' described above – then besets this development of routinisation.

6   It should be noted that while Weber's main examples of the charisma/routinisation paradox come from his religious studies, he also plainly wants to make the more generalised point that this is the fate of any charismatic episode (IEEWR: 297), as we will see below with politics.

The West

Apart from this analysis of paradox as a common experience of religion and the fateful overturning of meaning, Weber's explicit use of the term 'paradox' is most evident in his accounts of modernity and the Western trajectory of scientific and religious – especially Protestant – rationalisation. Although this Western development is but a specific example of the means/end paradox just outlined, it occupies much of Weber's work and constitutes the core of the argument on the relationship between meaning and paradox, with the Puritan case at the very centre of the theory. Weber does not want to stay at the level of abstract theory about the nature of unintended consequences, but to ask what this paradox actually entails, i.e., what are the consequences for modern human beings in terms of their ideal interests?[7] The basic, crucial discovery that marks Weber's overall theory of meaning is that the Western search for an answer to the meaning of life and the universe paradoxically empties the world of any possibility of an ultimate meaning. How does this happen? The overall paradoxical loss of meaning in the West partly[8] takes place through, on the one hand, religious rationalisation and on the other, the development of scientific reason. It should be noted that in the following discussion only the paradox of meaning at the level of ideal interests will be emphasised, but Weber always stresses the many complex causes of Western rationalisation and the links between religion and other social, economic and, indeed, geographical forces (see, for example, 'Author's Introduction' and *General Economic History* (e.g., GEH: Ch. XXII)). This qualification should always be borne in mind with what is to follow.

Let us examine religious rationalisation first.

The Paradox of Puritanism's Search for Meaning

In religion, Puritanism is the key and Weber uses it to unlock two 'doors' of paradox. The first door opens up into the most famous and visited room in Weber's mansion: the Protestant Ethic thesis.

As the secondary literature emphasises, the pivotal example of paradox in Weber's work is this most famous thesis: the relationship between capitalism and Protestantism. In essence, the Protestant means of exhibiting grace – rationalised labour in the world with wealth as proof of one's devotion – would itself become the end without the need of religious meaning, i.e., the capitalist spirit that would come to dominance had its origins and had been ethically sanctioned by the very religion it would come to replace. As this has been noted many times by Weberian scholars, and the thesis itself is the subject of seemingly endless accounts and

---

7 He will return to these consequences in more detail in his Vocation lectures, as we shall see in later chapters.

8 And such partial explanation is common in every one of Weber's theorisations.

criticisms, a detailed analysis of this example will not – indeed cannot – be undertaken here. Just two points will be made.

Firstly, we need to examine the ways that Weber himself labels the relationship between capitalism and Protestantism 'paradoxical'. For example, in his comparison of Confucianism with the Puritan vocational ethic, Weber writes:

> [N]o intermediate link led from Confucianism and its ethic – as firmly rooted as Christianity – to a civic and methodical way of life. This was all-important. Puritanism did create it and unintentionally at that. This strange reversion of the 'natural', which is strange only on first, superficial glance, instructs us in the *paradox* of unintended consequences: i.e., the relation of man and fate, of what he intends by his acts and what actually came of them.[9] (China: 238, emphasis added)

These unintended results of Puritan religious ethics and action are reiterated by Weber in the following:

> But only the Puritan rational ethic with its supramundane orientation brought economic rationalism to its consistent conclusion. This happened merely because nothing was further from conscious Puritan intention. It happened because inner-worldly work was simply expressive of the striving for a transcendental goal. (China: 247–8)

The Puritan ethic brought forth the most rationally consistent of all economic, worldly systems as part of its 'supramundane orientation'; but this religious value or end would ultimately be replaced by the very form of economic labour that had been created only to serve such a 'transcendental goal' (see also ES: 587–8).

This point is put more forcefully by Weber in *The Protestant Ethic and the Spirit of Capitalism* in terms of the spirit needed for capitalism:

> We thus take as our starting-point in the investigation of the relationship between the old Protestant ethic and the spirit of capitalism the works of Calvin, of Calvinism, and the other Puritan sects. But it is not to be understood that we expect to find any of the founders or representatives of these religious movements considering the promotion of what we have called the spirit of capitalism as in any sense the end of his life-work. We cannot well maintain that the pursuit of worldly goods, conceived as an end in itself, was to any of them of positive ethical value. Once and for all it must be remembered that programmes of ethical reform never were at the centre of interest for any of the religious

---

9 Weber here clearly sees this paradox as an example of a more general notion of unintended consequences. That it can be seen this way is not in dispute. What becomes troublesome is when the general debate itself takes precedence over, and so leads away from, the historical-cultural theory that Weber is actually arguing.

reformers (among whom, for our purposes, we must include men like Menno, George Fox, and Wesley). They were not the founders of societies for ethical culture nor the proponents of humanitarian projects for social reform or cultural ideals. The salvation of the soul and that alone was the centre of their life and work. Their ethical ideals and the practical results of their doctrines were all based on that alone, and were the consequences of purely religious motives. We shall thus have to admit that the cultural consequences of the Reformation were to a great extent, perhaps in the particular aspects with which we are dealing predominantly, *unforeseen* and even *unwished* for results of the labours of the reformers. They were often far removed from or even in *contradiction* to all that they themselves thought to attain. (PE: 89–90, emphasis added)

Note here Weber's stress on religious concerns such as salvation as the only motivation for these Protestants so that the 'consequences of the Reformation' are 'predominantly, unforeseen and even unwished for'. In this expression of religious meaning, Puritanical labour and the resultant 'worldly goods' are valued, but only as the means to grace and salvation. However, the pursuit of this religiously inscribed value of labour will have consequences that will lead to the abandonment of this religious worldview itself – it will lead to the spirit of capitalism.

The second point to be made flows from these quotations from Weber. Certainly the paradox of the Protestant Ethic thesis can be understood in the way it is taken up in the more standard interpretations of Weber, where the unforeseen result is just capitalism as today's dominant economic system with the question of meaning simply absent, i.e., the result is 'victorious capitalism' which partly has its origins in 'the spirit of religious asceticism' but 'needs its support no longer' (PE: 181–2). But, on the other hand, the argument can be seen to be about meaning, and the Protestant Ethic thesis might then be appreciated as providing the basic model of paradox that will be repeated throughout Weber's mature works. On this basis capitalism is meaningless in terms of religious questions of death and salvation but, crucially, its origins lie not just in religion itself but, more specifically, in the way that Protestantism will come to pursue the meaning of salvation through rationalised, mundane labour that will, partly, lead to the meaningless economic world of modernity. In *The Protestant Ethic and the Spirit of Capitalism* – the foundational text of Weber's most fecund period of theoretical production – we can therefore see the prime example of how the very pursuit of meaning will fatefully lead to the loss of that meaning.

At this stage we must turn back to the second long paradox of Western religion. Beyond this famous paradox of Protestantism and capitalism, Western religion is also consumed in a further, fateful paradox of extinguishing the aims of religion itself via the means used in the very pursuit of those ends. This is the second 'door' or sense of paradox that comes with Protestantism. The search for an answer to the problems of meaning – and here we will talk of life, death and suffering – is lost in the ultimate consistency of Calvinism. Only in the West would the means deployed to achieve the goal of comprehending the meaning of the cosmos ultimately result in a cosmos whose meaning cannot be known. Ascetic Protestantism is again the key element, not just because of its links to capitalism, but also because it will unleash a paradox on the level of meaning that is highly determinant of both the loss of religious meaning in modernity and the consequent shape of how ideal interests have to be met within modernity's meaninglessness. To understand why this specific example of paradox is so important to Weber, and Puritanism's role in such paradox, it is necessary to return to Weber's analysis of the world religions.

As stated in the last chapter, Weber's starting point is that there is a universal human need that initiates all religious rationalisation – humanity's quest for 'meaning' as it emerges from the:

> ... metaphysical needs of the human mind as it is driven to reflect on ethical and religious questions, driven not by material need but by an inner compulsion to understand the world as a *meaningful* cosmos and to take a stand towards it (ES: 499, emphasis added[10]).

Again, to repeat, these 'ethical and religious questions' will tend to revolve around the meaning of death and the presence of unjust suffering in the world (i.e., the 'problem of theodicy'), especially in the West. Nearly all religions will attempt to address these questions and will try to find some consistency in their outlooks, particularly when there is a strong intellectual influence in theological development (IR: 324).

With increasing rationalisation and the elimination of primitive magical notions, under 'the imperative of consistency', the problem of theodicy, in particular, became acute. In fact, 'the metaphysical conception of God, which the ineradicable demand for a theodicy called forth could produce only a few systems of ideas on the whole ... only three' (IEEWR: 275). Weber considered that Hinduism (with its many deities and the karma/caste relation), the clear dualism of Zoroastrianism, and the predestination of Calvinism, provided the only consistent solutions to the problem of theodicy (IEEWR: 275; IR: 358–9).

Much of Weber's empirical writings on religion can be regarded as an examination of the religious solutions to the questions of suffering and death, and their ramifications on life-conduct in their respective societies. His analyses suggest that, unlike other civilisations, the religious solution adopted in the West via Calvinism created paradoxes which would eventually deny the very possibility of asking the great religious questions regarding the meaning of the universe.

In the *Intermediary Reflection*, whilst discussing the tension between the ethic of brotherliness (the Christian ethical ideal) and the economic sphere, Weber tells us of another, deep 'paradox of the Puritan ethic of "vocation"':

> There have only been two consistent avenues for escaping the tension between religion and the economic world in a principled and *inward* manner: First, *the*

---

10 Also, as previously quoted, see: IEEWR: 281; IR: 353; Method: 81.

paradox of the Puritan ethic of 'vocation'.[11] As a religion of virtuosos, Puritanism renounced the universalism of love, and rationally routinised all work in the world into serving God's will and testing one's state of grace. God's will in its ultimate meaning was quite incomprehensible, yet it was the only positive will that could be known. In this respect, Puritanism accepted the routinisation of the economic cosmos, which, with the whole world, it devalued as creatural and depraved. This state of affairs appeared as God-willed, and as material and given for fulfilling one's duty. In the last resort, this meant in principle to renounce salvation as a goal attainable by man, that is, by everybody. It meant to renounce salvation in favour of the groundless and always particularised grace. *In truth, this standpoint of unbrotherliness was no longer a genuine 'religion of salvation'.* (IR: 332–3, emphasis added)

The paradox of Puritanism outlined here seems to imply that Puritanism, ostensibly a Christian doctrine, has most 'unchristian' consequences. Both brotherly love and the universality of salvation have been turned upside down in the Puritan, especially Calvinist, answer to the great religious questions. This solution – that God must already know who 'The Elect' are, that there is nothing one can do on this earth to alter this decision, that God's plan cannot really be known, that there can be no means of gaining access to God on this mundane earth (especially not through the offices of some church) – was a remarkably consistent answer when the basic Western assumptions of a unitary, all-powerful God in a disenchanted world are fully taken into account.[12]

---

11 The second avenue is via the mystical, acosmic (world-denying) disregard of economic reality. Weber also explicitly calls this alternative paradoxical – 'an acosmistic paradox' (ES: 633; also China: 185 on the 'paradoxes' of Taoism). Essentially, this paradox consists of the unconditional concern or love of the suffering other being pursued for the 'selfish' reasons of personal salvation (See ES: 632–3, 589; IR: 333). Again, at least from a Western, Christian perspective, the basic values of brotherliness are reversed in being consistently developed in these theologies. Mystic brotherliness will be discussed in detail in a following chapter.

12 These assumptions were developed at the very beginning of Western religious rationalisation in *Ancient Judaism*. Even at this early stage, paradoxes were becoming clear in Western religious rationalisation. For example, Judaism is involved in the: 'stupendous paradox that a god does not only fail to protect his chosen people against its enemies but allows them to fall, or pushes them himself, into ignominy and enslavement, yet is worshipped all the more ardently' (AJ: 364). Here the suffering of the Jewish people is made theologically problematic both because of the unique circumstances of the Jewish fate in Exile, but also under the momentum of disenchantment (AJ: 219, 222, 245) and the belief in a unitary God, which, for Weber, again explicitly results in 'paradox' due to 'the increasing universalisation of the conception of god' (AJ: 341–2). The basic twin parameters of Western religion are thus again stressed by Weber as crucial determinants of paradox. Also, these paradoxes will directly lead to an ethic of brotherliness (AJ: 342), as well as the consistent post-Exilic theodicy of Deutero-Isaiah where suffering, humility

Such a wonderfully consistent Christian worldview could not, however, provide a meaning for death which had to be renounced 'in principle ... as a goal attainable by man'. All that could be provided was a psychological certainty of grace as an answer to the fundamental question: 'Am I one of the elect?' (PE: 110). This certainty was made up of two factors: firstly, an unshakeable 'duty to consider oneself chosen, and to combat all doubts as temptations of the devil' (PE: 111); and secondly, such anxiety could be overcome through 'devotion to intense worldly activity' (PE: 112), or, in other words, vocational mundane labour. In such a situation, one of the most essential religious, human dilemmas is left unresolved through the search for meaning undertaken via religious rationalisation in the West. The question of the meaning of death, to which Christianity had always provided salvation and eternal life as the answers, is actually renounced as unknowable once the logic of Christian doctrine unfolds into its Calvinist form.

It is not the case that a sense of meaning is absent of course – quite the opposite. There is a clear injunction on how to lead a meaningful life: through the calling and mundane, rationalised labour. Tolstoy's question of 'What shall we do and how shall we live?' is given an unequivocal answer. Yet this life-conduct is undertaken because access to God's meaning about the path to salvation has been lost – the question of death is not answered. Indeed, the very fervour of the Puritan way of life is due to the overall meaninglessness for humanity of the world in which such a dutiful life has to be followed. This is how the paradox plays out in the case of Calvinist consistency: meaning as life-conduct in the mundane world depends on the meaninglessness of death.

The second great religious question, the problem of suffering, is treated similarly. Under Puritanism, paradoxically, the problem of suffering which began the long road of religious rationalisation will not be recognised as a problem at all, and the former Christian solution of an ethic based on brotherly love will be regarded as unethical. This process requires close scrutiny. We will briefly mention it here but brotherly love will be extensively examined in following chapters.

In the *Intermediary Reflection*, and elsewhere, the Christian tradition (at least) is said to have developed a universal ethic of brotherliness in the face of the suffering of the world (IR: 330). This constituted its answer to the question of how to deal with suffering within this increasingly disenchanted world under the rule of a unitary God. For Weber, the ethical content of this brotherliness depended on the maintenance of 'personal' as opposed to 'impersonal' relations between people. The actual person and their suffering are the immediate, direct concern in this ideal of love. Impersonality is at its most brutally unethical in the economic relations of

---

and the redeemer will become central and the covenant relegated to the periphery (AJ: 367–75). Weber has identified within this religion of salvation the paradoxical cracks that will expand so destructively in Puritanism. The model of paradox which he stressed in *The Protestant Ethic and the Spirit of Capitalism* and the *Intermediary Reflection* is shown in its nascent form in *Ancient Judaism*. Of all the secondary works on *Ancient Judaism*, only that of Schroeder (1992) analyses this important link.

capitalism (see ES: 636, 584–5; IR: 331). However, the impersonality of capitalism is almost matched by the internal logic of Protestantism, where, in religion itself, brotherly love can change into an impersonal, unbrotherly form. The result is that brotherliness has turned from an ethic of love into its opposite (IR: 338–9). Under Puritanism, the Elect would consider 'the sin of one's neighbour', not in terms of 'sympathetic understanding', but through 'hatred and contempt for him as an enemy of God bearing the signs of eternal damnation' (PE: 122).

The reversal of the Judaic/Christian ethical tradition can occur because this severely consistent solution to the problem of theodicy no longer recognises that there is such a problem to be solved. Protestantism leads to '[t]he complete elimination of the theodicy problem and of all those questions about the meaning of the world and life, which have tortured others' (PE: 109). The same logic of predestination which resulted in the paradox of salvation and drove the devout towards hard work and self-certainty of grace, also results in the idea that to help the suffering of others would be to question God's plan on earth (which ultimately cannot be known). In other words, there is no problem of suffering to prompt an ethical response of love. It must be God's will that this is so, and the right way of acting is only to devote oneself to vocational labour. Indeed, love is a distraction from such duty. It is in this sense that we can understand 'the paradox of the Puritan ethic of "vocation"' as a 'standpoint of unbrotherliness [that] was no longer a genuine "religion of salvation"'.

We might also now be able to grasp the sense and importance of some of the last words of the *Intermediary Reflection*, where these very themes are most clearly emphasised, before Weber launches into his long study of India. After briefly discussing the dualism of Zoroastrianism, he touches on Calvinism's response to the existence of evil within Christian doctrine:

> This less consistent form of dualism is the popular, world-wide conception of heaven and hell, which restores God's sovereignty over the evil spirit who is His creature, and thereby believes that divine omnipotence is saved. But, willy-nilly, it must then, overtly or covertly, sacrifice some of the divine love. For if the omniscience is maintained, the creation of a power of radical evil and the admission of sin, especially in communion with the eternity of hell's punishments for one of God's own and finite creatures and for finite sins, simply does not correspond to divine love. In that case, only a renunciation of benevolence is consistent.
>
> The belief in *predestination* realises this renunciation, in fact and with full consistency. Man's acknowledged incapacity to scrutinise the ways of God means that he renounces in a loveless clarity man's accessibility to any meaning of the world. This renunciation brought all problems of this sort to an end. (IR: 358–9, Weber's emphasis)

In 'loveless clarity' the world has become meaningless for humanity, and all these religious problems are no more. The questions of meaning, the very basis of

Western religion, are left behind by the sheer intellectual rigour and logical power of the religious solution. The very status of Calvinism as a religion is questionable once the fundamental religious anthropology has been transcended in this way. It is here that the depth of the paradox is most manifest. At the end of the Western rationalisation of religion, religion itself is dissolved in its own consistency.

A reminder must be made that this is only the fate of the most radically consistent form of Protestantism, and that, of course, other forms of Western religion still retain meaning. But from within the perspective of meaning, it should be clear why Weber gives so much emphasis to Protestantism, and Calvinism in particular – it is here, in religion itself, that one can further trace the threads in the weave of Western meaninglessness.

As a final note to this section on Protestant meaning, the two paradoxes that have been so far identified need to be drawn together. The strand of internal religious rationalisation can be isolated and has its own particular trajectory as an example of the paradox of meaning, but it is also tied together with the first paradox that we have examined: the Protestant/capitalist relation. As mentioned, one of the ways that the unbearable doctrine of predestination could be borne was through devoted, worldly labour, which promoted a self-confident certainty of grace; such mundane labour and its material results acted as a *demonstration* of a meaning for death – of salvation – within a world whose meaning could only lie with God and was, necessarily, beyond human comprehension. This paradox of meaning in Puritan theology, and its practical implications, resulted, then, in the dedicated, meaningful labour that would help establish capitalism – where any religious meaning, of course, would prove to be almost wholly absent. In other words, the very Protestant labour that, in part, would paradoxically lead to meaningless capitalism, was being pursued, with all its famous puritanical rigour, because it was the only way that ideal interests might be psychologically met within a world where, paradoxically, meaning could no longer be found.

It also follows, from within the perspective of meaning, that if the calling is still part of how meaning still manages to exist in modernity (as we will examine in the next few chapters), then this paradox of religion in the West, which spawned such an ethical regard for rationalised labour, is an important component in the shaping of how ideal interests are met in the modern world. The fate of meaning in our contemporary world is, partly, the outcome of this Puritan paradox.

So, the two paradoxes do complement each other; and both separately and together they help establish Weber's overall theory of Western meaning. Now, in order to add to this picture, we need to leave the religion of the West and consider another paradox of Western meaning.

The Paradox of Western Reason

Besides religion, the other long paradox of Western meaning occurs in reason itself, with its origin in Ancient Greece.

'Science as a Vocation', as we have seen, famously places science in contrast with Tolstoy in terms of the meaning of death (SV: 139) and the accompanying question of how life should be lived (SV: 143). In this lecture, Weber attempts to demonstrate how the development of science/intellectual reason itself leads to this state of ultimate meaninglessness.

Weber begins with the Greek discovery of the *concept*, which gave tremendous logical power and was pursued in the belief that it could provide the way to 'eternal truth', 'true being', 'how to act rightly in life and, above all, how to act as a citizen of the state. [It was] for these reasons one engaged in science' (SV: 141). Weber stresses here that science/intellectual reason, in its initial phases, was undertaken to answer Tolstoy's very question. After the 'concept', Weber lists the 'rational experiment' as 'the great tool of scientific work' (SV: 141). The Renaissance raised experiment 'to a principle of research' (SV: 141) and with Leonardo and musical innovators of the time, it provided the way to 'true art', 'true nature' and to 'the meaning of life' (SV: 142). Also, in the hands of the Puritans and other Protestants, it could even 'show the path to God' (SV: 142). It is, therefore, in the search for meaning that science began to unfurl its potent display of analytic power.

Today, however:

> Who – aside from certain big children who are indeed found in the natural sciences – still believes that the findings of [the natural sciences] could teach us anything about the *meaning* of the world? (SV: 142, Weber's emphasis)

Weber demonstrates in 'Science as a Vocation' that the great achievements in the early history of science were developed as part of the attempt to provide solutions to the Tolstoyan questions of life and death. Yet, as with the religious logic of consistent Protestantism, science has lost the ability to ask the very questions that began its development. The sheer logical power and consistency of the answers leave the questions behind. As in the Western religious sphere, science pursued the meaning of the world, and by its brilliantly argued conclusions, eliminated any rational basis for such a meaning. Weber has repeated the paradoxical view of the religion of the Occident in this account of science; indeed they will mesh at times and, in their final moments, combine to help form the overarching senselessness of modernity.

This dual paradox in religion and reason – of achieving meaninglessness in the very pursuit of meaning – can be looked at from another angle: disenchantment.[13]

---

13 As Schluchter (1979a: 46) notes, 'Weber tends to explain disenchantment in terms of the paradox of consequences in relation to intention – a perspective that plays a central role in his sociology'. Note also that the idea of disenchantment, and attempts to overcome it in modernity, will be discussed more fully in a later chapter. At this stage it is assumed that the complete removal of meaning from the cosmos is the full extent of scientific disenchantment, but sometimes disenchantment is understood more narrowly as just the removal of magic from the world. 'Science as a Vocation', arguably, makes the more comprehensive interpretation of disenchantment abundantly clear.

These wonderfully consistent, rationalised attempts at meaning were, to use the phrase already quoted: 'driven not by material need but by an inner compulsion to understand the world as a *meaningful* cosmos'. To be meaningful the cosmos must contain some presence of a purpose, of a comprehensible reason why things are as they are. In the radical disenchantment of the world found in Protestantism the meaning of the world exists beyond human comprehension; and with scientific disenchantment the world is finally stripped of anything that lies beyond the potential understanding of science/intellectual reason and in this way is rendered utterly meaningless (SV: 139).

Weber emphasises that this process happens in all religions through a process of intellectualisation by privileged strata. Under rationalised religious worldviews, life's meaning becomes a matter of life-conduct rather than magic.[14]

> As intellectualism suppresses beliefs in magic, the world's processes become disenchanted, lose their magical significance and henceforth simply 'are' or 'happen' but no longer signify anything. As a consequence, there is a growing demand that the world and the total pattern of life [life-conduct] be subject to an order that is significant and meaningful. (ES: 506)

Crucially, it is only in the West that demagicalisation becomes radically complete as opposed to the continuation of the 'magical garden' of the East (India: 336; China: 227; ES: 630; AJ: 222). The movement begins in ancient Judaism (AJ: 4, 219, 222, 394; also GEH: 360f) and gathers weight under the logic of the Christian, unitary, universal god with ethical demands. Yet compromises exist until Protestantism challenges the magic of the Catholic Church.

> That great historic process in the development of religions, the elimination of magic from the world which had begun with the old Hebrew prophets and, in conjunction with Hellenistic scientific thought, had repudiated all magical means to salvation as superstition and sin, came here to its logical conclusion. The genuine Puritan even rejected all signs of religious ceremony at the grave and buried his nearest and dearest without song or ritual in order that no superstition, no trust in the effects of magical and sacramental forces on salvation, should creep in. (PE: 105)

Calvinist predestination will take this process to its logical and paradoxical conclusion. As we have seen, 'Man's acknowledged incapacity to scrutinise the

---

14 Magic tends to be left to the non-privileged but remains part of the overall cosmic order, and might still play a limited role for the intellectual strata. In *The Religion of China* Weber shows how Confucianism in China is aligned with Greek polis beliefs on this point (China: 175ff, 194, 229); and, in *The Religion of India*, Weber discusses how the Brahman caste in Hinduism has a complex mixture of incorporation and rejection of magic (e.g., India: 139, where Confucian and Greek attitudes are again included).

ways of God means that he renounces in a loveless clarity man's accessibility to any meaning of the world'. The world is without any magical or enchanted means to meaning when God's ways cannot be known.

However, there is still the idea that the world is God-created and that labour in this mundane world can exhibit grace – there is a divine meaning to the cosmos even if it now lies beyond any human understanding. The parallel, and sometimes interlinked, process of scientific disenchantment loses even this last place for God:

> The tension between religion and intellectual knowledge definitely comes to the fore wherever rational, empirical knowledge has consistently worked through the disenchantment of the world and its transformation into a causal mechanism. For then science encounters the claims of the ethical postulate that the world is God-ordained, and hence somehow [a] *meaningfully* and ethically orientated, cosmos. (IR: 350–51; also ES: 450–51, Weber's emphasis)

In principle nothing now exists beyond the possibility of rational understanding. As Weber puts it:

> The increasing intellectualisation and rationalisation do *not,* therefore, indicate an increased and general knowledge of the conditions under which one lives.
>
> It means something else, namely, the knowledge or belief that if one but wished one *could* learn it at any time. Hence, it means that principally there are no mysterious incalculable forces that come into play, but rather that one can, in principle, master all things by calculation. This means that the world is disenchanted. (SV: 139, Weber's emphasis)

Part of the story of the Western search for meaning, therefore, tells how the use of reason and science will so radically disenchant the world that the very idea of a meaningful cosmos becomes nonsensical and 'irrational'.

Conclusion

In sum, there are fundamental, unresolvable paradoxes to be found in Western religion and science so that, Weber argues, the pursuit of meaning results in meaninglessness, or, to put it another way, the way ideal interests were met in fact led to the inability to meet those very ideal interests. The universal paradoxes of religion – of monks and charisma – lose meaning to various degrees, and this loss can be appreciated within a lifetime. However, in the West these long paradoxes in science and Protestant religion do much more – the result is capitalism, and meaninglessness on a scale larger than ever previously experienced. Modernity for Weber is, partly, to be understood in these terms.

Chapter 3
The Economic Value-Sphere

Introduction to the Value-Spheres

The paradoxical outcomes of the search for meaning in Western history have played a significant part in rendering modernity meaningless. It does not follow, however, that the concepts found in Weber's work, such as ideal interests and culture, no longer apply. Rather, Weber provides an understanding of modernity based on the continuing paradoxical outcomes found in modern searches for meaning.

Without the unifying effect of enchanted, cosmic meaning the modern world is structured as a series of five competing, separate value-spheres: the economic, intellectual, political, aesthetic and erotic.[1] It is through this theory of the value-spheres that Weber will try to understand the continuing search for meaning in modernity. Essentially, instead of a coherent life-conduct based on religion and set within the parameters of a meaningful cosmos, different sections of the social whole – the value-spheres – offer a new, if limited and conditional, sense of meaning.

There are different levels of meaning that can be achieved by following the values on offer in each of the spheres. Many common engagements with the value-spheres exist where meaning is absent or notional, e.g., in shopping or negotiating a bank loan in the economic sphere; or renewing a driver's licence through the state bureaucracy in the political sphere. The value structure of each sphere must still be adhered to even at this low level, but what Weber displays for us are those engagements with the value-spheres when, to its maximum extent, meaning can be gained by pursuing the varied values on offer. So, the examples of this maximised, if paradoxical, meaning that Weber provides are: the artist (and, to a slightly lesser degree, the connoisseur of high cultural taste) in the aesthetic sphere; the vocational scientist/academic in the value-sphere of science/intellectual reason; the elected politician in the value-sphere of politics; and romantic lovers within the erotic value-sphere. Weber also gives an account of the maximum meaning still available in the value-sphere of the economy, i.e., within capitalism, but it is shown to be relatively weak in comparison with the others.[2]

---

1   The family might also be regarded as a value-sphere (see IR: 328–30). However, it is scarcely developed by Weber and will have to be left out of the current analysis.

2   Note that, as is usual in Weber, these accounts are all 'ideal-types' and are given a rational purity that will not be found in empirical reality. Also, the idea of 'meaning' being discussed is oriented to those ultimate questions of death and suffering, even when the religious context, wherein such topics can be made explicit, is absent.

The values of meaning that are followed in each sphere are themselves the result of two processes that result from the rationalisation process that has rendered the world disenchanted and meaningless.

Firstly, new kinds of meaning are formed in modernity:

> ... [the] fate of an epoch which has eaten at the tree of knowledge is that it must know that it cannot learn the *meaning* of the world from the results of its analysis, be it ever so perfect, it must rather be in a position to create this meaning itself. (Method: 57, Weber's emphasis)

If intellectual reason can no longer give answers to the questions of meaning – it has lost religious meaning and, in this sense, has 'eaten at the tree of knowledge' – then this age must conjure up some replacements. To this effect, in the argument to follow we will see: how a new form of 'polytheism' arises (represented, in part, by the competing value-spheres); how politics gives meaning to the 'cause'; as well as how new kinds of 'salvation' develop in the aesthetic and erotic value-spheres.

Secondly, since such rationalisation is always necessarily incomplete, the irrational residues of the long intellectual path to meaninglessness are, partly, these values that must be followed in each of the spheres of modernity. In *Introduction to the Economic Ethic of the World Religions* Weber indicates how this process has played out:

> The general result of the modern form of thoroughly rationalising the conception of the world and of the way of life, theoretically and practically, in a purposive manner, has been that religion has been shifted into the realm of the irrational. This has been more the case the further the purposive type of rationalisation has progressed, if one takes the standpoint of an intellectual articulation of an image of the world. This shift of religion into the irrational realm has occurred for several reasons. On the one hand, the calculation of consistent rationalism has not easily come out even with nothing left over. In music, the Pythagorean 'comma' resisted complete rationalisation oriented to tonal physics. The various great systems of music of all peoples and ages have differed in the manner in which they have either covered up or bypassed this inescapable irrationality or, on the other hand, put irrationality into the service of the richness of tonalities. The same has seemed to happen to the theoretical conception of the world, only far more so; and above all, it has seemed to happen to the rationalisation of practical life. The various great ways of leading a rational and methodical life have been characterised by irrational presuppositions, which have been accepted simply as 'given' and which have been incorporated into such ways of life. What these presuppositions have been is historically and socially determined, at least to a very large extent, through the peculiarity of those strata that have been the carriers of the ways of life during its formative and decisive period. The *interest* situation of these strata, as determined socially and psychologically, has made for their peculiarity, as we here understand it. (IEEWR: 281, Weber's emphasis)

In this statement Weber is indicating how a practical, methodical life in modern times, with religion pushed away from the dominant social structures such as the economy, law and the academy, must necessarily fall back on irrational assumptions that themselves have been formed during the great intellectualisation of the West. To put this point in slightly different Weberian terms, the long paradox of Western meaning has left behind a set of separate values that will help to form the content of ideal interests in meaningless modernity.

The most important of these irrational elements that must be assumed in the practical life of the rationalised value-spheres comes from the history of Protestant rationalisation. This religious source of modernity is understood as an ongoing determinant of meaning, for not only is the Protestant tradition one of the significant factors behind modern meaninglessness, as we have just seen, but it also provides a source of ongoing meaning at the level of the internal workings of the value-spheres. The crucial factor here is, of course, the vocation or calling. As against the notion that ideal interests can only be met through a return to religion that can only now reside within the irrational borderlands of modernity, Weber will stress that the calling can still provide meaning to routinised, everyday life in terms of methodical, rationalised work and in terms of certain deeds or tasks. Protestantism, then, is not just a source of the senselessness of modern life, but it provides an ongoing tradition of meaning in tasks and ordinary work, even when a religious framework is no longer present. A more detailed account of the calling will be given immediately below and then in this chapter and the two to follow all the value-spheres will be considered in terms of how they have been affected by the Protestant heritage, either by incorporating some notion of the calling, or by reacting against the methodical, rational patterns of work that vocation entails.

However, before the calling and the value-spheres can be discussed in detail, a crucial division in the way meaning is manifested in this structure has to be initially stated. On the one hand, within each value-sphere there will be ways that the ideal interest in the problem of death and how to live in the world will be given some expression, and this is what we will consider in this chapter and the next two. On the other hand, the problem of theodicy – of unjust suffering in the world – will in fact be excluded by each of the value-spheres, and, consequently, the ethic concerned with such suffering will have a quite different presence in modernity. This second area of meaning – the ethic of brotherliness – will be taken up in a later section of the argument.

So, with this division in mind, we will concentrate on the first way ideal interests are expressed, or partly met, within the various value-spheres: giving meaning to those basic Tolstoyan questions of death and how to live in the world. Paradox is still the key and works in these cases on a double level. Ideal interests and meaning will be pursued, in different ways, in each of the value-spheres but on the first most general level such pursuit must fail to recover the meaning of death and life that only religion can usually provide. On this level the striving for meaning must always end in meaninglessness – yet on the second level some measure of meaning will be found and followed. Indeed, the value-sphere structure is set up by Weber to exhibit such meaning within meaninglessness. Now death can still be regarded as the orientating ideal interest on this level – even when death is meaningless – in two senses: first, the meaning still present in some of the spheres will be based around the calling which has its origins in Puritan notions of salvation from death; and, second, a new, fake form of 'death' is in fact formed in modernity which will offer a sense of salvation within meaningless modernity itself. What we will then find is that these different glimpses of meaning within each sphere will themselves be subject to even further paradoxical loss, i.e., meaning will be lost in its very pursuit even within the overall meaninglessness of the modern world, although the degree of paradox will vary sharply between the various spheres. It is in this sense that paradox might be seen as the very logic of modernity for Weber.

A brief comment needs to be given on how Weber's texts will be used. Although the value-sphere structure is laid out most plainly in the *Intermediary Reflection* and *Economy and Society* within his explicit sociology of religion, this commentary is so densely and incompletely put that one has to go beyond such texts to make sense of Weber's argument. As we have noted, the usual tendency, even amongst those interpreters concerned with meaning, is to repeat the formulas and terms of the *Intermediary Reflection* and then leave Weber behind in search of explanation through the ideas of other theorists. In contrast, to repeat the point, Weber's ideas will be understood through reference to what Weber himself has said on these topics throughout his writings. An overall theoretical unity will be assumed that permits us to pull together these, often scattered, remarks in order to see what Weber himself has argued. This is in no way a straightforward exercise, but it will be shown that Weber does in fact display a remarkable consistency that allows a coherent, complex theory to be constructed.

For this chapter and the next, besides the *Intermediary Reflection* and sections from *Economy and Society*, the texts that will provide most of the content are *The Protestant Ethic and the Spirit of Capitalism*, 'Science as a Vocation' and 'Politics as a Vocation'. It will be assumed that in the way each of these texts specifically targets the economy, science/intellectual knowledge and politics, they are talking about a particular value-sphere.[3] We will see that when all these texts are considered together they lay out how meaning in modernity becomes this logic of paradox.

The value-sphere that will be taken up in this chapter is the economic, then, in the next chapter, the scientific and political spheres will be examined, and the last two – the irrational spheres of art and the erotic – will be considered in the

---

3   However, it should be noted that there is an assumption being made here that the 'science' ('*Wissenschaft*') of 'Science as a Vocation' is talking about the same thing as the intellectual sphere ('*Reich des denkenden Erkennens*') that is specified in the *Intermediary Reflection*. It is usually accepted that both texts are discussing the same area, though with very different emphases. There is considerable theoretical overlap between the texts, and even occasional word for word mirroring between 'Science as a Vocation' and the *Intermediary Reflection* in this regard.

chapter that follows. Note that for reasons of clarity this ordering of the value-spheres is slightly different to the one used by Weber.[4] So, after a brief excursion on the nature of vocation, we will first turn our attention to the value-sphere of the economy.

The Calling

The Protestant idea of the calling or vocation (*Beruf*) still has a meaningful presence at the very heart of the secular modern world. As noted, we are just taking Weber at his word here since the calling is the very *spirit* of *The Protestant Ethic and the Spirit of Capitalism*, and the two famous lectures on science and politics specify in their titles that *vocation* will be their concern.

The Protestant Ethic and the Spirit of Capitalism spends a good deal of time mapping out this notion (which, as with all of Weber's ideas, is the subject of widespread critical commentary). There are two basic aspects to the Protestant calling which need careful delineation for the modern presence of *Beruf* to be more easily appreciated: firstly, the calling is a task set by God for worldly activity; and, secondly, the calling is rational, methodical labour for the glory of God. Weber will emphasise one of these aspects over the other in his discussion of each of the value-spheres of the economy, science and politics. However, Weber does us no favours in that he does not clearly delineate the two meanings of the vocation and we will have to fill in some of the gaps in Weber's actual account in order to construct an overall argument on the nature of the calling. For this reason it is easy to understand the hostile reception that this area of Weber's theory has sometimes received from within the secondary literature.

It should also be noted here that each part of the calling is manifested in the two common ways that vocation is understood and expressed in ordinary, modern life: the God-given task as the finding of one's vocation in terms of a specific job which seems somehow to have been pre-ordained on an individual, internal level; and the value of hard, mundane work in the commonly termed 'Protestant work ethic'. In a way, the following argument is just an explanation of these two

---

4 There are problems that face any use of the *Intermediary Reflection* and its theory of the value-spheres. The English translators have consistently tried to add headings to the various sections in the text. The value-sphere headings are clear until the end when the intellectual sphere comes after the aesthetic and erotic and tends to blur into other arguments about cultural values. Gerth and Mills label the whole section 'The Intellectual Sphere' but other translators such as Whimster have divided the section into two (Whimster, 2004, 238ff). Also, the variation in the order that will be used, in contrast to the way it is presented in *Intermediary Reflection* itself, is to put the intellectual sphere before the aesthetic and erotic spheres and thus link the intellectual to the economic and political spheres as part of rationalised modernity. This strategy uses 'Science as a Vocation' as part of the value-sphere theory, and 'Science as a Vocation' clearly links the intellectual value-sphere into the rationalised world more clearly than in the *Intermediary Reflection*.

everyday notions, (and, whose current expression, it should also be noted, is almost certainly reflexively derived, in part, from Weberian theory itself.) The fact that the vocation has this common understanding might help explain the relative lack of theoretical attention that Weber gives to this issue. In the Vocation lectures especially, Weber can assume the audience has this common knowledge so he has no need to say anything more about it.

So, how does Weber theorise the concept of vocation? On the first aspect – the task given by God – Weber states:

> Now it is unmistakable that even in the German word *Beruf*, and perhaps still more clearly in the English *calling*, a religious conception, that of a task set by God, is at least suggested. The more emphasis is put upon the word in a concrete case, the more evident is the connotation. And if we trace the history of the word through the civilised languages, it appears that neither the predominantly Catholic peoples nor those of classical antiquity have possessed any expression of similar connotation for what we know as a calling (in the sense of a life-task, a definite field in which to work) … [and which] speedily took on its present meaning in the everyday speech of all Protestant peoples.[5] (PE: 79, Weber's emphasis)

Here the religious origins of the German and English terms are emphasised as having an ongoing, everyday connotation. The central point that Weber goes on to stress about the calling as the God-given task is the Protestant shift to mundane, worldly activity as the way to achieve grace. Instead of prayer to saints, or monastic devotion separated from the world of ordinary human affairs, it is in this world itself that the most godly life should be lived. There had been different forms of the calling before the Reformation:

> But at least one thing was unquestionably new: the valuation of the fulfilment of duty in worldly affairs as the highest form which the moral activity of the individual could assume. This it was which inevitably gave every-day worldly activity a religious significance, and which first created the conception of a calling in this sense. The conception of the calling thus brings out that central dogma of all Protestant denominations which the Catholic division of ethical precepts into *command* and *recommendation* discards. The only way of living acceptably to God was not to surpass worldly morality in monastic asceticism, but solely through the fulfilment of the obligations imposed upon the individual by his position in the world. That was his calling. (PE: 80, Weber's emphasis)

The first part of the calling – which is still with us – is the task given by God which can be fulfilled only in worldly activity.

---

5 It is unclear how far this everyday understanding might be restricted just to 'Protestant peoples'.

The second aspect of the calling emerges when, in order to reach the pertinent sense of the calling that will inform the spirit of capitalism, Weber moves on from this initial definition past Luther's traditional understanding to Calvinist predestination and its emphasis on a particular form of labour in the world as an exhibition of one's state of grace.

> What God demands is not labour in itself, but rational labour in a calling. In the Puritan concept of the calling the emphasis is always placed on this methodical character of worldly asceticism, not, as with Luther, on the acceptance of the lot which God has irretrievably assigned to man. (PE: 161–2)

Such methodical, rational labour must be self-monitored, life-long and is necessary for all who would show certainty of their own salvation:

> On the other hand, though the means by which it was attained differed for different doctrines, it could not be guaranteed by any magical sacraments, by relief in the confession, nor by individual good works. That was only possible by proof in a specific type of conduct unmistakably different from the way of life of the natural man. From that followed for the individual an incentive methodically to supervise his own state of grace in his own conduct, and thus to penetrate it with asceticism. But, as we have seen, this ascetic conduct meant a rational planning of the whole of one's life in accordance with God's will. And this asceticism was no longer an *opus supererogationis*, but something which could be required of everyone who would be certain of salvation. The religious life of the saints, as distinguished from the natural life, was – the most important point – no longer lived outside the world in monastic communities, but within the world and its institutions. This rationalisation of conduct within this world, but for the sake of the world beyond, was the consequence of the concept of calling of ascetic Protestantism.
>
> Christian asceticism, at first fleeing from the world into solitude, had already ruled the world which it had renounced from the monastery and through the Church. But it had, on the whole, left the naturally spontaneous character of daily life in the world untouched. Now it strode into the market-place of life, slammed the door of the monastery behind it, and undertook to penetrate just that daily routine of life with its methodicalness, to fashion it into a life in the world, but neither of nor for this world. (PE: 153–4)

Undertaken for other-worldly ends – 'neither of nor for this world' – this labour tended to be set within the economy because the creation of wealth could in fact be understood as for the glory of God. Wealth was certainly a danger and capitalism a clear source of moral degradation, as Wesley has reminded us, but the gaining of wealth, if it was based on and did not alter this methodical duty, was a sign of being one of the Elect, and conversely, poverty a sign of potential damnation.

> Wealth is thus bad ethically only in so far as it is a temptation to idleness and sinful enjoyment of life, and its acquisition is bad only when it is with the purpose of later living merrily and without care. But as a performance of duty in a calling it is not only morally permissible, but actually enjoined. The parable of the servant who was rejected because he did not increase the talent which was entrusted to him seemed to say so directly. To wish to be poor was, it was often argued, the same as wishing to be unhealthy; it is objectionable as a glorification of works and derogatory to the glory of God. (PE: 163; also PE: 118)

The calling under this Puritan determination is about the devotion to economic labour as part of a methodical, self-scrutinising life which will be taken up, without its religious meaning, in the maxims of Benjamin Franklin and will come to form the core of the ongoing 'spirit of capitalism'. It is this sense of the calling that Weber is using when he so famously states that the 'Puritan wanted to work in a calling; we are forced to do so' (PE: 181), as will be discussed further in the next section. Moreover, the now common notion of the Protestant work ethic is what is on display here. However, what is no longer explicitly present is the calling as the God-given task.

This second sense of the calling marks the fateful character of the economic order of capitalism but is extended as a presence to the social order more widely:

> One of the fundamental elements of the spirit of modern capitalism, and not only of that but of all modern culture: rational conduct on the basis of the idea of the calling, was born – that is what this discussion has sought to demonstrate – from the spirit of Christian asceticism. (PE: 180)

The implications of this extension of the vocation into culture more generally will be shown as the pieces of Weber's overall theory of meaning start to fall into place.

The Economic Sphere

The understanding of modernity in terms of value-spheres comes late in Weber's life in the *Intermediary Reflection* and *Economy and Society*. Yet it is part of his sociology of religion and undoubtedly assumes *The Protestant Ethic and the Spirit of Capitalism* (with the 1920 version published in *GARS* with the *Intermediary Reflection*). To comprehend how the economic value-sphere works we need to return to *The Protestant Ethic and the Spirit of Capitalism*. In this famous text we have seen how the long paradoxes of religion have unfolded, but what meaning has become as a result of this process needs now to be explained, and to do this we will have to address a phrase that has long been known for being troublesome: 'the spirit of capitalism'.

Before taking on this task let us just sum up the theoretical background of this topic. The economic value-sphere – a concept that is part of Weber's understanding of meaning – is the partial result of the long paradox of religion with the calling as its central concept. The religious meaning of death has been lost but a sense of vocational meaning still lingers within the value-spheres of modernity. However, in the economic value-sphere Weber will only stress the rational labour part of the calling, and the God-ordained task is left out of what pure economic labour might be able to salvage from the Protestant, vocational heritage of meaning. The argument in *The Protestant Ethic and the Spirit of Capitalism* had put the stress on the Calvinist view of the calling as that which can be seen as active in capitalism, and in the Calvinist worldview the calling will predominantly be about the ascetic life-long devotion to mundane, routinised work, as we have seen, and where the holy task fades away, on Weber's account. The calling that is inherent in the capitalist economy – the *spirit* of capitalism – will therefore contain only this limited sense of vocational meaning when compared to the value-spheres of politics and science where, as we will see, it is the task, not the labour, that is predominant. So, bearing this point in mind, how does labour in the economic value-sphere work in terms of the paradox of meaning?

The paradox here can be understood in terms of means and ends. Economic activity in the West had meaning but this has been lost in the very pursuit of that meaning. Without the meaning provided by religion (however this is itself caught up in its own paradoxical development), the economic labour that has emerged from Protestantism is just the means without its former ends – and these means now become the ends as part of this separate value-sphere of the economy. These ends of the economy – once the means to meaning in Protestantism – are summed up with the maxims of Benjamin Franklin that Weber lists at the start of *The Protestant Ethic and the Spirit of Capitalism* (such as 'Time is money'). That is, money-making through methodical dutiful labour becomes the end to be followed (PE: 53, 70).

Two quotes from *The Protestant Ethic and the Spirit of Capitalism* plainly make this point.

> The peculiarity of this philosophy of avarice appears to be the ideal of the honest man of recognised credit, and above all the idea of a duty of the individual toward the increase of his capital, which is assumed as *an end in itself*. Truly what is here preached is not simply a means of making one's way in the world, but a peculiar ethic. The infraction of its rules is treated not as foolishness but as forgetfulness of duty. That is the essence of the matter. It is not mere business astuteness, that sort of thing is common enough, it is an ethos. (PE: 51, emphasis added)

Also:

> In fact, the *summum bonum* of this ethic, the earning of more and more money, combined with the strict avoidance of all spontaneous enjoyment of life ... is

thought of so purely *as an end in itself*[6] that from the point of view of the happiness of, or utility to, the single individual, it appears entirely transcendental and absolutely irrational. Man is dominated by the making of money, by acquisition as the ultimate purpose of life. (PE: 53, emphasis added)

Yet this economic labour, although now meaningless in terms of religious salvation from death, is still determined by its religious formation in Protestantism. It cannot but be a striving for meaning; it cannot lose the fact that these ends of capitalism were once the means to grace. This is why Weber calls this economic duty an ethic or ethos in the above quote; and it is especially why he devotes so much time to understanding this modern economic ethic in terms of vocation or calling.

So, for Weber:

The earning of money within the modern economic order is, so long as it is done legally, the result and the expression of virtue and proficiency in a calling; and this virtue and proficiency are, as it is now not difficult to see, the real Alpha and Omega of Franklin's ethic. (PE: 53)

This devotion – in the sense of the calling – to the duty of honest hard work and the making of money as an end in itself is the spirit of capitalism.

From these points the economic value-sphere can be seen as a place of paradox. Meaning and ideal interests are still at work in the economic sphere, but, within the fateful meaninglessness of modernity, work and money will be pursued as if they are meaningful ends in themselves, but such values have only had meaning as the means to a now lost end of religious meaning. So this notion that the means have become the ends is an indication of not only meaninglessness, but also the continuation of a diminished form of meaning as vocation; or, in other words, the calling is sustained into modern economic life in a reduced form, yet to retain the term 'calling' is to indicate that a sense of meaning is still part of what capitalist labour has become.

This means/ends paradox might be further understood by looking at the justifications that are given for these values of endless labour and money-making, and the accompanying sense that this ethos is worthwhile. In other words, this work is still done in terms of spirit and vocation, in the sense that it must mean something, and Weber traces out the justifications that have been given for this pursuit of meaning beyond its original religious understanding. What Weber shows is that there has been a diminution of meaning, even at this level of means as ends; that is, even after the loss of religious meaning the values of the economic sphere were still followed and talked about as if they still had significant meaning. But even this restricted sense of meaning is itself lessened so that by Weber's day justifications for the capitalist ethos are almost impossible to give, and the

---

6 Also Weber sees the calling of capitalism as involving 'labour as an end in itself' (PE: 63).

vocational sense of labour is more assumed rather than followed as an articulated ethical duty. This is one way that the economic value-sphere suffers a paradox of meaning from within – how meaning is diminished/lost within meaninglessness.

In this regard, *The Protestant Ethic and the Spirit of Capitalism* begins with the confident articulations of the capitalist ethos exhibited in Franklin's series of maxims. Weber tells us how Franklin, who had just emerged from the time of religious understanding, gives a justification for this dutiful life:

> Benjamin Franklin himself, although he was a colourless deist, answers in his autobiography with a quotation from the Bible, which his strict Calvinistic father drummed into him again and again in his youth: 'Seest thou a man diligent in his business? He shall stand before kings'. (PE: 53)

Franklin is harking back to the religious beliefs of his youth that he has outgrown, although the stated Biblical quotation, it might be interpreted, gives promise of highly secular honours. Weber goes on to list other ways that Franklin will validate the following of his ethos. For example, Franklin will admit to the 'irrational sense of a job well done' (PE: 71); and there are often-stated economic benefits to the community:[7]

> Labour in the service of a rational organisation for the provision of humanity with material goods has without doubt always appeared to representatives of the capitalistic spirit as one of the most important purposes of their life-work. It is only necessary, for instance, to read Franklin's account of his efforts in the service of civic improvements in Philadelphia clearly to apprehend this obvious truth. And the joy and pride of having given employment to numerous people, of having had a part in the economic progress of his home town in the sense referring to figures of population and volume of trade which capitalism associated with the word, all these things obviously are part of the specific and undoubtedly idealistic ['*idealistisch*'] satisfactions in life to modern men of business. (PE: 76)

Here, at the beginning of the spirit of capitalism, there is a strong sense of meaning, with an accompanying emotional state ('joy', 'pride', satisfaction'), as well as a series of well-articulated justifications and prescriptions formulated by Franklin. The religious sense is still near and able to be called upon, despite the fact that it cannot be the basis for the new ethos. So, even though the means are now the ends, these ends are understood and talked about as if they still had something like the meaning of old.

However, despite the continuation of some of these reasons for a lifetime of devotion to the capitalist ethos (e.g., in the benefits to the community), this early

---

7 'Of course, the desire for the power and recognition which the mere fact of wealth brings plays its part' (PE: 70).

exuberance of meaning, however misplaced, is overtaken by something much less. Any links with religion will be foregone and it will become difficult to give any validation for this pursuit of money and endless work. Indeed, by Weber's time, such labour and wealth might, perhaps, be given a hard-pressed justification in terms of an ethic benefitting the family. Weber states that:

> Any relationship between religious beliefs and conduct is generally absent, and where any exists, at least in Germany, it tends to be of the negative sort. The people filled with the spirit of capitalism today tend to be indifferent, if not hostile, to the Church. The thought of the pious boredom of paradise has little attraction for their active natures; religion appears to them as a means of drawing people away from labour in this world. If you ask them what is the meaning of their restless activity, why they are never satisfied with what they have, thus appearing so senseless to any purely worldly view of life, they would perhaps give the answer, if they know any at all: 'to provide for my children and grandchildren'. (PE: 70)

Increasingly then, the 'restless', 'senseless' nature of this economic activity is becoming more apparent; the confident proclamations of Franklin are in decline; and, importantly, the capitalist ethos is more and more something that is unquestionably assumed rather than consciously undertaken. These points are emphasised when this last quote goes on to say:

> But more often and, since that motive is not peculiar to them, but was just as effective for the traditionalist, more correctly, simply: that business with its continuous work has become a necessary part of their lives. That is in fact the only possible motivation, but it at the same time expresses what is, seen from the view-point of personal happiness, so irrational about this sort of life, where a man exists for the sake of his business, instead of the reverse. (PE: 70)

At the end of *The Protestant Ethic and the Spirit of Capitalism* this is put bluntly:

> Where the fulfilment of the calling cannot directly be related to the highest spiritual and cultural values, or when, on the other hand, it need not be felt simply as economic compulsion, the individual generally abandons the attempt to justify it at all. In the field of its highest development, in the United States, the pursuit of wealth, stripped of its religious and ethical meaning, tends to become associated with purely mundane passions, which often actually give it the character of sport.[8] (PE: 182)

---

8   Weber's footnote here is worth quoting: '"Couldn't the old man be satisfied with his $75,000 a year and rest? No! The frontage of the store must be widened to 400 feet. Why? That beats everything, he says. In the evening when his wife and daughter read together, he wants to go to bed. Sundays he looks at the clock every five minutes to see when the day

Here at the end, the 'fulfilment of the calling', which has been 'stripped of its religious and ethical meaning', is, generally, not able to be given any vindication, or it becomes regarded as just a game. In a sense, there is a truth in this self-understanding of the spirit of capitalism: these economic ends finally cannot escape the fact that they are only the means to ends that are now lost. Moreover, the paradox of meaning is in evidence: from Franklin's confident, ethical prescriptions of how to conduct one's life, meaning has been fatefully lost as it has still been pursued in the economic activity itself. Or, to put it another way, vocational, rationalised labour is still undertaken but not only is the original religious meaning lost, but further attempts to provide ethical meaning for such work have necessarily faded.[9]

If this lessening of ethical validation from Franklin's time suggests one paradox of meaning within the meaninglessness of the economic value-sphere, a second paradox is also present in Weber's account in *The Protestant Ethic and the Spirit of Capitalism*. This paradox starts to become apparent in the last quotation when Weber gives a three-fold approach to the calling in capitalism. Firstly, there are some who will undertake such mundane labour with the 'highest spiritual values' still intact, i.e., those very few who still maintain religious beliefs that are in some manner allied with the original Puritan worldview. Secondly, there are the businessmen and businesswomen who take up and follow this kind of work as meaningful, but who now cannot give any worthwhile justification for following such a 'restless' ethos, as we have just discussed. And thirdly, there are those who follow this way of work because of 'economic compulsion' – and it is here that the second paradox can be identified. What is being indicated is an aspect of the economic value-sphere that increases as religious and ethical meaning fades: the fateful, necessary nature of this 'spirit' that forces itself upon those who labour in capitalism. This point is even more plainly stressed by Weber when he states:

> Still less, naturally, do we maintain that a *conscious* acceptance of these ethical maxims on the part of the individuals, entrepreneurs or labourers, in modern capitalistic enterprises, is a condition of the further existence of present-day capitalism. The capitalistic economy of the present day is an immense cosmos into which the individual is born, and which presents itself to him, at least as an individual, as an unalterable order of things in which he must live. It forces the individual, in so far as he is involved in the system of market relationships, to conform to capitalistic rules of action. The manufacturer who in the long run acts counter to these norms, will just as inevitably be eliminated from the

---

will be over – what a futile life!" In these terms the son-in-law (who had emigrated from Germany) of the leading dry-goods man of an Ohio city expressed his judgment of the latter, a judgment which would undoubtedly have seemed simply incomprehensible to the old man. A symptom of German lack of energy' (PE: 283n).

9 Although, as noted, some of these validations are, of course, still employed, e.g., the benefit to society and family.

economic scene as the worker who cannot or will not adapt himself to them will be thrown into the streets without a job. (PE: 54–5, emphasis added)

Some famous words at the end of *The Protestant Ethic and the Spirit of Capitalism* reiterate this point:

> The Puritan wanted to work in a calling; we are forced to do so. For when asceticism was carried out of monastic cells into everyday life, and began to dominate worldly morality, it did its part in building the tremendous cosmos of the modern economic order. This order is now bound to the technical and economic conditions of machine production which today determine the lives of all the individuals who are born into this mechanism, not only those directly concerned with economic acquisition, with irresistible force.[10] (PE: 181)

For Weber the calling is no longer a matter of choice and agency, as it was at the time of its Puritan origins – it is part of the fact of capitalism. If the world was changed – albeit unintentionally – by the Puritan's conscious devotion to work as a vocation, the unalterable economic value-sphere that resulted now demands the calling as a condition of entry (at least ideal-typically).

However, it is not just the loss of Puritan meaning that is at stake here; it also applies to the first paradox of meaning within meaninglessness – from the time of Franklin's maxims to the diminished, often mute, acceptance of the calling. With the loss of the religious Puritan meaning, coupled with the fading of the later ethical validations that follow from Franklin, the fateful character of capitalism increases for Weber. Although this 'economic compulsion' would have always applied to some degree, stripped bare now of almost all justification, the vocation of work is increasingly 'forced' upon all who enter the economic sphere – one must 'conform to capitalistic rules of action'. This fateful characteristic of the calling extends the paradoxical loss of meaning to its limit: for those who have vocational duty forced upon them and feel no sense of the vocation as something that, in some sense, is still their own (even if it cannot be articulated or can only by understood as sport) the meaninglessness of the vocation is at its most extreme. Weber gives the clearest example when he discusses the fate of this meaning for labourers in capitalism:

> Furthermore, one may well doubt to what extent the joy of the mediæval craftsman in his creation, which is so commonly appealed to, was effective as a psychological motive force. Nevertheless, there is undoubtedly something in that thesis. But in any case asceticism certainly deprived all labour of this

---

10 Also, Weber notes: 'Whoever does not adapt his manner of life to the conditions of capitalistic success must go under, or at least cannot rise. But these are phenomena of a time in which modern capitalism has become dominant and has become emancipated from its old supports' (PE: 72).

worldly attractiveness, today for ever destroyed by capitalism, and oriented it to the beyond. Labour in a calling as such is willed by God. The impersonality of present-day labour, what, from the standpoint of the individual, is *its joyless lack of meaning*, still has a religious justification here. Capitalism at the time of its development needed labourers who were available for economic exploitation for conscience' sake. Today it is in the saddle, and hence able to force people to labour without transcendental sanctions. (PE: 282n; emphasis added)

Although somewhat clumsily translated, the essential point is that while the original labour in the calling had 'religious justification', now, with capitalism 'in the saddle', there is just a 'joyless lack of meaning'.

Yet something more needs to be added to try and make sense of this rather extraordinary claim that 'we are forced' to follow the calling once chosen by the Puritans – it is not just the businessmen playing the game of money-making, nor the workers and their utter lack of meaning, but 'we' who are affected. Although the compulsory nature of rationalised labour is now a structural, institutionalised aspect of the capitalist system, it is still not the case that all meaning has been squeezed out of such labour. How does meaning work here in this final version of the vocation in the capitalist economic order? Two possibilities suggest themselves.

Firstly, as part of capitalist culture more widely, the Protestant judgement on the worth of work is seemingly inescapable and, almost, unquestionable; this is, perhaps, the most common understanding of the 'Protestant work ethic', and it applies to 'not only those directly concerned with economic acquisition'. Hard work – anywhere – is itself assumed to have value, because such work still bears the trace of the now forgotten salvation, which it was once believed to have provided. This sense of meaning, therefore, is a classic example of the paradox of the means becoming the ends, but such meaning is forced upon us as a pervasive fact of work itself.

Its expansive presence can be witnessed in the legitimation of achievement in modernity. That is, a Franklinesque ethos can still be seen as prevalent, and is commonly exemplified, in various forms of success, e.g,. in sport, with the winner's standard, irrational appeal to hard work as both explanation and justification, or in the way any position of superiority is routinely legitimated in terms of the amount of mundane labour undertaken.[11] Indeed, 'we are forced' to follow this ethic in such a way that the Protestant view is mimicked quite closely: work cannot guarantee success, as it once could not guarantee being one of the elect; but it is certain that the slothful will be condemned to failure, as they were once condemned to the fires of hell.

Secondly, a related, but more difficult sense of this enforced vocation might be seen when labour within the value-sphere of the economy is again considered.

---

11 An obvious example is the often reported case of 'those hard working royals'. Although largely written from a class perspective, see Seabrook (1988) for a long list of further instances.

Some assistance in clarifying this particular point of meaning can be found in the way that Weber understands the value-sphere structure as a form of polytheism.

> We live as did the ancients when their world was not yet disenchanted of its gods and demons, only we live in a different sense. As the Hellenic person at times sacrificed to Aphrodite and at other times to Apollo, and, above all, as everybody sacrificed to the gods of his city, so do we still nowadays. (SV: 147)

Weber seems to be saying that the diverse values that are necessarily followed in modernity should be considered as akin to ancient religion; however there are similarities and differences between ancient and modern polytheism that should be noted. The similarities lie not just in the continuation of the perspective of meaning, which obviously comes with the idea that the many values of modernity might be compared with the many gods of the ancient polis, but also in the common enforced nature of these practices of meaning. For the intellectual strata of the Greek polis, belief in the gods was optional at best, but the performance of the rituals of sacrifice to the city gods was unquestionable:

> The Hellenic state gave ample leeway to metaphysical and social-ethical speculations. The state merely demanded the observance of the cultic duties which were bequeathed, for neglect of them could bring misfortune to the polis. The Greek philosophical schools corresponded to Confucianism in their social-ethical orientation and the main representatives of the classical period, like the Chinese intellectuals of the Confucian school, essentially left the gods aside. On the whole they simply went along with the transmitted rites, as the circles of genteel intellectuals in China did and as such circles generally do with us. (China: 175)

To enter the ancient temple and observe the traditional rites was compulsory even when there was no longer any belief in the god itself. Similarly today, Weber seems to be suggesting, we must follow older practices of meaning despite the fact that the originating religious belief has been displaced through a process of rationalisation. This point is particularly pertinent for the economic sphere in the sense that capitalism will demand certain practices be followed that once had great meaning but now are simply enforced; any continued belief – even if reduced to the level of a game – is simply unnecessary and not expected.

The obvious major difference between the polis and modernity in this regard, as noted above by Weber, concerns disenchantment. God/s and religion have been completely eradicated from modern capitalism, partly due to Protestant belief itself. Consequently, entering the economic sphere to work will almost certainly be understood only in terms of material interests, and the fact that it is also a place of meaning – the site of ideal interests as well – will necessarily be forgotten, as opposed to the non-believing Hellenic intellectual entering a temple to Athena.[12] However, the point here, as Weber constantly seeks to remind us, is that the vocational aspect of capitalism provides a link back to religion that cannot be undone.

This claim can be seen to be reinforced when Weber states:

> ... the idea of duty in one's calling prowls about in our lives like the ghost of dead religious beliefs. (PE: 182)

It cannot be justified, it cannot be avoided and it is now meaningless but the vocation has the smallest of traces from its origin in religion that still linger. The brutal meaninglessness of capitalism is not completely cut off from its religious past; in other words, ideal interests must still be at work even here, and they will call upon this older meaning. For Weber to retain the name of 'vocation' for this labour and call it the 'spirit'[13] of capitalism is to seek to preserve some sense of that meaning.

As the ancient Greeks had to worship the gods of the polis, so the modern economy demands its rituals be performed; and when one enters these sites of devotion, even as a conscripted non-believer, the sense of meaning can be tangible if only within the particular space that has been dedicated to each of the polytheistic powers.[14] So, when Weber tells us that we are forced to follow the calling, he is saying, in part, that the *meaning* of the vocation has been forced upon us. It is meaningless in terms of religion, and such meaninglessness will be recognised once we leave the economic value-sphere and reflect back on our restless, perhaps joyless labour,[15] but in the work itself – when it is being done – meaning can

---

12 It is important to remember that the Greek cults were political not religious, in the sense that classical antiquity was dominated by the ideals of citizenry and war, there were no priestly castes with power, and no sense of an afterlife gained through religious salvation (e.g., AS: 158, 187, 346, 358). As opposed to the dominance of religion in the medieval era, this brings the Greek and modern worldviews into a kind of alignment that might be seen to more easily allow the polytheism comparison that Weber makes here.

13 The connotation of the divine that adheres to the term '*Geist*' cannot be ignored.

14 Consideration of a contemporary problem of labour might aid our understanding of such enforced vocational meaning and this view of the value-spheres as a kind of polytheism. What Weber's theories here might partly serve to explain is the question of why long working hours have not been lessened as overall material wealth rises in advanced capitalist nations, despite the many predictions about an increase in leisure time (See, for example, Keynes's 1930 essay (Keynes, 1963) for an early expression of this idea). An explanation of this dilemma in terms of ideal interests, amongst many other factors, might argue that such work forces some minimal sense of meaning onto the labourer, and so will be pursued for this reason and not just because of material interests or structural reasons of the economy.

15 As reflected in the current ubiquitous notions that only family really matters, and/or no-one on their deathbed wishes they had spent more time at the office. The contrast with the Puritan worldview is made plain when Weber mentions how Christian, in Bunyan's *Pilgrim's Progress*, leaves his wife and children upon hearing the call to take up his pilgrimage – only salvation mattered (PE: 107).

be present. Even if there is a conscious ethical rejection of the capitalist spirit, when the economic sphere has been entered and the routines of mundane labour engaged, then the meaning of the Puritan calling is a fateful, determining presence – it cannot be so completely eradicated that meaning is simply absent.

To put this in terms of interests: ideal interests will be touched and, perhaps, followed, when the practices of rationalised labour are engaged, even though such labour can only be understood in terms of material interests. However, despite the fact that they might be teasingly invoked, so tiny is the measure of meaning that ideal interests cannot be *met* in any discernible sense at all. Even the debased, mute ethos of those who still do willingly follow the vocation of labour is much more than can be achieved when the vocation is forced upon us. In this last iteration of the vocation in capitalism meaning is reduced as far as it can go. Within the overall meaninglessness of modernity, partly occasioned by the long paradoxes of Western religion and science, the meaning that is still recognisable within the economic value-sphere has diminished to the point of being just the barest trace that is only discernible within the practices of labour itself and which makes no sense at all once this sphere is left. Yet, even at this final stage, Weber does not want to abandon the perspective of ideal interests; rather he wishes to show how such minimal meaning within meaninglessness actually works in capitalism.

The calling that we are forced to follow is the second way that meaning exists within the meaninglessness of the economic value-sphere, and it is understandable as part of the pattern of paradoxes that Weber has laid out as constitutive of this sphere. Most clearly Weber tells us that this diminished sense of the calling is to be contrasted with the originating Puritan form: meaning has been lost as it has been pursued. In this sense the long paradox that associates religious meaning with the advent of capitalism is being invoked. However, when we consider how this enforced vocation now operates within the capitalist order as an example of meaning within meaninglessness, it can be recognised how meaning is caught in this impossible paradox of being pursued – in fact, having to be pursued – and being lost at the same time. The very idea that we are forced to work in the calling both puts forward the idea of meaning and withdraws it at the same moment.

A summary of what has been said concerning the economic value-sphere might be given as follows, and when we put all these factors together the spirit of capitalism might be understandable in terms of the paradox of meaning. There are two levels of meaning at work. Firstly, there is the great story of the paradoxical relation of the Protestant religion and capitalism, where without the religious foundation the means are now the ends – so such economic activity is meaningless in terms of some of the great questions which ideal interests have to meet, i.e., how one should live and the meaning of death (the question which became pre-eminent in the West). Yet the spirit of vocation is preserved in a non-religious form, and it is here that a second level of the paradox of meaning is apparent, and on this second level there are two forms of interlinked paradox at work. Firstly, the non-religious validation of vocation runs from Franklin's explicit ethos with its backwards glance to his nurturing religion, to the inability to give any sense of meaning except as a kind of sport; and, secondly, with such a fading of ethical justification for this life-conduct, the compulsory aspect of the calling is made more manifest in our age of triumphant capitalism. Here there is a final sense of paradox offered by Weber in the idea of enforced vocational meaning that is only found in the very practices of the meaningless capitalist economy. To put all this more generally, it might now perhaps be seen how the Protestant legacy for Weber – from the perspective of meaning – is not just capitalism, as it is so often interpreted, but capitalism as the economic value-sphere, which is constituted by ideal interests into a complex pattern of paradoxes.[16]

Conclusion

The chapter has tried to articulate Weber's understanding of the value-spheres, vocation and the specific paradoxes of the economic sphere. Now, although this understanding of capitalism in terms of meaning might be seen as important in its own right, of even more significance, it might be argued, is the way Weber extends the concept of the calling into the value-spheres beyond the economic. It is to these sites of meaning that we now turn.

---

16 It should also be noted that this perspective is one that is from within the value-sphere of the economy. As we will see, other perspectives will regard such economic activity as not just senseless in the most complete sense but what in fact has to be rejected in order to achieve meaning.

Chapter 4
The Scientific and Political Value-Spheres

Introduction

This chapter will deal with the paradox of meaning as it is displayed in the intellectual/scientific and political values-spheres. Before an analysis of the intellectual sphere begins, some comparisons with the economic value-sphere need to be put.

Western meaning has a peculiar, overarching characteristic for Weber: economic, mundane activities, which were not a means to salvation in any other religion, were given meaning in Protestantism and became in fact the path to grace; and reason/intellectual life, which had always been one of the roads to religious meaning, became itself a path that led away from the meaning of death and life. Due, in part, to these differences, meaning and meaninglessness in the modern world of value-spheres are put into tense relationships by Weber, and the paradox of meaning will take different shapes in the intellectual and economic spheres respectively.

Two general points can be made about the differences between these spheres. Firstly, the difference can be seen in the way the calling in the economic sphere comes to be unable to be justified, except perhaps as sport, and that it tends to ever more meaninglessness as it becomes just the practices of capitalist labour. That is, on one level money-making reverts to meaninglessness, but, on another level, because of the Protestant Ethic, the spirit of capitalism will be pursued, or enforced, as if it still had meaning. In the intellectual sphere, however, reason continues to consider itself meaningful. The sense of vocation in this value-sphere is one where, instead of struggling to find the justification for following the values of this sphere (reason rather than money), the tendency is that science will give itself meaning that papers over its state of meaninglessness in modernity.

The second general point concerns the concept of the vocation. 'Science as a Vocation' and 'Politics as a Vocation' do not place much emphasis on vocation in terms of mundane, rationalised labour – all the stress is on vocation as the special task that, in its religious formulation, was set by God. However, we might assume that the mundane routines are a necessary, accompanying part of this sense of vocation as the divinely inspired task if the conclusions to *The Protestant Ethic and the Spirit of Capitalism* are remembered, as we have just discussed, i.e., where the imperative for such worldly, routinised work applies to all ('*We* are forced to do so'), and applies throughout modern culture. For example, early on, Weber writes:

> And in truth this peculiar idea, so familiar to us today, but in reality so little a matter of course, of one's duty in a calling, is what is most characteristic of the social ethic of capitalistic culture, and is in a sense the fundamental basis of it. (PE: 53–4)

So, let us assume the labour side of the calling, and concentrate on the side of the 'vocation' which, for the case of the intellectual sphere, is displayed in 'Science as a Vocation' as the once divinely ordered task where there is an '*inward* calling of science' (SV: 134, Weber's emphasis).[1] Weber does not emphasise the Protestant heritage of this sense of vocation in either lecture, but again, it can be safely assumed given the initial definitions of the calling provided in *The Protestant Ethic and the Spirit of Capitalism*. If this quite common view of the vocational attraction of a particular field of work has this originating religious meaning, the question Weber puts is what meaning does such vocation now have when the religious setting has been stripped away as must happen in the modern world of disenchantment.

The Intellectual/Scientific Sphere

The overall pattern of meaning is one where the vocation for science is set within the meaninglessness of science:

> Science today is a 'vocation' organised in special disciplines in the service of self-clarification and knowledge of interrelated facts. It is not the gift of grace of seers and prophets dispensing sacred values and revelations, nor does it partake of the contemplation of sages and philosophers about the meaning of the universe. This, to be sure, is the inescapable condition of our historical situation. (SV: 152)

To try to understand the particular kind of vocation Weber begins his account with the psychological state that must be part of any such meaningful pursuit. It is in this sense that the 'inner devotion to the task' (SV: 137) within intellectual sphere has great emotional consequences:

> And whoever lacks the capacity to put on blinders, so to speak, and to come up to the idea that the fate of his soul depends upon whether or not he makes the correct conjecture at this passage of this manuscript may as well stay away from science. He will never have what one may call the 'personal experience' of science. Without this strange intoxication, ridiculed by every outsider; without this passion, this 'thousands of years must pass before you enter into life and thousands more wait in silence' – according to whether or not you succeed in making this conjecture; without this, you have *no* calling for science and you

---

1 '*von dem* inneren *Berufe zur Wissenschaft*' (WB: 80, Weber's emphasis).

should do something else. For nothing is worthy of person as person unless he can pursue it with passionate devotion. (SV: 135, Weber's emphasis)

Such passionate experience is a *sine qua non* of the calling of science, and is an inheritance from the psychological state of salvation for the Protestant in their calling. Weber had stressed that religion of all kinds has this quality.

> Psychologically considered, man in quest of salvation has been primarily preoccupied by attitudes of the here and now. The puritan *certitudo salutis,* the permanent state of grace that rests in the feeling of 'having proved oneself', was psychologically the only concrete object among the sacred values of this ascetic religion. The Buddhist monk, certain to enter Nirvana, seeks the sentiment of a cosmic love; the devout Hindu seeks either Bhakti (fervent love in the possession of God) or apathetic ecstasy. The Chlyst with his radjeny, as well as the dancing Dervish, strives for orgiastic ecstasy. Others seek to be possessed by God and to possess God, to be a bridegroom of the Virgin Mary, or to be the bride of the Saviour. The Jesuits' cult of the heart of Jesus, quietistic edification, the pietists' tender love for the child Jesus and its 'running sore', the sexual and semi-sexual orgies at the wooing of Krishna, the sophisticated cultic dinners of the Vallabhacharis, the gnostic onanist cult activities, the various forms of the *unio mystica,* and the contemplative submersion in the All-one – these states undoubtedly have been sought, first of all, for the sake of such emotional value as they directly offered the devout. In this respect, they have in fact been absolutely equal to the religious and alcoholic intoxication of the Dionysian or the soma cult; to totemic meat-orgies, the cannibalistic feasts, the ancient and religiously consecrated use of hashish, opium, and nicotine; and, in general, to all sorts of magical intoxication. They have been considered specifically consecrated and divine because of their psychic extraordinariness and because of the intrinsic value of the respective states conditioned by them. (IEEWR: 278)

Puritan certitude and Dionysian intoxication are linked together in terms of the emotional state of religious meaning. Moreover, Weber reminds us that the meaning of the Greek beginning of Western reason had this emotional end as part of reaching the divine. At least this is the case with Plato's philosopher-king leaving the cave in *The Republic* to discover a divine 'pulsating' reality, which was 'the tremendous experience which dawned upon the disciples of Socrates' (SV: 141).

Without the meaning of salvation the emotional potential of the calling in the scientific sphere of modernity must be lesser than the religious past. However, it still has sufficient force for Weber to write, as we have just seen, about the intellectual/scientist in terms of the 'fate of his soul' depending 'upon whether or not he makes the correct conjecture at this passage of this manuscript'. It is clear that, not only is the religious heritage still a presence in this modern manifestation of the calling, but also, more generally, ideal interests can be seen to be at work when such descriptions are employed.

This emotional state of the calling must be present, but the meaning of this vocational labour is put under some heavy restrictions by Weber. Firstly, there is the necessity of specialisation (SV: 134–5; Method: 112); and, secondly, there is the temporary nature of all scientific results.

> In science, each of us knows that what he has accomplished will be antiquated in ten, twenty, fifty years. That is the fate to which science is subjected; it is the very *meaning* of scientific work, to which it is devoted in a quite specific sense, as compared with other spheres of culture for which in general the same holds. Every scientific 'fulfilment' raises new 'questions'; it *asks* to be 'surpassed' and outdated. Whoever wishes to serve science has to resign himself to this fact. Scientific works certainly can last as 'gratifications' because of their artistic quality, or they may remain important as a means of training. Yet they will be surpassed scientifically – let that be repeated – for it is our common fate and, more, our common goal. We cannot work without hoping that others will advance further than we have. (SV: 138, Weber's emphasis)

The vocation of science has these limitations, but Weber is yet to reach the major paradox of science and meaning. The endless nature of scientific findings in fact throws up the question of meaning directly.

> ... this progress goes on *ad infinitum*. And with this we come to inquire into the *meaning of* science. For, after all, it is not self-evident that something subordinate to such a law is sensible and meaningful in itself. (SV: 138, Weber's emphasis)

It is at this stage in 'Science as a Vocation' that Weber introduces his account of the history of scientific/intellectual Western meaning that we have discussed in a previous chapter – where meaning was the point of rational inquiry and was lost in the very success of reason as science. An extended version of the previously cited quotation on Tolstoy and meaning makes the point that science has indeed ended in senselessness.

> Tolstoi has given the simplest answer, with the words: 'Science is meaningless because it gives no answer, the only question important for us: "what shall we do and how shall we live?"' That science does not give an answer to this is indisputable. The only question that remains is the sense in which science gives 'no' answer, and whether or not science might yet be of some use to the one who puts the question correctly. (SV: 143)[2]

---

2 'Die einfachste Antwort hat Tolstoj gegeben mit den Worten: 'Sie ist sinnlos, weil sie auf die allein für uns wichtige Frage: "Was sollen wir tun? Wie sollen wir leben?" keine Antwort gibt.' Die Tatsache, daß sie diese Antwort nicht gibt, ist schlechthin unbestreitbar. Die Frage ist nur, in welchem Sinne sie 'keine' Antwort gibt, und ob sie statt dessen nicht doch vielleicht dem, der die Frage richtig stellt, etwas leisten könnte' (WB: 93).

At this point, on how 'science gives "no" answer', comes the important paradox of meaning for modern vocational duty in the value-sphere of science. Here is science revealed as meaningless, and it is on this disenchanted view of the world that its very success depends. Yet as a vocation there must be some meaning, and the Protestant vocational aspect of science has to be added to through the use of now irrational assumptions that provide this extra dimension.[3] The vocation of science builds upon its necessary Protestant base in the following way:

> Today one usually speaks of science as 'free from presuppositions'. Is there such a thing? It depends upon what one understands thereby. All scientific work presupposes that the rules of logic and method are valid; these are the general foundations of our orientation in the world; and, at least for our special question, these presuppositions are the least problematic aspect of science. Science further presupposes that what is yielded by scientific work is important in the sense that it is 'worth being known'. In this, obviously, are contained all our problems. For this presupposition cannot be proved by scientific means. It can only be *interpreted* with reference to its ultimate meaning, which we must reject or accept according to our ultimate position towards life. (SV: 143, Weber's emphasis)

'All our problems' centre on this assumption of meaning, which will vary between the scientific/intellectual disciplines.

> Furthermore, the nature of the relationship of scientific work and its presuppositions varies widely according to their structure. The natural sciences, for instance, physics, chemistry, and astronomy, presuppose as self-evident that it is worthwhile to know the ultimate laws of cosmic events as far as science can construe them. *This is the case not only because with such knowledge one can attain technical results*[4] *but for its own sake, if the quest for such knowledge is to be a 'vocation'*. Yet this presupposition can by no means be proved. And still less can it be proved that the existence of the world which these sciences describe is worthwhile, that it has any 'meaning', or that it makes sense to live

---

3   Also, it should be noted here that this additional layer of meaning will feed the passion that should be part of the scientific task. Once the vocation is understood to have this extra dimension of meaning, beyond the Protestant heritage, Weber's stress on passion becomes far more understandable. The work will be undertaken with some fervour, in part, because the meaning it once did have is still assumed.

4   In 'Objectivity in the Social Sciences and Social Policy' Weber says that with specialisation science will come to consider analysis of data as an end in itself, discontinue its link to ultimate values and lose the idea that it is rooted in such values at all. And this can in fact be considered a good thing (Method: 112). However this is, again, part of the overall paradox of meaning for science – the means become the ends – and must run counter to science considered as a vocation.

in such a world. Science does not ask for the answers to such questions. (SV: 143–4, emphasis added)

Those disciplines in the intellectual/scientific sphere that might be imagined as the most objective, rationalised and free from the heritage of religious meaning in that they deal in the pure disenchantment of the physical world, even these natural sciences are still tied to the pursuit of meaning: they presuppose that their knowledge is 'worthwhile'.[5] Science is undertaken on the assumption that it has some worthy value or end, but, of course, this cannot be proved, and nor can the ultimate meaning of the world from which such presuppositions derive be part of any scientific inquiry. The meaning that science once had is therefore still present, but now as a necessary irrational presupposition.

Weber says here that if the natural sciences are not tied to such irrational assumptions of meaning then the only products are technical results for their own sake. This is the way instrumental reason, or the way the means become the ends, is manifested in the intellectual sphere. With the final point of meaning lost in the long paradox of science in the West, the means to such meaning – technical results and the values of 'self-clarification and knowledge of interrelated facts' – are now the only ends that can be pursued. This is correct but incomplete. As a vocation these means as ends do have to be followed, but as a vocation they must also be assumed to be doing something more. Here is the fateful paradox of meaning at work in this value-sphere, i.e., it is how meaning works within meaninglessness, or how ideal interests still have an inevitable role to play even here. Science still has to be pursued as having meaning but the only possible results are meaningless, with any elements of presupposed meaning absent from the final scientific findings.

In the case of the natural sciences the effect of this paradox might seem small, but Weber next uses the example of medicine where the effects are of greater consequence:

> Consider modern medicine, a practical technology which is highly developed scientifically. The general 'presupposition' of the medical enterprise is stated trivially in the assertion that medical science has the task of maintaining life as such and of diminishing suffering as such to the greatest possible degree. Yet this is problematical. By his means the medical person preserves the life of the mortally ill man, even if the patient implores us to relieve him of life, even if his relatives, to whom his life is worthless and to whom the costs of maintaining his worthless life grow unbearable, grant his redemption from suffering. Perhaps a poor lunatic is involved, whose relatives, whether they admit it or not, wish and must wish for his death. Yet the presuppositions of medicine, and the penal code, prevent the physician from relinquishing his therapeutic efforts. Whether life is worthwhile living and when – this question is not asked by medicine. Natural

---

5 Following Lassman and Velody, who note this aspect of scientific culture as a paradox (Lassman and Velody, 1989: 96).

science gives us an answer to the question of what we must do if we wish to master life technically. It leaves quite aside, or assumes for its purposes, whether we should and do wish to master life technically and whether it ultimately makes sense to do so. (SV: 145)

The 'trivially' stated assumptions of preserving life and alleviating suffering – which give meaning to the vocation of medicine – are necessarily lost in the medical pursuit of these values as *science*. In so far as medicine is part of the scientific value-sphere, the means will become the ends and the questions of meaning cannot be asked. Life is preserved by the 'means' of medical science, i.e., all that can be done is to try to master life technically because medicine as part of the scientific value-sphere cannot ask questions of meaning and the irrational assumptions of its meaning must be abandoned or lost as the means as ends are necessarily followed. Yes, life is preserved, but it is done so, and overrides the alleviation of suffering, for purely technical reasons.[6] Of course, there will be exceptions to this ideal-typical depiction of medicine where different values are followed and life ended in the face of suffering – but the essential paradox will not therefore be overcome. All that will have happened is that medicine has left science behind and the realm of the irrational entered. Medicine will be given meaning, but its whole status as science will have been necessarily compromised.

If this is indeed how the paradox of scientific meaning plays out in modernity, it might be suggested that it is not only the religious sense of vocation that allows meaning to be extended into meaninglessness; rather, and Weber does not quite say this in 'Science as a Vocation', the history of meaning that is part of science itself still has a resonance in the modern scientific enterprise in addition to the religious effect. Science, despite its rationalised disenchanted meaninglessness, has its history of meaning imperfectly and precariously present in the assumptions of meaning that must accompany science as a vocation. Fragments of its past answers are still sustained in its modern, inescapable assumption of being meaningful; or, in other words, whatever its current state of meaninglessness science cannot completely escape its past of once being part of a some kind of divinely ordered cosmos.

Such an interpretation of the intellectual sphere and its assumptions of meaning would seem to be an example of how (as quoted): 'irrational presuppositions, which have been accepted simply as "given" ... have been historically and socially determined during its formative and decisive period'. (IEEWR: 281). And the point is emphasised in terms of science when Weber continues this section of the *Introduction to the Economic Ethic of the World Religions* to say that:

---

6 Since Weber's time, it might be argued, this problem has become exacerbated to the point that, in the case of old age care, medicine has extended life to such an extent that suffering has in fact been increased.

> Furthermore, the irrational elements in the rationalisation of reality have been the *loci* to which the irrepressible quest of intellectualism for the possession of supernatural values has been compelled to retreat. That is the more so the more denuded of irrationality the world appears to be ... (IEEWR: 281–2)[7]

This passage suggests that not only is intellectualism pursuing 'supernatural values' but that it must increasingly assume those elements that cannot be rationally accounted for the more it is rationally successful in disenchanting the world. To put this in the terms of 'Science as a Vocation', science will be undertaken as a vocation because it is assumed to have meaning – to be 'worthwhile' at the most minimum level; but these irrational assumptions are what could not be rationally accounted for in its intellectual quest for meaning. These presuppositions are in fact about 'ultimate meaning' (as above, SV: 143), which is precisely what had to be left out of the scientific rationalisation of reality, even though the quest began with the goal of accounting for reality as possessing this meaning.

In sum, the problem of the assumption of meaning shows how meaning is still present in the intellectual sphere, once this value-sphere is understood in terms of the vocation. It is paradoxical in that science will be pursued as meaningful, but the ultimate meaning of life and death can never be gained by science.

We now turn to another side of the paradox of intellectual meaning. This particular dilemma of meaning arises, again, from the fact that the '*meaning* of scientific work ... in reality never comes, and never can come, to an end' (SV: 138, Weber's emphasis). In both 'Science as a Vocation' and the *Intermediary Reflection*, this point is developed when Weber writes of death and science in the somewhat wider context of modern culture:

> You will find this question raised in the most principled form in the works of Leo Tolstoi. He came to raise the question in a peculiar way. All his broodings increasingly revolved around the problem of whether or not death is a meaningful phenomenon. And his answer was: for the civilised person death has no meaning. It has none because the individual life of civilised man, placed into an infinite 'progress', according to its own imminent meaning should never come to an end; for there is always a further step ahead of one who stands in the march of progress. And no person who comes to die stands upon the peak which lies in infinity. Abraham, or some peasant of the past, died 'old and satiated with life' because he stood in the organic cycle of life; because his life, in terms of its meaning and on the eve of his days, had given to him what life had to offer; because for him there remained no puzzles he might wish to solve; and therefore he could have had 'enough' of life. Whereas civilised man, placed in the midst of the continuous enrichment of culture by ideas, knowledge, and problems, may become 'tired of life' but not 'satiated with life'. He catches only

---

7 Although it should be noted that Weber will then go on to give examples only from religion.

the most minute part of what the life of the spirit brings forth ever anew, and
what he seizes is always something provisional and not definitive, and therefore
death for him is a meaningless occurrence. And because death is meaningless,
civilised life as such is meaningless; by its very 'progressiveness' it gives death
the imprint of meaninglessness. (SV: 139–40; see also IR: 356–7)

Death is meaningless for 'civilised man' and for intellectual cultivation (IR: 356)
because of the endlessness of modern culture. A cosmos of older meaning could
sustain 'organic cycles of life', as opposed to the patterns of modern intellectual
culture where such a sense of 'satiation' must be denied. The paradox lies in how
the modern striving for 'self-perfection, in the sense of acquiring or creating
"cultural values"' (IR: 356) is never-ending.

The advancement of cultural values, however, seems to become a senseless
hustle in the service of worthless, moreover self-contradictory, and mutually
antagonistic ends. (IR: 357)

Values, such as perfection in the cultivation of the self, or truth and reason in
science (or beauty in art), are sought but are necessarily incomplete and provisional.
There can be no completion in modernity, only 'devastating senselessness'
with 'culture's every step forward' (IR: 357). The intention of modern culture
(especially science) is to find some finality, some answer, but the very process of
this attempted realisation means that every result necessarily fails (IR: 356). To
put it more plainly, the labour of the intellectual, despite the passionate vocational
commitment, contains a disquieting sense that what is achievable in terms of
science as a vocation is going to be necessarily lesser than what is necessarily part
of the intention of the task – why labour so long on what we know is provisional
and never-ending? Weber might be interpreted here as saying that every modern
cultural act is trying to regain the meaning that is only possible within the structure
of an ancient, enchanted cosmology – in its very leaving of the past, modern
culture is also trying to return – but the intellectual way forward leads only further
away from this cosmic meaning.

To expand on this same point in slightly different terms, the fateful nature of
this paradox is able to be understood in the way this endlessness of modern culture
is the only possibility within the intellectual sphere. In Weber's understanding of
science as a vocation, meaningfulness, and the old enchanted world where that
was possible, are what have to be sought, but the only way this can be done is
through following the intellectual values which lead to increased or reinforced
disenchantment and heightened specialisation.[8] The only path to be followed in

---

8 What Weber in one sense understands as 'intellectualism' might be added to this
list. Weber specifically mentions his own hatred of this 'devil' that besets intellectual
work – where the game of the academy takes over and arcane, internal debates come to the
fore. He is in sympathy with the reaction of youth against science on this ground. But this

the vocation of science is rational 'progress' which leads away from the end of meaning – but it is towards this end of meaning that the progress of modern reason is necessarily still trying to work.

There is, however, another layer to this particular paradox which comes with the idea of the vocation. Weber writes that:

> The advancement of cultural values appears the more meaningless the more it is made a holy task, a 'calling'. (IR: 357)

Weber does not spell out what is meant here but two speculative points might be made when considering the vocation of science/intellectual reason. Firstly, the calling of science sustains a trace of the 'holy' meaning of religion, so that the paradox of both striving for and losing that meaning is more acute the deeper the sense of vocation is felt. Secondly, if science is undertaken under the influence, however distant and partial, of the Protestant calling, then the injunction is always towards more hard, rationalised labour in order to gain some level of meaning. We have seen how the Puritan paradox resulted in the prescription for endless labour in order to gain the psychological state of grace; and for those who can nowadays follow science as a vocation there is the imperative to work even harder in order to gain the presupposed meaning that is always out of reach. Yet such labour only ties the bonds of paradox even tighter; the scientist must work to free herself through more science, but it is science itself that is the problem. The vocation gives a sense of meaningful labour but to work even harder to try to reach the unreachable only increases the overall state of meaninglessness.

So, with the endlessness of modern culture, the logic of paradox is again in evidence within the intellectual value-sphere. Weber shows how the meaninglessness of modernity operates through his sociology of meaning – modern senselessness is not the absence of meaning but the paradox of meaning as fate.

Finally a point should be noted here that will be taken up more thoroughly in a later chapter. 'Science as a Vocation' is famous for advocating the following: a clear choice between religion and science; that only 'big children' think that they can combine the two again;[9] that to enter into religion is to have to accept a

---

paradox has to be faced, for if the calling is to be followed: 'It means that if one wishes to settle with this devil, one must not take to flight before him as so many like to do nowadays. First of all, one has to see the devil's ways to the end in order to realise his power and his limitations' (SV: 152).

9 The quotation has already been given that for Weber it is only 'certain big children' that still hold that science/reason 'could teach us anything about the *meaning* of the world' (SV: 142, Weber's emphasis). On this point – that science and religion are still in a sympathetic relation – Weber is scathingly dismissive: '... the need of some modern intellectuals to furnish their souls with, so to speak, guaranteed genuine antiques. In doing so, they happen to remember that religion has belonged among such antiques, and of all

'sacrifice of the intellect' (SV: 155); that 'intellectual integrity' (SV: 155) demands maintaining a position within science; and that modernity is meaningless and disenchanted. Weber does say all this in 'Science as a Vocation' but this is clearly not all that he says, as we have seen. As a vocation, there must be more to science in terms of meaning. Moreover, there is no problem maintaining all these aspects of 'Science as a Vocation' together as long as the concept of paradox as meaning is preserved. To be able to ask the questions of meaning – as religion can do – is to leave reason as science behind. There is no alternative here – it is part of the fate of modernity. Yet to remain in science is not to leave religion and meaning behind. There is meaning within meaninglessness, but it is always lost in its very pursuit, with meaninglessness always the final outcome. The idea of vocation allows the mundane labour of science a sense of meaning and the accompanying psychological state, but the content of this meaning is never able to be gained even though it has a necessary presence. This is the paradox that Weber offers. The temptation is to try to resolve the paradox in one way or the other, that is, to give science meaning in the sense that it can still answer the questions of religion, or reject all meaning in science and proclaim a complete division between religion and science. Certainly, at one level, the very internal technical values of intellectual reason are pressing for just such a resolution, for example, in terms of consistency. However, for Weber this paradox is our fate; and the very idea of fate includes attempts to escape its hold and believe that such escape has succeeded. Perhaps such an understanding can help to fill out Weber's statement that it is only a 'hair-line which separates science from faith' (Method: 110)

If this is indeed how the paradoxes of meaning are manifested within the scientific/intellectual realm, a quite different set of paradoxes is apparent in Weber's account of the political value-sphere.

The Political Sphere

> The use of force within the political community increasingly assumes the form of the *Rechsstaat*. But from the point of view of religion, this is the merely the effective mimicry of brutality. All politics is oriented to *raison d'*état [reasons of state], to realism, and to the autonomous end of maintaining the external and internal distribution of power. These goals, again, must necessarily seem completely senseless from the religious point of view. Yet only in this way does the realm of politics acquire a peculiarly rational mystique of its own ... (ES: 600–601)

---

things religion is what they do not possess. By way of substitute, however, they play at decorating a sort of domestic chapel with small sacred images from all over the world, or they produce surrogates through all sorts of psychic experiences to which they ascribe the dignity of mystic holiness, which they peddle in the book market. This is plain humbug or self-deception' (SV: 154; also ES: 517).

The necessities of the state – power and violence – are meaningless for religion, especially as religion develops into its universal salvation forms (IR: 334–5). There have been tense compromises between politics and religion, for example, in the cosmic worldview of medieval Catholicism (IR: 338–9),[10] but, unlike the economic and intellectual realms, politics is not part of the paradox of religious meaning – it has not been seen as a way to salvation. So, it is basically meaningless, but Weber hints here that there is something more on offer as the state develops its own 'peculiarly rational mystique'. How this transpires can be understood when we contemplate politics as a value-sphere of modernity?[11]

Weber discusses politics as in fact a source of meaning within meaninglessness. That is, his concern is with understanding – as his famous lecture is titled – 'Politics as a Vocation' (*Politik als Beruf*) within the overall senselessness of modernity. The concept of vocation, as we have seen is, firstly, the continuation of religious meaning into the paradoxes of modernity in the sense that duty in mundane labour sustains, in different ways, some measure of meaning; and, secondly, beyond the economic value-sphere, such meaningful labour can be 'value-added' to provide a greater sense of vocation in terms of the pre-ordained task, as is the case with the value-sphere of science/intellectual reason. This expanded concept of vocation will also be found in the political value-sphere. However, whereas in the economic and scientific spheres this sense of meaning in the vocation has been fundamentally determined by the religious and scientific paradoxes of the West – so it is a question of how the means to meaning are now themselves the ends – this is not the case with the political sphere. The growth of the modern state in its rationalised form seems to provide an increase in the possibility of vocational meaning as compared to past forms, even though the political value-sphere will offer up perhaps the greatest force for meaninglessness in the whole of modernity. Meaning has therefore been created in the sphere of modern politics, in addition to, and as part of, the sense of the Protestant calling.

Firstly, it has to be noted that politics in the modern state can still bring forth charismatic leaders who experience the '"calling" in the most genuine sense of the word' (PV: 80), or as its 'highest expression' (PV: 79). Such leaders have emerged throughout history and command a personal devotion from their followers. Here is the sense of the calling as part of some sort of divine plan, with meaning heightened accordingly, although this is the extraordinary case.

More important is the way a range of 'professional politicians' come to the fore with the rise of the power of the state, which Weber summarises in the following way:

---

10 We will look at this period more closely in a following chapter.

11 A significant qualification must be made here. The political sphere, and the state's monopoly on the legitimate use of violence, offer an unambiguous, non-paradoxical meaning to death and suffering: war. War is a direct rival to religion in this regard because soldiers on the battlefield can experience a meaningful death and do form a brotherly bond in the face of suffering (IR: 335ff).

> ... the modern state is a compulsory association which organises domination. It has been successful in seeking to monopolise the legitimate use of physical force as a means of domination within a territory. To this end the state has combined the material means of organisation in the hands of its leaders, and it has expropriated all autonomous functionaries of estates who formerly controlled these means in their own right. The state has taken their positions and now stands in the top place.
>
> During this process of political expropriation, which has occurred with varying success in all countries on earth, 'professional politicians' in another sense have emerged. (PV: 82–3)

These professional politicians do not necessarily want to rule as do charismatic leaders, but to serve. They emerge with the rule of the prince but only in the West is there found 'this kind of professional politician in the service of powers other than the princes' (PV: 83).

Within the modern political sphere it is not just politicians who can follow a vocation, there is also the vocation of the administrator.

> According to his proper *vocation* [emphasis added], the genuine official – and this is decisive for the evaluation of our former regime – will not engage in politics. Rather, he should engage in 'impartial administration'. This also holds for the so called 'political' administrator, at least officially, in so far as the *raison d'état*, that is, the vital interests of the ruling order, are not in question. *Sine ira et studio*, 'without scorn and bias', he shall administer his office. Hence, he shall not do precisely what the politician, the leader as well as his following, must always and necessarily do, namely, *fight*. (PV: 95; see also IR: 334; and ES: 958, 975)

Weber's concern in 'Politics as a Vocation' is with the politician not the administrator, and he will stress this passion as part of the politicians' vocational meaning. He goes on to say:

> To take a stand, to be passionate – *ira et studium* – is the politician's element ... (PV: 95; also PV: 127)

This 'passionate devotion' (PV: 115), as with science as a vocation, indicates the presence of a motivating psychological state that can be traced back to all religious belief, and the origin of such passion in modern rationalised labour is partly, as discussed, the Protestant calling as the devotional task. Politics as a vocation must include this great feeling of the meaning of such duty. However, the vocation of politics, as with science, has something more than a Puritan-derived sense of passion and meaning. But what is the added meaningful content of this vocation in politics, and how is it subject to paradox in modernity? The idea that the politician must 'take a stand' gives an indication of a part of what constitutes this created, extra vocational content.

In 'Politics as a Vocation' Weber does not take political sides. Rather, he talks of vocational meaning in terms of the 'cause'. This is one of the vital additional components which make up the vocation of politics. It adds to the meaning of labour in the once divinely given task that harks back to Protestantism, and feeds the passion that should accompany such work.[12] Hence the politician 'nourishes his inner balance and self-feeling by the consciousness that his life has *meaning* in the service of a "cause"' (PV: 84, Weber's emphasis). Yet if the cause must be present for meaning in politics, it faces inevitable paradoxes:

> The final result of political action often, no, even regularly, stands in completely inadequate and often even *paradoxical* relation to its original meaning. This is fundamental to all history, a point not to be proved in detail here. But because of this fact, the serving of a cause must not be absent if action is to have inner strength. Exactly what the cause, in the service of which the politician strives for power and uses power, looks like is a *matter of faith*. The politician may serve national, humanitarian, social, ethical, cultural, worldly, or religious ends. The politician may be sustained by a strong belief in 'progress' – no matter in which sense – or he may coolly reject this kind of belief. He may claim to stand in the service of an 'idea' or, rejecting this in principle, he may want to serve external ends of everyday life. However, some kind of *faith* must always exist. (PV: 117, emphasis added)

Political results have always had a paradoxical relationship with their originating intention, but, despite this inevitability, the serving of the cause gives meaning. Ideal interests are seen to be at work in this sphere, with religious meaning at least to some degree recalled, when Weber states that is a matter of 'faith'. However, for the case of the meaningful cause in modernity, the bigger picture of meaninglessness must be remembered: it is meaning within meaninglessness (although this is not a point stressed in 'Politics as a Vocation'). What *is* stressed by Weber, as indicated by this quotation, is how this meaning within the value-sphere of politics is itself subject to paradox. Weber shows us how a set of paradoxes is fatefully present

---

12 Barbalet (2008) criticises Weber's concept of the vocation as being inconsistent between its use in *The Protestant Ethic and the Spirit of Capitalism* and the Vocation lectures. He argues that the emotional content is far more pronounced in the later lectures. However, if this point is put within the wider argument of the paradox of meaning, such alleged inconsistency might be explained in the way science and politics have added dimensions of meaning compared to the economic/capitalist sphere, where any vocational meaning has been reduced to the level of sport or compulsion and is tied to mundane labour – with the 'task' seemingly absent. That is, in its sense of vocation the economic value-sphere has only the fading Protestant tradition of meaningful labour to fan emotional enthusiasm, whereas science and politics have extra factors to prompt the necessary passion.

within the political sphere as a threat to this meaning; he details how the 'cause' as meaning will 'regularly' be lost or diminished, to varying degrees, in the very pursuit of that meaning.

The 'cause', then, provides the crucial content for politics as a vocation. Remarkably, the vocation of politics will then be broadened to include not only the devotion to, or faith in, the cause, but also the understanding that the cause will, in all likelihood, be lost, to some degree, through the fateful presence of these paradoxes. The paradox of meaning within the value-sphere of politics is inscribed into vocational meaning itself; it is not just that vocational meaning will be lost, or diminished, in being pursued, as we witnessed in the economic and intellectual spheres, but an appreciation of this paradoxical loss is itself constitutive of having the vocation for politics. This paradox of meaning is the second vital element, along with the cause, that has to be added to the Protestant calling to make up what Weber takes to be the vocation for politics.

Let us consider the paradoxes that Weber specifies as the fate of politics. There are four in all, with the first two stemming from factors that occur in all political forms – 'all history', and the second two tied into factors that arise more predominantly in modernity. It needs to be noted that when Weber discusses all these paradoxes in this lecture he clearly has the example of the modern vocation of politics in mind – where the meaning of the cause is present.

Firstly, there are the unavoidable necessities or reasons of state: power and violence. These inescapable values of the state must be followed, or at least bowed down to, and they must nearly always undermine and lessen whatever cause is being followed; and they might well lead to the cause being entirely forsaken. This is another example of how the means (here power and violence) can become the ends. So, with the case of power in modernity, there is the danger that this means will come to overwhelm the end of the vocational cause; that is, the necessary means of power will become the end itself and whatever meaning that is possible in politics will be lost.

> The sin against the lofty spirit of his vocation, however, begins where this striving for power ceases to be objective and becomes purely personal self-intoxication, instead of exclusively entering the service of 'the cause' ... Although, or rather just because, power is the unavoidable means, and striving for power is one of the driving forces of all politics, there is no more harmful distortion of political force than the parvenu-like braggart with power, and the vain self-reflection in the feeling of power, and in general every worship of power per se. The mere 'power politician' may get strong effects, but actually his work leads nowhere and is senseless. (PV: 116)

With regard to violence, Weber gives several examples of this 'decisive means for politics' and 'its tension between means and ends' (PV: 121). Because violence is the core *raison d'état* it cannot be avoided, and such means must threaten grave paradoxical consequences for any meaningful end. His position can be summed up in the following two quotations:

> ... whosoever contracts with violent means for whatever ends – and every politician does – is exposed to its specific consequences. (PV: 124).

> Whoever wants to engage in politics at all, and especially in politics as a vocation, has to realise these ethical *paradoxes*. He must know that he is responsible for what may become of himself under the impact of these paradoxes. I repeat, he lets himself in for the diabolic forces lurking in all violence. (PV: 125–6, emphasis added)

Power and violence are the factors of politics that have always been antipathetic to the ends of salvation religions, but they are factors that must always affect – perhaps even destroy – every cause as part of politics as a vocation in modernity. So, for Weber, the very reasons of state are understood in terms of the paradox of meaning.

A second paradox that arises again in politics is that of charisma/routinisation. As noted, charisma can be an obviously important part of political leadership, and it can be tied to the very strongest sense of politics as a calling. However, as we saw in a previous chapter in terms of religion, charisma, despite its stated intentions, must eventually give way, in the name of discipline and predictability, to routinisation. Hence, in politics the plans of charismatic leaders diminish: 'Emotional revolutionism is followed by the traditionalist routine of everyday life; the crusading leader and the faith itself fade away ...' (PV: 125). In so far as the cause is upheld and followed because of the charisma of the leader, this meaning, and the faith in the cause, will necessarily diminish with the inevitability of routinisation.

The two paradoxes listed so far depend on factors that occur in all politics, but the political sphere in modernity adds two other levels to the paradox of meaning.

The third paradox invokes a problem of modern democratic politics in that, to gain power for whatever cause, two forces, or means to the end of the cause, have to be engaged. Firstly, there is the need to deal with the party 'machine' that raises money, and, often, chooses candidates and determines policy (PV: 102ff), as especially seen in American politics (PV: 108–11). Here: '"Professional" politicians *outside* the parliaments take control of the organisation' (PV: 102). And, secondly, politicians must cater to the 'human machine' (PV: 125) and meet the basest of their followers' motives. Weber makes this point in terms of the extremes of class-based politics where revolutionary force and violence are present,[13] but the point might be qualified and widened to include democratic politics more widely. Weber states:

---

13 As was present in Germany in 1919, when 'Politics as a Vocation' was given as a lecture.

> Under the conditions of the modern class struggle, the internal premiums consist of the satisfying of hatred and the craving for revenge; above all, resentment and the need for pseudo-ethical self-righteousness: the opponents must be slandered and accused of heresy. (PV: 125)

The paradox here is that the vocation of modern democratic politics is necessarily set within these forces that can undo the cause, and, almost certainly, must at least compromise it. The democratic party must be accompanied by the power of its machine; and popular support for a cause or leader has a price attached – these 'machines' are part of the paradoxical fate of the political sphere.

But the fourth and last example of paradox in modern politics is the one for which Weber is most famous, and is the one that has definitional status for the paradox of modern meaning: bureaucracy.[14] For Weber the modern state has bureaucracy as its defining quality:

> The bureaucratic state order is especially important; in its most rational developments, it is precisely characteristic of the modern state (PV: 82; also IR: 333–4)

The paradox emerges here via the contradiction of how a large and powerful bureaucracy, a necessary component of the administrative means of the nation-state (or any large organisation), will itself become a force of such dominance that it threatens the very aims of that state or organisation. For Weber, this occurs in two ways. Firstly, when the state aims for democracy, bureaucratic power will ensure that all are democratically levelled before the democratic state (ES: 985). Providing power and resources to bureaucracy to achieve this end raises it to new levels of authority and social control. Democracy is dependent on a means that is in contradiction to its egalitarian ends. Secondly, and more generally, the power and position of the bureaucracy entail that the ends of government (or any large organisation) will be doubtfully realised because the ends of the bureaucracy itself will become pre-eminent (ES: 990).

Weber considered that these bureaucratic threats had an immediate political presence in two examples – one from either end of the political spectrum. The first danger (democratic levelling) reaches an extreme pitch for Weber in left-wing politics, since part of Weber's rejection of Marxism is that the necessary central control of the economy would create a power for inequality greater than that which Marxism sought to overcome (for example, ES: 1394, 1402).

---

14 Merton, in his study of bureaucracy, says that when 'the adherence to the rules, originally conceived as a means, becomes transformed into an end-in-itself; there occurs the familiar process of displacement of values whereby an instrumental value becomes a terminal value'; and this is described in the accompanying footnote as one of Weber's paradoxes (Merton, 1968: 253). Note also that 'Politics as a Vocation' only hints at this paradox, but it is strongly apparent elsewhere.

The necessary means undermine the intended result. The more general second problem, the administration controlling the ends of an organisation, constitutes a large part of his specific concern about the actuality of more standard, right-wing German politics, i.e., the dangers that then inhered in the uncontrolled power of the bureaucracy created by Bismark (for example, ES: 1393, 1404, 1413; PV: 95, 111).[15]

It is clear that bureaucracy epitomises the paradox of Western rationalisation for Weber. It is merely means, with no ends, problems or values of its own, except efficiency and those values that cluster around the hierarchy of the office, and bureaucratic training and procedure. Either the power of bureaucracy will deny the ends of democracy, and/or, more simply, the bureaucratic means themselves become the ends.

Now these are the extreme examples for Weber, but to bring this account of bureaucracy back to the present argument in 'Politics as a Vocation', it is clear that the vocational meaning of political causes must be threatened by the paradox of modern state bureaucracy. Whatever the cause, it will pass beneath the grindstone of the bureaucratic mill if it is to have political existence in the modern world – the cause, as the end that is being pursued, will be determined by the bureaucratic means that must be employed in the pursuit of meaning. At the extreme, the cause as end will be wholly lost or reversed, but in almost every case, at some level, the means will become the ends and the cause will be lessened as a result.[16]

In fact, the rise of bureaucracy might be seen as the final phase of the paradoxical logic of Western religious rationalisation. The rise and expansion of the capitalist economy, and the nature of the democratic nation-state are, in terms of the current analysis, partly determined by the paradox of the search for ultimate meaning since the realisation of the values of these spheres is still caught up in the pursuit of ideal interests that have been influenced by the religious history of the West – even if that influence is now at a minimal level. In the end, however, even these

---

15   A variant of this problem was played out within the German party structure where, with the decline of, or absence of, charismatic leaders, there arose 'the rule of professional politicians without a calling' (PV: 113). This paradox can be seen as the extreme case of the previously discussed paradox of the compromises demanded by the party machine; the vocational meaning is now not just lessened by necessary compromise with the machine but, perhaps, wholly lost when officials come to power. Weber gives an example from left-wing politics when, with the death of Bebel, 'the rule of officials began' in the Social Democratic Party (PV: 112). Robert Michels's 1911 work on parties should be noted here. A pupil of Weber, Michels spelt out the paradoxes of power inherent in the democratic party machine. Also, see Mommsen (1985, 1992) for a detailed analysis of Weber's fears and actions regarding the political situation of Germany in his time; and Goldman on politics and the 'Caeserist' solution (Goldman, 1992: Ch. 6).

16   Note that there is not necessarily something sinister at work here. The practical institutionalisation of a cause, and/or its compatibility with democratic, impersonal principles may well be reasons why the bureaucratic administration of a cause will undermine the intended meaning.

values of capitalism and democratic politics are in danger of being eclipsed by the very means they must use in their own realisation, i.e., bureaucracy. The questions of meaning are here left as far behind as, perhaps, is possible, when the values of these spheres are potentially dissolved in this final decisive paradox of modernity. The endlessness and senselessness of modern culture are actually increased when the answers appear to lie in even more administration.

In sum, the 'ethical paradoxes' (as quoted, PV: 125) of politics in modernity clearly involve the means undermining or defeating the ends: the meaning of the cause is lost in varying degrees. On top of this, however, Weber also includes the understanding of this fact of paradox into the vocation of politics itself, since it is highly unlikely that the cause will be able to be achieved unless there is this appreciation of the political reality. On this point he says:

> ... the fact that in numerous instances the attainment of 'good' ends is bound to the fact that one must be willing to pay the price of using morally dubious means or at least dangerous ones – and facing the possibility or even the probability of evil ramifications. (PV: 121)

So, the fact of paradox is something that is included into Weber's view of what it takes to have a vocation for politics. To engage in politics as a vocation, Weber warns, is not just to have a cause to which one is passionately devoted but, most importantly, it is to understand the probable paradoxical fate of that cause: in its very pursuit in the value-sphere of politics the cause will be fatefully diminished, or perhaps lost.

To view the political sphere in this paradoxical light might also go some way towards illuminating Weber's famous dichotomy in 'Politics as a Vocation' between an ethics of responsibility and an ethics of ultimate ends or 'convictions'. As usual, the commentary on this section of Weber is immense, with the strong tendency to try to bring the two sides into some sort of *ethical* resolution.[17] However this section should not be considered in terms of resolution and ethics, but in terms of paradox and meaning – as part of the vocation of politics. From this perspective, convictions, or causes, must be passionately maintained as a necessary part of vocational meaning, but this passion must also combine with a 'cool sense of proportion' to make 'responsibility to this cause the guiding star of action (PV: 115)'. In fact, to emphasise that this specific discussion is part of the overall meaning of politics as vocation, Weber begins this debate by saying that his concern is with 'the *ethos* of politics as a "cause"' (PV: 117, Weber's emphasis), and concludes his argument on the two ethical postures with the statement that:

> ... an ethic of ultimate ends and an ethic of responsibility are not absolute contrasts but rather supplements, which only in unison constitute a genuine man – a man who *can* have the 'calling for politics'. (PV: 127, Weber's emphasis)

---

17   See, for example, Schluchter (1979b: 85ff) for a discussion of how difficult this is.

Weber has in fact devoted a great deal of 'Politics as a Vocation' to telling us what this ethical dilemma entails as a 'calling for politics': one has to accept the fateful paradox of meaning within the value-sphere of politics. The vocation of politics, then, includes not just the ethic of absolute ends (the emotional pursuit of the cause as meaning), but also, the ethic of absolute ends combined with the ethic of responsibility (an appreciation of the fateful, paradoxical pursuit of the cause as meaning).

Finally, in the last paragraphs of 'Politics as a Vocation' Weber tells his audience how difficult it is to live the vocational life of politics. Weber acknowledges the great internal and international political challenges that faced Germany at the time: its 'polar night' (PV: 128). However, perhaps the greatest difficulty – and the one that is threaded throughout the entire text of 'Politics as a Vocation' – is the problem of the vocational life itself. The hard, routinised, mundane labour of the Protestant calling is recalled by Weber when he tells us that politics as a vocation demands measuring up 'to the world as it really is in its everyday routine' and necessitates 'the strong and slow boring of hard boards' (PV: 128). Indeed, it might be said that the inherent paradoxes of the value-sphere of politics demand such labour if the task of the cause is to be realised in its likely diminished form (if at all). So, if all the elements that Weber lists in 'Politics as a Vocation' are present – the passionate devotion to the task as political cause, the awareness of the paradoxes that await such a meaningful task, and the dutiful labour that the paradoxical realisation of the cause entails – then, perhaps, what has been 'experienced [is] the vocation for politics in its deepest meaning' (PV: 128). Arguably, it is in this sense that one can understand the famous last lines of 'Politics as a Vocation':

> Only he who in the face of all this can say 'In spite of all!' has the calling for politics. (PV: 128)

Conclusion

When the last two chapters are considered together, a pattern of paradox can be seen to arise from these three value-spheres based on the Protestant heritage of the calling. Each sphere will have its own specific way of expressing, or giving content to, this sense of vocation: the economic sphere gains its minimal vocational meaning from Protestantism itself and the calling as just rationalised labour; science/intellectual reason has its own history of meaning from the very beginning which gives content to the Protestant notion of the pre-ordained task; and the modern political sphere seems to have been able to create its own content for the Protestant-derived task with the cause. This pattern of modern paradox can only be recognised once the greater weave of Western meaninglessness has already been appreciated in terms of religion and intellectual reason.

If the result is an understanding of paradox as 'meaning within meaninglessness' it should be remembered that this expression and concept are not something externally imposed on the texts but are how Weber himself – quite explicitly in fact – sets up his account of the value-spheres. This is at its most apparent in 'Science as a Vocation' where there are the description and explanation of modern *meaninglessness* and disenchantment, and there is also the account of the *meaning* of intellectual work as a vocation, as has been recounted above. Using these terms from 'Science as a Vocation', we can reflect back on *The Protestant Ethic and the Spirit of Capitalism* to understand how religious meaning has been lost as part of the formation of modern meaninglessness, but how the 'spirit' of capitalism is the ongoing presence of meaning in the form of the calling within the economic value-sphere. With 'Politics as a Vocation' the overall meaninglessness of the modern world has to be assumed, and then the cause as meaning is taken up with its own set of paradoxes clearly indicated by Weber. The phrase 'meaning within meaninglessness', then, arises from Weber's own terminology and is fairly readily comprehensible once the strategy of sticking to what Weber himself had to say on these topics is sustained.

The pattern of paradox is not complete, however. Two more spheres need now to be considered.

Chapter 5
The Aesthetic and Erotic Value-Spheres

Introduction: From the Rationalised to the Irrational Value-Spheres

For Weber, the value-sphere theory of meaning can help explain the extraordinary status of art and erotic love in modernity. In order for us to understand his arguments here we need to step back and consider the emerging pattern of meaning/meaninglessness that can so far be discerned.

Although vocational meaning is a possible presence in the spheres that we have considered, the value-spheres of the economy, politics and science are the prime sites that have determined, and continue to sustain the overarching senselessness of the modern world. The meaninglessness of modernity in terms of the basic questions that have informed Western religion – death and theodicy – is the result of the processes of rationalisation that have led to capitalism, the bureaucratic state and a disenchanted universe. These are the factors that combine to give the grim, hard picture of Weber's modernity that has so often been described in the commentary. So, whatever meaning might be found through a sense of vocation in these spheres, it has to be remembered that an overall senselessness is still the common fate – it is only meaning within meaninglessness after all. This is especially the case with work in the capitalist economy where, as argued, the calling we are 'forced' to follow has reduced meaning to the barest of levels, so that all that this rationalised world would usually seem to offer in terms of ideal interests is a life of senseless routine.

If the focus is on this structure of meaninglessness and it is recognised how rationalisation is the ongoing basic process at work that has constituted this formation, then we might call the spheres of the economy, politics and science the 'rationalised' value-spheres. 'Rationalisation' is certainly a concept in Weber that has been subject to widespread critical review, but this particular application will be made more understandable as the contrasting value-spheres of art and the erotic start to become more clearly delineated.

Weber understands the aesthetic and erotic spheres as fatefully tied to the rationalised value-spheres, and this relationship provides a new sense of meaning that in fact rivals religion. Indeed, for Weber, this part of the pattern of meaning in modernity contains within it a new understanding of salvation and even 'death'. It is an ersatz, mock, unreal 'death' but Weber's theory of how ideal interests function at the centre of modern senselessness offers this remarkable extra dimension to the sociology of meaning/meaninglessness in modernity.

How this works can be seen in the following way. As the end point of the disenchanting logic of Western reason, these rationalised value-spheres, individually and in combination, are, to repeat, meaningless in terms of the ultimate questions, and whatever vocational meaning remains is, as it has been argued, caught in a web of means as ends. Yet over and above the remnants of vocational meaning present within these spheres, and in the face of this hard, disenchanted world, a sense of salvation and redemption arises in *escaping* this fate of extreme rationalisation: it is from the rationalised spheres themselves that one has to be saved. It is in this sense of 'salvation from' that a new, pale, mock idea of 'death' emerges. Weber does not explicitly call it 'death', but the imagery used points to how ideal interests are at work to create a modern form of this ultimate problem of meaning.

In 'Science as a Vocation' Weber compares the ancient Platonic view of reason, which did provide meaning, with today.

> Well, who today views science in such a manner? Today youth feels rather the reverse: the intellectual constructions of science constitute an unreal realm of artificial abstractions, which with their bony hands seek to grasp the blood-and-the-sap of true life without ever catching up with it. (SV: 140–41)[1]

Also, in the *Intermediary Reflection* there is this statement (among others, as we will see below) on the erotic experience:

> The lover realises himself to be rooted in the kernel of the truly living, which is eternally inaccessible to any rational endeavour. He knows himself to be freed from the cold skeleton hands of rational orders, just as completely as from the banality of everyday routine. (IR: 347)[2]

In these quotes the impersonal, rationalised world constitutes a sort of death – the repeated image is of skeletal hands – as opposed to the kernel of life. Moreover, to escape this fate is to gain salvation and redemption. This is clearly stated in 'Science as a Vocation':

---

1 '*Ja, wer steht heute so zur Wissenschaft? Heute ist die Empfindung gerade der Jugend wohl eher die umgekehrte: Die Gedankengebilde der Wissenschaft sind ein hinterweltliches Reich von künstlichen Abstraktionen, die mit ihren dürren Händen Blut und Saft des wirklichen Lebens einzufangen trachten, ohne es doch je zu erhaschen*' (WB: 89). Note that '*dürren*' might have been translated as scrawny, thin or scraggy, and the syntax is a little confusing. But the wider meaning is, in fact, better captured by the Gerth and Mills rendering of the German here, and any confusions are, arguably, clarified in the quote that follows.

2 '... *weiß sich der Liebende in den jedem rationalen Bemühen ewig unzugänglichen Kern des wahrhaft Lebendigen eingepflanzt, den kalten Skeletthänden rationaler Ordnungen ebenso völlig entronnen wie der Stumpfheit des Alltages*' (Zw: 561).

And today? 'Science as the way to nature' would sound like blasphemy to youth. Today, youth proclaims the opposite: redemption from the intellectualism of science in order to return to one's own nature and therewith to nature in general ...

And finally, science as a way 'to God'? Science, this specifically irreligious power? That science today is irreligious no one will doubt in his innermost being, even if he will not admit it to himself. Redemption from the rationalism and intellectualism of science is the fundamental presupposition of living in union with the divine. This, or something similar in meaning, is one of the fundamental watchwords one hears among German youth, whose feelings are attuned to religion or who crave religious experiences. They crave not only religious experience but experience as such. The only thing that is strange is the method that is now followed: the spheres of the irrational [*Sphären des Irrationalen*], the only spheres that intellectualism has not yet touched ... (SV: 142–3)

Redemption from science's intellectualism is found in religion, but also in 'experience as such' and this is most clearly sought in the 'spheres of the irrational'. These irrational spheres are the aesthetic and erotic. In the *Intermediary Reflection* Weber plainly emphasises how these value-spheres are characterised by this opposition between the rational and the irrational. 'The spheres of aesthetic and erotic life':

> ... are "this-worldly" life-forces, whose character is essentially non-rational or basically anti-rational. (IR: 341)

These 'non-rational', 'anti-rational' spheres are regarded by Weber in terms of humans pursuing ideal interests as part of his sociology of meaning; they are salvations from the rationalised spheres. So, it is in this context that we can turn to consider these last two of Weber's value-spheres.

A qualification has to be added here. Although Weber clearly wants to contrast these essentially irrational spheres from the rationalised,[3] it is not a clear-cut distinction. The rationalised spheres in fact contain important and necessary irrational elements, as we have seen, for example, in terms of passion and meaning; and these irrational spheres themselves only arise from a long history of intellectual rationalisation and must include rational elements (that in fact constitute a paradoxical threat, as we will see). So, as always with Weber, it is a relative not absolute contrast that is being made.

---

3 Brubaker (1984: 85) and Scaff (1991: 102ff) use the terms 'objective' and 'subjective' spheres. But this is not Weber's terminology here and, especially in the case of Scaff's argument, the stress on subjectivity leads away from meaning and religion, and into the terminology of modernity.

The Aesthetic and Erotic Spheres

We will first discuss the common features of art and the erotic and then treat each value-sphere separately.

Initially it should be stressed that Weber's account of these spheres only occurs within his sociology of religion. The question that forms his understanding here is the one of meaning. In *Economy and Society* and the *Intermediary Reflection* Weber discusses the history of the tense relationship between religion and art/the erotic. However, his point is to show how, as value-spheres in modernity, art and the erotic have become rivals to religion in terms of meaning and salvation.

The pursuit of meaning in these spheres is almost wholly formed by what is opposed; and what is opposed is the ultimately rationalised world of the economy, science and politics. A list can be compiled of what Weber says the irrational spheres provide salvation from: 'intellectual constructions of science [as] an unreal realm of artificial abstractions', 'the rationalism and intellectualism of science', 'rational endeavour', 'rational orders', 'the banality of everyday routine' (all given above in the stated quotations), 'routines of everyday life, and especially from the increasing pressures of theoretical and practical rationalism' (IR: 342), 'the unavoidably ascetic trait of the vocational specialist type of man' and 'rationalisation' (IR: 346), 'purposive–rational conduct' (IR: 341), 'mechanics of rationalisation' (IR: 345), and just plain 'rationality' (IR: 346).

In opposition, then, the values in the aesthetic and erotic spheres are irrational and emotional (where the level of emotional intensity attainable can be tremendous); they proffer supposed links back to non-disenchanted nature; and they give a sense of salvation through this very escape from the rationalised world. As has been stressed already, this last point is the crucial one – the mundane world of rationalised senselessness becomes a pair of 'skeletal hands' which can be escaped by entering these alternative value-spheres.

Clearly for Weber, these spheres are understood as meeting ideal interests, but these interests are being met within the overall meaninglessness of the modern world not from outside as with the irrational return to religion. Nor, in contrast to the rationalised spheres we have just discussed, is meaning gained in fragmentary form from the Protestant heritage of vocation, or from the sphere's own history of lost meaning. Further, whereas the economic, intellectual and political spheres each have their own history of non-meaningful internal values[4] (that is, making money, logic and self-clarification, power and violence) the irrational spheres will clearly develop nearly all of their own values only within modern times – but these internal values will be formed as meaningful, that is, as salvation from the ersatz 'death' of the rationalised spheres themselves. It is inside modern meaninglessness, then, that the aesthetic and erotic spheres each actually create their own inner 'cosmos' of values.

---

4 Some of which were the means to a meaningful end, as we have seen.

Art can be seen to be constituted as a value-sphere in this way:

> The development of intellectualism and the rationalisation of life change this situation.[5] For under these conditions, art becomes a cosmos of more and more consciously grasped independent values which exist in their own right. Art takes over the function of a this-worldly salvation, no matter how this may be interpreted. It provides a *salvation* from the routines of everyday life, and especially from the increasing pressures of theoretical and practical rationalism. (IR: 342, Weber's emphasis).

In the case of the erotic value-sphere:

> The last accentuation of the erotical sphere occurred in terms of intellectualist cultures. It occurred where this sphere collided with the unavoidably ascetic trait of the vocational specialist type of man .... A tremendous value emphasis on the specific sensation of an inner-worldly *salvation from* rationalisation thus resulted. (IR: 346, emphasis added)

So, these value-spheres developed as separate (especially in breaking from religion) only within, and in opposition to, intellectualised, rationalised culture, with the modern West being the most developed form of such culture. Of course, eroticised sexual satisfactions, and artistic pleasure might well be said to occur beyond such a modern determination, but the point for Weber is that these spheres develop as separate and gain their place in modernity because they are able to rival religion in terms of meaning – they provide a form of salvation within meaninglessness.

If the aesthetic and erotic values-spheres are, in this way, understood in terms of meaning, then the meaning pursued within these spheres is necessarily cast into paradox. This occurs on a general level – as the search for meaning within a broad sense of the value-spheres structure of senseless modernity – in two ways. Firstly, and obviously, the salvation and 'death' involved here are not meeting the problem of death itself. Ideal interests have formed this fake meaning as a substitute for the religious meaning and to gain this salvation is, in fact, to gain meaninglessness, whatever the level of emotional satisfaction and intensity. The drive to meet ideal interests, again, follows a logic of paradox in the modern West. We will see how this general paradox is substantiated in the content detail of the erotic values.

Secondly, this general level of paradox is evident in the way the rationalised spheres are left intact by these oppositional irrational value-spheres, and in fact these contrary spheres cannot exist without the rationalised realms on which they

---

5   This refers to art and religion still being tied together. Yet modernity in fact is the key element in separating the two because art can exist as a separate value-sphere in this state of opposition. This recalls part of Hegel's understanding of the end of art.

rely for their content.[6] So, when this mock meaning is gained within these spheres through achieving aesthetic and erotic values, this very achievement confirms, and indeed enhances the rationalised senselessness of modernity. This is how the structure of the value-spheres works for Weber. Since art and the erotic are really only optional value-spheres that one might choose to enter, they also must be left and the inescapable fact of rationalised meaninglessness re-engaged. This adds to our sense of how modernity functions as a kind of 'polytheism', where the 'gods of [the] city' (SV: 148; also PV: 123) must be worshipped. That is, even if the rationalised spheres are not entered in terms of a vocation, the disenchanted world of capitalism, science and bureaucracy is the unavoidable determination of modern existence – one has to follow the rituals demanded at these altars.[7] Indeed, it is this necessary condition that will continually regenerate the escape to the redemption of the irrational spheres. Again, to gain such meaning confirms this fate of modernity for Weber. Ideal interests, in their quest for meaning, serve to reproduce the value-sphere structure of meaninglessness.

If these general paradoxes of meaning exist, the inner 'cosmos' of values that constitutes these spheres provides a seemingly non-paradoxical structure of meaning within meaninglessness, as opposed to the rationalised spheres where fragmentary components of meaning (which arose, for example, from the metaphysical history of these very spheres) produced the set of paradoxes we have just examined. There is a stronger coherence within the realms of the aesthetic and erotic, the emotional states are obviously more intense and, to a large degree, unqualified by the necessities of mundane labour; but paradox is still present within such a cosmos of meaning. So let us now consider each of these irrational value-spheres in turn, and try to understand the way these spheres work as both internal worlds of 'cosmic' meaning, and, at the same moment, as sites where the logic of paradox is inescapably still present.

The Aesthetic Sphere[8]

In some brief, dense passages from the *Intermediary Reflection* and *Economy and Society* religion and art are distinguished from each other on the grounds of meaning. In fact rival kinds of salvation are said to be at stake. Weber writes that:

---

6 Following Scaff who notes, in his terms, the subjectivist dependence on objectivist culture; and, strikingly, he uses the term 'paradox' to describe this relation (Scaff, 1991: 110).

7 So to deal with a bank, or the education system, or the state bureaucracy/law – as we all must do – is to enter the rationalised spheres and follow their fateful, unalterable values. We will return to this understanding in a later chapter.

8 A note on vocation is needed at this point. It might seem that the aesthetic is also an obvious place for vocational meaning. After all, artists seem to be perhaps the loudest champions of a sense of calling in modern times. We will take up this point in a later chapter.

Indeed, religion violently rejects as sinful the type of salvation within the world that art *qua* art claims to provide. (ES: 608)

The aesthetic value-sphere achieved this capacity for meaning 'within the world' based on a new set of three values: taste, the creative subject and form.[9]

Firstly, judgement becomes based on taste as opposed to ethics.

> As a matter of fact, the refusal of modern men to assume responsibility for moral judgments tends to transform judgments of moral intent into judgments of taste ('in poor taste' instead of 'reprehensible'). (IR: 342; also ES: 608)

Secondly, the artist, and those who are aesthetically receptive, have an inner subjectivity – 'subjectivist needs' (IR: 342; also ES: 608) – that must reject all other norms as restrictive of their creative originality and sensitivities:

> To the creative artist, however, as well as to the aesthetically excited and receptive mind, the ethical norm as such may easily appear as a coercion of their genuine creativeness and innermost selves. (IR: 342; also ES: 608)

Thirdly, within the value-spheres of art, form or style triumphs over content (with form having a long history of tension with religious meaning):

> The sublimation of the religious ethic and the quest for salvation, on the one hand, and the evolution of the inherent logic of art, on the other, have tended to form an increasingly tense relation. All sublimated religions of salvation have focused upon the meaning alone, not upon the form, of the things and actions relevant for salvation. Salvation religions have devalued form as contingent, as something creaturely and distracting from meaning. (IR: 341; also ES: 610)

Weber contrasts the inner world of artistic form with religious, particularly mystic, experience:

> The most irrational form of religious behaviour, the mystic experience, is in its innermost being not only alien but hostile to all form. Form is unfortunate and inexpressible to the mystic because he believes precisely in the experience of exploding all forms, and hopes by this to be absorbed into the 'All-oneness' which lies beyond any kind of determination and form. For him the indubitable psychological affinity of profoundly shaking experiences in art and religion can only be a symptom of the diabolical nature of art. Especially music, the most 'inward' of all the arts, can appear in its purest form of instrumental music as an irresponsible *Ersatz* for primary religious experience. The internal logic

---

9   It might be noted here how closely Weber's account aligns with Kant's understanding of the aesthetic in the *Critique of Judgement*.

of instrumental music as a realm not living 'within' appears as a deceptive pretension to religious experience …. Art becomes an 'idolatry', a competing power, and a deceptive bedazzlement … (IR: 342–3)

This comparison with religion is indicative of the salvation value of art in modernity and the opposition here is between the 'internal' or 'inherent logic' of artistic form over the content of salvation religions.[10]

In sum, the irrational escape from the rationalised world creates the separate aesthetic sphere in terms of the values of taste, subjective originality and form. On this basis a work of art can achieve a 'fulfilment'. In comparison to science:

> A work of art which is genuine 'fulfilment' is never surpassed; it will never be antiquated. Individuals may differ in appreciating the personal significance of works of art, but no one will ever be able to say of such a work that it is 'outstripped by another work, which is also 'fulfilment'. (SV: 138)

There is emotional fulfilment if the standard of taste is met through the irrational subjective experience, or original creation, of the form of the artwork.[11] Yet in this very mode of fulfilment as salvation from rationalisation lies a return to a paradox of the rationalised world itself. Note that in order to make sense of these remarks on art we will have to fill in some points of argument that are not quite explicit in Weber's own writing.

Despite the internal sense of fulfilment and salvation that is achieved by following the aesthetic values in contrast to scientific progress, art is still prone to the general paradox of cultural values that we have noted with regard to science and the intellectual sphere. In other words, the artwork can be returned to as a source of emotional fulfilment, and so is not so easily surpassed as intellectual theory, but it is still not immune from the paradox of cultural endlessness that is the fate of scientific values.

In the *Intermediary Reflection* Weber talks of the cultivation of the cultural values of mind and taste in modernity:

> [the] 'cultural values' which usually rank highest … have proved to be bound to the charisma of the mind or of taste. The barriers of education and of

---

10 There has long been a tension between art/the erotic and religion, which Weber describes in the *Intermediary Reflection*. However, the point is that it is only in modernity that these irrational forces become competing spheres of meaning with religion.

11 Also, it might be added, romanticism in particular offers a subjective return to a new form of enchanted nature. But Weber only fleetingly makes reference to this point (for example, to 'romantic irrationalism' (SV: 143); to Rousseau (ES: 506); and in the quote: '… redemption from the intellectualism of science in order to return to one's own nature and therewith to nature in general …' (SV: 142).

aesthetic cultivation are the most intimate and the most insuperable of all status differences. (IR: 354)

In this meaningless, intellectualist[12] culture the values of the rational mind and its irrational aesthetic opposite gain charisma and status.

However, as we have seen, the pursuit of these cultural values in modernity is subject to the logic of paradox. The long and famous quote from 'Science as a Vocation', where this point is made about intellectual values, has already been given. Here is a parallel quotation from the *Intermediary Reflection*, where:

> ... under the very conditions of 'culture', senseless death has seemed only to put the decisive stamp upon the senselessness of life itself ...
>
> ... the 'cultivated' man who strives for self-perfection, in the sense of acquiring or creating 'cultural values', ... can become 'weary of life' but he cannot become 'satiated with life' in the sense of completing a cycle. For the perfectibility of the man of culture in principle progresses indefinitely, as do the cultural values ... (IR: 356)

The pursuit of cultural values is endless and senseless because it cannot regain the meaningful, organic cosmos, with the result that every new idea or book or work of art is always 'provisional' and has to be immediately left behind. This endlessness is the fate of the aesthetic sphere's combination of the values of taste, subjectivity/ originality and the progress of form, since these cultural values have the in-built paradox of gaining fulfilment and 'salvation' that is necessarily temporary – more is always demanded. New experiences are needed for this emotional fulfilment of the aesthetic sphere, and the empty values of style and subjective creativity are in fact the means of meeting this demand; or, to put is slightly differently, form, or style, is necessarily always changing, especially under the pressure of the demand for creative originality. And originality, as the mark of the genuine inner self, is a value that, by definition, can only be met by creating the new. Further, to regard art in terms of meaning and ideal interests, as Weber does, is to understand that because artistic fulfilment is a kind of salvation from the rationalised world then these aesthetic values are, of necessity, insatiable – there is no completion, no rest, no meaningful death.

The Erotic Sphere

If this is the way Weber understands the workings of the aesthetic sphere in terms of the paradox of meaning, let us now turn to the other sphere of 'salvation' – the erotic. Weber wants to stress how the modern erotic sphere is shaped by and

---

12 '... the advance of intellectualism ... may be described as quasi-aesthetic' (ES: 608).

against religion and modern rationalised/intellectualised life as part of a long and complex cultural history. The values that emerge in this value-sphere centre around nature/the natural and the emotional state of religious salvation, and these ends are gained by the means of sexual activity itself. Indeed it is within this sphere that the overall pattern of meaning in modernity is most clearly exemplified, since, within the internal cosmos of the erotic, meaningful nature and even religion itself are what is said to be regained.

A point of difference needs to be noted concerning the state of paradox in this sphere. Like the other value-spheres the internal cosmos of erotic values is shaped by the overall paradoxes of the West, and each of its values will have a paradoxical history, but, in contrast to the other spheres, this example of meaning within meaninglessness proves itself to be less prone to such inner meaning being lessened or lost as it is pursued. Meaning, then, is more able to be sustained within the bounds of the erotic cosmos.

Let us now consider the values at work in this sphere. Firstly, on the value of the natural/nature (the 'kernel of the truly living', as we have seen above), Weber states:

> The extraordinary quality of eroticism has consisted precisely in a gradual turning away from the naive naturalism of sex. The reason and significance of this evolution, however, involve the universal rationalisation and intellectualisation of culture ...
>
> The total being of man has now been alienated from the organic cycle of peasant life; life has been increasingly enriched in cultural content, whether this content is evaluated as intellectually or otherwise supra-individual. All this has worked, through the estrangement of life-value from that which is merely naturally given, toward a further enhancement of the special position of eroticism. Eroticism was raised into the sphere of conscious enjoyment (in the most sublime sense of the term). Nevertheless, indeed because of this elevation, eroticism appeared to be like a gate into the most irrational and thereby real kernel of life, as compared with the mechanisms of rationalisation. (IR: 345)

This point is repeated in the following expansion of a quotation already given:

> The last accentuation of the erotical sphere occurred in terms of intellectualist cultures. It occurred where this sphere collided with the unavoidably ascetic trait of the vocational specialist type of man. Under this tension between the erotic sphere and rational everyday life, specifically extramarital sexual life, which had been removed from everyday affairs, could appear as the only tie which still linked man with the natural fountain of all life. (IR: 346)

The 'natural fountain of life' and 'gate into most irrational and thereby real kernel of life' suggest a return to nature in terms of finding some pure originating life as opposed to the loss of life, or some sort of artificial life. And we have seen how this explicitly entails the salvation from 'the mechanics of rationalisation' as a form of 'death', or, more specifically here, as the loss of 'real' life. The natural therefore acquires meaning within the erotic sphere as salvation from the rationalised spheres: sex in modernity is a means of snatching an originating (fountain, kernel), naturally pure life away from the 'skeletal hands' of rationalisation.

This value of the erotic sphere can be seen to have its own specific, paradoxical, historical formation, as an illustration of the overall patterns already described. It is because of the intellectualised disenchantment of nature, and in fact the leaving behind of the naïve naturalism of 'the peasant'[13] within the organic cycle of meaningful nature, that the erotic becomes the way to the irrational and a return to meaningful 'life' in terms of a new sense of the natural.

Weber maps out a history of the development of the erotic in the West where these internal values become intellectually and consciously formed, and on this basis the irrational path is opened (IR: 344ff). So, the 'peasant' reference is one that invokes a meaningful cycle of nature that has been lost through disenchantment; but it also suggests a 'naïve', lower class, agricultural naturalism that intellectualised urban culture will necessarily surpass. This process has had a number of historical manifestations (from the Greeks to the Renaissance) which mark changing worldviews of meaning in which the erotic is placed. This Western intellectualisation that forms the erotic is in contrast to the distinctly un-erotic peasant naturalism, where sex has meaning only as part of the overall worldview of organic cycles. However, it is in modernity (against the 'vocational specialist') that it will be most accentuated. The erotic, then, is a 'consciously cultivated ... non-routinised sphere' (IR: 344) in which:

> ... man had now been completely emancipated from the old, simple and organic existence of the peasant. (IR: 346)

At this point there is 'a joyous triumph over rationality', 'an inner-worldly salvation' and the 'highly valued erotic sensation ... reinterprets and glorifies all the pure animality of the relation' (IR: 346–7).

Weber sums this up:

> ... this mature love of intellectualism reaffirms the natural quality of the sexual sphere, but it does so consciously, as an embodied creative power. (IR: 347)

What is in evidence is how the value of the natural in the erotic sphere lies in the specific intellectualised leaving of the peasant form of nature/sex so that, consciously, an irrational return to nature ('pure animality') is opened. The intellectual process itself will understand its own limits of rationalised

---

13 It is to be remembered that the '*peasant*, like Abraham, could die satiated with life' (IR: 356, emphasis added; also SV: 140), as opposed to the endless senselessness of modern culture.

senselessness and consciously form the erotic as an irrational alternative. The basic condition of salvation from rationalisation must be stressed. But the content of the erotic sphere itself – its irrational valuing of the natural – is formed by the intellectualised conscious West that the erotic values must in fact deny. The paradoxical gestation of the erotic sphere might be stated in the following way: in the pursuit of meaning in the intellectualised, disenchanting West a meaningful nature is lost; but this intellectualisation itself will prove meaningless; as a result, a vastly diminished form of the natural is intellectually regained as meaningful against intellectualisation itself; and this new sense of nature becomes constitutive of the irrational erotic value-sphere. Here, as opposed to the naïve naturalism of the peasant, sex will be the site of meaning and nature.[14]

This value of nature/life is woven into a pattern of meaning in the erotic value-sphere with another value of the greatest possible meaning: religion itself. We have already discussed how both of the irrational value-spheres are cast in terms of religious meaning by Weber, as *salvation* and *redemption* from some sort of anti-life/'death'. Also, it might be added here, within the value-sphere of art, the aesthetic experience is often expressed in religious terms.[15] However, Weber accords the erotic sphere a further explicit dimension of religiosity.

> … the erotic relation seems to offer the unsurpassable peak of the fulfillment of the request for love in the direct fusion of the souls of one to the other. This boundless giving of oneself is as radical as possible in its opposition to all functionality, rationality, and generality. It is displayed here as the unique meaning which one creature in his irrationality has for another, and only for this specific other. However, from the point of view of eroticism, this meaning, and with it the value-content of the relation itself, rests upon the possibility of a communion which is felt as a complete unification, as a fading of the 'thou'. It is so overpowering that it is interpreted 'symbolically': as a sacrament. (IR: 347)

The lovers' erotic embrace takes on all the characteristics of religious meaning as 'communion' and 'sacrament'. Further, the sexual experience of the lovers is 'equivalent to the having of the mystic' (IR: 347), says Weber. In this way the irrationality of the erotic works as a form of salvation from 'all functionality,

---

14 Scaff recognises this natural escape with the erotic and, again, labels as a 'paradox' the intellectualism that is part of this process (Scaff, 1991: 109–10).

15 There are numerous cases, but one example might be given. In 2010 the philosopher and art critic Arthur Danto, in a response to an astonishingly popular piece by the performance artist Marina Abramovich in New York, used the following phrases: 'a charmed space'; 'it was a shamanic trance'; 'magic'; 'fraught with meaning'; 'a ritual moment'; 'a spiritual exchange'; 'a pilgrimage'; 'The spiritual wiring of the human soul remains to be diagrammed. That is what art is for'; 'the sacredness [of] the performance'; and 'For a wild moment I thought my physical ailments would fade away, as if I were at Lourdes' (Danto, 2010a; Danto, 2010b).

rationality and generality'; and this is a further reason for its extraordinary status and character in modernity.

Because of this value of religious sensibility Weber stresses how the erotic sphere is in direct conflict with forms of religion itself:

> A principled ethic of religious brotherhood is radically and antagonistically opposed to all this. From the point of view of such an ethic, this inner, earthly sensation of salvation by mature love competes in the sharpest possible way with the devotion of a supra-mundane God, with the devotion of an ethically rational order of God, or with the devotion of a mystical bursting of individuation, which alone appear 'genuine' to the ethic of brotherhood. (IR: 347–8)

If religion does then become a value in the erotic, a problem about the term 'religion' is immediately apparent. Within the erotic sphere, at this altar in the modern polytheism, irrational salvation from rationalisation gains religious meaning, but it is only meaning within the value-sphere structure. It might be argued, therefore, that it should not properly be called 'religion' if this is the case. This point is obviously correct at the level of ultimate metaphysical meaning, however even if the newly concocted 'death' is fake, the sense of salvation, and the religiosity of the erotic emotions, are drawing on, and sustaining, religious understanding. Like the specific continuation of Protestant meaning in terms of the calling, the erotic will adopt part of the religious worldview within its internal, non-religious cosmos of the value-sphere.

The inner cosmos of the erotic is constructed with these twin, interwoven values of nature/life and religiosity. And the obvious emotional intensity of the erotic sphere is understood by Weber in these terms. So, Weber will stress that the 'euphoria of the happy lover' (IR: 348) is due to the emotional impact of this meaningful nature and religious experience. It is not the physical pleasure of the sexual act that is important; what is added to the physical act to constitute the erotic value-sphere is meaning, and it is this which enables the increase of sexual pleasure to a state of such heightened happiness within the overall rationalised meaninglessness of a disenchanted world. A psychological state of salvation is achieved that rivals religion and is understandable in religious terms. This is why the erotic achieves such status in modernity.

The erotic, then, forms itself as an internal cosmos of independent values against both religion and the rationalised spheres. Cocooned in the erotic value-sphere, a sense of religious meaning and meaningful nature, with their attendant emotional intensity, can be regained. Further, the values of this sphere, which enable the sense of salvation, are explained by Weber as specific parts in the overall pattern of paradoxes that form modernity: there is a sense of meaningful 'nature' that is the product of an intellectualised rejection of the natural; and there is a religious, emotional sense of mystic salvation that must be non-religious. Both meaningful nature and religion are gained, but in a diminished form within the sphere, and on the condition that 'real' meaningful nature and religion are themselves excluded, or lost to, the rationalised structures of modernity beyond this sphere. Again, we can start to appreciate more of the detail of Weber's pattern for meaning within meaninglessness.

To conclude this section on the irrational spheres one further paradox, or potential paradox, needs mentioning.

The irrational spheres work as 'salvation' as long as they can maintain their integrity as spheres separate from the rationalised routines. Yet it may well be that in pursuing their values/ends they will have this integrity compromised by the very value-spheres they exist to oppose. Paradox is, in this way, a constant threat.

For Weber the most immediate danger lies with the intellectual sphere:[16]

> The only thing that is strange is the method that is now followed: the spheres of the irrational, the only spheres that intellectualism has not yet touched, are now raised into consciousness and put under its lens. For in practice this is where the modern intellectualist form of romantic irrationalism leads. *This method of emancipation from intellectualism may well bring about the very opposite of what those who take to it conceive as its goal.* (SV: 143, emphasis added)

Intellectualist culture creates the irrational values both as opposition to reason, and also in setting the agenda on what sort of 'nature' is allowed to be regained (as we saw with the erotic; but this might also be said of romanticism). That is, these two irrational spheres are themselves partly shaped by intellectual developments of their values – it is not the case that the irrational and rationalised spheres are ever wholly differentiated. However, Weber's point in this quote is that in seeking 'emancipation from intellectualism' these irrational values will themselves come under the determination of reason and the intellectual sphere. This paradoxical outcome will occur as art and the erotic try to further themselves by being understood intellectually – reason will increasingly be used as a means to gain the values of the irrational. The result is that what has value as a release from the rationalised world will itself be caught in those 'skeletal hands'.[17]

---

16 Weber's point here can be added to by noting that a common critique of modern art is that its pure ideal form has been compromised by the art market, that is, the economic value-sphere. Also, with regard to the political value-sphere, political determination by totalitarian regimes usually means that such art is, at least, suspect as 'art'. With the case of the erotic sphere, economics, perhaps aided by technological tools like the web, might be regarded as a cause for the erotic sphere losing some of its salvation quality by becoming mere pornography.

17 Following Brubaker, who makes this point about the threat and presence of 'intellectualising rationalisation' within the value-spheres of the erotic and aesthetic; and, it should be stressed, he calls this a further example of a 'paradox of unintended consequences' in Weber (Brubaker, 1984: 79). Further on this point, Weber remarks in 'Science as a Vocation' that for aesthetics *within* the value-sphere of art: 'aesthetics does not ask whether there *should* be works of art' (SV: 144, Weber's emphasis). However, it is at least arguable whether this point about art and aesthetics has been upheld since Weber's

Conclusion

The last three chapters have tried to show how meaning works in modernity for Weber – as a set of competing value-spheres in the shadow of cosmic meaninglessness. The many arguments that Weber has on these complex issues are linked together through his persistent and consistent use of a specific concept of paradox for which the Protestant ethic thesis provided the model: the pursuit or development of meaning will fatefully result in that meaning being diminished or lost. This concept of paradox is different to that used by other social theorists, most notably in the way paradox, for Weber, is the fate and logic of modernity. It cannot be overcome.

In each value-sphere some sense of meaning was shown to be possible, as opposed to the overall meaninglessness of modern existence in terms of death and life-conduct. These fragments of polytheistic meaning within meaninglessness were formed within a complex structure of paradox that combined the long paradoxes of Western meaning with a series of paradoxes that arose within the various spheres. A theory of meaning as paradox was thus able to be pieced together, and it was done so by maintaining a methodology of, firstly, persisting with Weber's perspective of the sociology of religion, and, secondly, only using Weber's own terms.

However, this picture is still incomplete. Although a considerable expanse of theory has been covered in this account of the paradoxes of meaning, we have only briefly discussed the ethic of brotherliness. This position can be explained in terms of ideal interests. The limited meaning possible in each of the value-spheres provided a semblance of how one could and should live in the world with death as the determining factor – either through some degree of preservation of the Protestant heritage of the calling, where salvation had been the dominant concern, or with the creation of an ersatz form of death with the irrational spheres. The ideal interest in finding some meaning to life and death was, in this way, partly met and was crucial in the determination of the value-sphere structure. But the problem of theodicy – of unjust suffering in the world – has not been accounted for in this structure of meaning in modernity. The ideal interest in finding some meaning for

---

time. Through intellectualisation within the art sphere the question of the very existence of the art object seems to have been put within art itself, for example, with, at least, the confrontation of Duchamp's ready-mades and the anti-art of dada. And, in aesthetic theory more widely, theorists like Arthur Danto have recently proclaimed 'the end of art' with the seeming extinguishing of the development of style and form, and the triumph of theory. These points cannot be fully explored here, but the argument might be made that art and its aesthetic theory indicate that the pursuit of taste, form and subjectivity/originality – values directly targeted by Duchamp – might well have expended itself in a paradoxical breaking apart of the value-sphere of art because of the intellectualisation of this irrational sphere, as Weber predicted. Salvation, it might be argued, is difficult to imagine with Duchamp's 'Fountain'.

this fact of human existence is absent. In the West at least, the religious account of suffering gave rise to the ethic of brotherly love, and Weber, especially in the *Intermediary Reflection*, tries to show how modernity both opposes and necessarily preserves this ideal interest and its resultant ethic. It follows that it is to the concept of brotherliness that we must now turn to complete our reconstruction of Weber's theory.

PART II
Meaning, Modernity and Brotherliness

Chapter 6
The Concept of Brotherliness

Introduction

In the previous chapters we have examined a concept previously under-examined in sociology's use of Weber's work, that of paradox. 'Brotherliness' is another concept which has also suffered the same fate and which is equally as important in understanding Weber's sociology of meaning. The fundamental problem of suffering in an imperfect world – the problem of theodicy – will have a variety of theological explanations; but a crucial response, which takes different forms in different cultures, is an ethic of care and compassion for the sufferer. This is the ethic of brotherliness. Brotherliness, or brotherly love, is formed as part of the wider problem of meaning for Weber and is also subject to paradox. An ideal of this ethic becomes a standard of goodness in the West, but is lost in being pursued within the religious sphere itself; however, it still acts as the ultimate ideal of virtue within modernity even though the value-spheres of the age are necessarily hostile to it. Here lies the underlying 'guilt' of modern times, according to Weber.

Brotherliness is the central idea of the *Intermediary Reflection*, and it is here that this ethic is most clearly set against the antagonistic value-spheres of modernity. After understanding these value-spheres as subject to the paradoxes of meaning in the previous chapters, we are now in a position to understand brotherliness and its embattled position in modernity. First, in this chapter, after using the *Intermediary Reflection* as a starting position, we will examine Weber's vast sociological studies of religion to make sense of the ethic of brotherly love; and then, in the next chapter, we can return to its fate in the *Intermediary Reflection*, that is, how the paradox of brotherliness has come to sit within the paradoxes of modern meaning.

As with the concept of paradox, the approach that will be adopted to understand brotherliness is one of searching through Weber's writings to piece together what this idea means, rather than using outside sources which lead away from Weber's own understanding. However, before going into Weber's writings on this topic a brief survey of what has been said in the secondary literature has to be given. It will become evident that the trend in the interpretations has been to acknowledge and then look past the concept of brotherliness.

Some Previous Commentaries on Brotherly Love

The importance of brotherly love or brotherliness in the works of Max Weber has been noted by many authors (see, for example, Nelson, 1969, 1976; Bryan Turner,

1996: 105; Brubaker, 1984: 3; Scaff, 1991: 97ff), but has rarely been examined beyond, what amounts to, just a passing remark. The most notable exceptions to this tendency are works by Bologh (1990), Bellah (1999) and, to a lesser extent, Schluchter (1981).

Schluchter (1981: 156–74) has traced Weber's concern with the cultural significance of brotherly love, as well as the influence of Troeltsch's work on Weber in this area. He has also stressed the effect of Protestantism on this brotherliness:

> ... consistent Calvinism has had above all two consequences: the inner loneliness of the individual and the treatment of 'brothers' as 'others'. We can say, then, that the religious ethic of ascetic Protestantism is a *monologic* ethic of conviction with *unbrotherly* consequences ... the autonomous vocational culture of Western modernity reveals the remnants of the religious elements which helped bring about its birth. They continue to haunt us in the secularised attitude of world mastery and the world domination of impersonality and lack of brotherhood. (1981: 172–4, Schluchter's emphasis)

Despite these insights (which we will explore further below), Schluchter's account of brotherliness in Weber's work remains relatively undeveloped and brief, a circumstance which is unsurprising given that this theme has never been his primary focus.

Bologh (1990: 165) discusses the idea of love as presented in the *Intermediary Reflection* as part of her overall critique of Weber, which is aimed at Weber's alleged advocacy of public 'greatness' over love as part of a feminine, private realm. Brotherliness is not discussed in detail beyond the terms of this critique. Bologh, then, will come to see Weber as supporting a form of brotherliness as an ethic of 'impersonal love', in opposition to her own position of a 'personal ethic of erotic love' or 'ethic of personal love' (Bologh, 1990: 168). The following argument promotes a substantially different interpretation of brotherliness and the personal/impersonal in Weber's texts to that of Bologh.

Bellah's (1999) essay is perhaps the most comprehensive and impressive examination of the question of love in the works of Max Weber yet composed. However, his analysis might be said to be limited by his concentration on just one kind of brotherliness: acosmic mysticism. The various meanings of brotherliness are, consequently, not clearly revealed within this discussion. Bellah also tends to concentrate too much on the *Intermediary Reflection*, so that the range of meanings exhibited by Weber in his empirical religious studies is somewhat understated. However a debt has to be acknowledged to Bellah's insights and references.

If these are the authors who start to conceptualise the idea of brotherliness, the question then arises as to why it has been so understated in the secondary literature, despite the fact that it is often mentioned by the commentators, is clearly a presence throughout Weber's sociology of religion, and is the key concept in one of the texts most favoured in post-1960s interpretations: the *Intermediary*

Reflection. One possible explanation, when an attempt is made to understand some part of Weber's theory of modernity, lies in the favoured intellectual strategy of placing Weber's texts within some academic debate, either of the time or soon after (Lassman and Velody, 1989; Mommsen and Osterhammel, 1987; Schluchter, 1996; Turner and Factor, 1984; Scaff, 1991; C. Turner, 1992); or within a wider, contemporary debate on modernity/postmodernity (C. Turner, 1992; Gane, 2002). A further overlapping tactic is to make sense of Weber's position through another thinker, such as Heidegger (Löwith, 1982; Turner and Factor, 1984), Marx (Löwith, 1982; Sayers, 1990; B. Turner, 1996), Freud (Bologh, 1990) and, especially, Nietzsche (e.g., Brubaker, 1984; Hennis, 1988; Stauth, 1992; B. Turner, 1993; Warren, 1994; and, as crucially important for the theme of meaning: Scaff, 1991; and Gane, 2002). All of these interpretations offer much scholarly insight, but none of these debates or theorists is concerned with Christian brotherliness so that this key concept is both necessarily a passing presence in these varied accounts of Weber, but it is also, understandably, consistently overlooked.[1]

As foreshadowed, it has to be said that the intellectualist framework which has most contributed to this process is the Nietzschean. Of course, the notion that Nietzsche had an important influence on many of Weber's views is not being contested.[2] However, to place Weber within some sort of Nietzschean theoretical setting is to begin from a position which – perhaps more than any other – is unlikely to consider the importance of something like an ethic of brotherliness.[3]

---

1 A further question might be asked about why these intellectual settings to Weber's work do not have a place for the very ethic that was so very much part of Weber's concern. Two possible answers flow from Weber's own arguments: firstly, such *Christian* love will be excluded from these modern intellectual solutions and pushed into the realm of the unconsidered irrational; and, secondly, as we have started to see and as will be articulated further below, the values and ideal interests at work within the scientific value-sphere help create an intellectual unbrotherly aristocracy which will tend to turn away from the problem at the heart of brotherliness: human suffering.

2 Turner (1996: Introduction) has provided a useful summary of these effects. The idea of a Nietzschean 'personality' has also been important.

3 For example, Hennis (1988) understands 'Politics as a Vocation' and 'Science as a Vocation' in terms of 'personality' and 'life-conduct' (1988: 71, 100). He makes the impersonal/personal theme explicit (1988: 96) but a Nietzschean perspective is dominant. Hence he says that Weber took over an understanding of Christianity from Nietzsche so that 'For Weber there is no human relationship, no "life order" that could not be defined by struggle' (1988: 159). Part of the task for Hennis is to show how Weber was not a liberal, and a Nietzschean influence is seen to be conclusive on this issue. Further, Hennis adds the ad hominem point that despite Weber's deeply imbued sense of Christian dignity he was a great hater full of heartfelt contempt (1988: 177). All these points add up to the ignoring or, in fact, denial of a possible place for brotherliness in the life-conduct appropriate for modernity. From the perspective of the argument being presented here, it is the placing of Weber in the intellectual debate over liberalism versus Nietzsche that

In fact, it is precisely on this ethical point that Weber distinguishes himself from Nietzsche. In the discussion of the origins of brotherly love within religious attempts to deal with the problem of suffering, Weber is at pains to contrast his position to the Nietzschean explanation of theodicy as being based upon the resentment of the 'inferior' peoples of history (IEEWR: 270ff; ES: 494; also ES: 934–5). His discussion of Nietzsche's work in this regard is easily his most sustained treatment of Nietzsche,[4] and is usually ignored by commentators who are more interested in seeking the commonalities between the two thinkers.[5]

Essentially, while admitting the power of Nietzsche's arguments in *The Genealogy of Morals*, Weber will argue against him for two reasons. Firstly, Weber believes that the resentment of the underprivileged is not the cause of all salvation religions, as demonstrated by the example of Buddhism where it arises from the privileged/intellectual strata. Secondly, in the only religion in which resentment does play a significant role, ancient Judaism, such a role is limited by a large range of other factors.[6] Weber also points out, against Nietzsche, that,

---

leads such interpretation, undoubtedly valuable in many ways, away from some of Weber's ethical understanding. Another example of this tendency is witnessed in Gane (2002). Gane will stress the *Intermediary Reflection*, the problem of meaning, and mentions and then must ignore brotherliness when he defines Weber's position on values as 'nihilistic' – with explicit reference to Nietzsche (Gane, 2002: 23ff).

4 And is, perhaps, the most lengthy, direct engagement with any theorist or text in the whole of Weber's works.

5 One major exception to the trend of not dealing with Weber's arguments against Nietzsche on resentment is Turner (1996). Turner claims that although Weber was critical of, and wanted to limit, the resentment thesis, Weber's arguments in *Ancient Judaism*, and elsewhere, have some correlation with Nietzsche, especially in agreeing on different types of theodicies and goodness. Turner also believes that Weber's own personal position was one of the (very Nietzschean) isolated prophet of doom (1996: 158–65). This may be correct to a degree, but, it might be argued, it tips the balance far too much in favour of Nietzsche and does not consider the more obvious rejection of the resentment thesis, especially when the dimension of brotherliness is included. However, it is undoubtedly correct that Weber did maintain the Nietzschean personality ideal as being necessary for undertaking the vocational task in modernity; but also, as we will see, Weber regards such heroic strength as needed in order to follow the ethic of brotherliness.

6 Some brief explanation of Judaism and the resentment thesis can be found in the *Introduction to the Economic Ethic of the World Religions* and *Economy and Society*, but, more obviously, it is in *Ancient Judaism* that Weber gives a highly detailed account of the development of Judaic beliefs. Resentment and revenge are certainly there as part of the explanation (e.g., AJ: 367, 404), but only amongst a large number of other determinants, including climate, civic culture and the internal logics of Judaic theology. Further, when resentment and its morality are discussed by Weber, their origins are not understood by him in the same manner as Nietzsche (see AJ: 365–77 on how the theodicy of Deutero-Isaiah developed suffering, humility and the redeemer as central to Judaism). Nietzsche is not mentioned by name in *Ancient Judaism*, but this absence and the relatively minor role resentment plays in this work should in themselves be regarded as constituting a sort

despite its obvious origins in Judaism, the teachings of Jesus are not reducible to *ressentiment* (ES: 498–9).

Weber sums up his position on Nietzsche's resentment thesis in the following way:

> The theodicy of suffering can be coloured by resentment. But the need of compensation for the insufficiency of one's fate in this world has not, as a rule, had resentment as a basic and decisive colour. Certainly, the need for vengeance has had a special affinity with the belief that the unjust are well off in this world only because hell is reserved for them later. Eternal bliss is reserved for the pious; occasional sins, which, after all, the pious also commit, ought therefore to be expiated in this world. Yet one can readily be convinced that even this way of thinking, which occasionally appears, is not always determined by resentment, and that it is by no means always the product of socially oppressed strata. We shall see that there have been only a few examples of religion to which resentment contributed essential features. Among these examples only one is a fully developed case. All that can be said is that resentment *could* be, and often and everywhere has been, significant as one factor, among others, in influencing the religiously determined rationalism of socially disadvantaged strata. It has gained such significance, in highly diverse and often minute degrees, in accordance with the nature of the promises held out by different religions. In any case, it would be quite wrong to attempt to deduce 'asceticism' in general from these sources. (IEEWR: 276)

This critique of the resentment thesis is important because it frees Weber from the Nietzschean reading of morality and religion. Suffering and love are allowed to be focal points for Weber once Nietzsche's condemnation of such morality as inferior and reducible to the psychology of slaves and weaklings has been critiqued. Let us now try to unravel this concept of brotherliness.

The Forms of Brotherliness in Weber's Sociology of Religion

A close reading of Weber's use of the term 'brotherliness' *throughout* his works indicates that it is a consistent, if sometimes implied, theme in Weber's most notable writings. Whilst the concept is prominently discussed in the *Intermediary Reflection* and has a strong, if sometimes assumed, presence in the *Introduction to the Economic Ethic of the World Religions*, it is also used in a subtle and multifaceted manner in his empirical studies of the world religions, in the sections on religion and political domination in *Economy and Society*, and briefly in both

---

of reply to Nietzsche's claims. It should also be remembered that the explicit dealing with Nietzsche's thesis comes in the general introduction (IEEWR) to the religious studies (*Gesammelte Aufsätze zur Religionssoziologie*) of which *Ancient Judaism* is a part.

of the Vocation lectures. In these works, a complex typology of brotherly love emerges, one that allows Weber to trace the paradoxical fates of a number of different empirical forms of brotherliness within different cultural rationalisation processes. Specifically, it will be shown that four main types of brotherliness are identified by Weber: Puritan brotherliness; mystic brotherliness; medieval Christian brotherliness; and charismatic communistic brotherliness.[7] These different types of 'brotherliness' are contrasted with each other by Weber, as well as with a more general, ideal-typical form. To understand this typology, and the different types of brotherliness it identifies, it is necessary to once again go back to the complex arguments of the *Intermediary Reflection*, and, to a lesser extent, the *Introduction to the Economic Ethic of the World Religions*.

The Ideal-Type, or 'Genuine Ethic of Brotherliness'

There is little doubt that Weber's use of the term 'brotherliness', and the way the various usages are related to each other throughout his works, pose a serious problem of consistency and opaqueness. However, greater clarity is obtained once Weber's favoured methodological starting point of the ideal-type is assumed. The aim of outlining such an ideal-type is that:

> They enable us to see if, in particular traits or in their total character, the phenomena approximate one of our constructions: to determine the degree of approximation of the historical phenomena to the theoretically constructed type. (IR: 324)[8]

For Weber, then, an ideal-type is a theoretical construction against which empirical examples can be compared; but it can also have an historical impact. Weber goes on to say:

> To this extent, the construction is merely a technical aid which facilitates a more lucid arrangement and terminology. Yet, under certain conditions, a construction might mean more. For the rationality, in the sense of logical or teleological 'consistency', of an intellectual-theoretical or practical-ethical attitude has and

---

7 As often mentioned, Weber did not complete an account of the religion of Islam, with the result that Islamic brotherliness is a notable absence from this typology.

8 In his methodological writings Weber defines the ideal-type as a: 'conceptual pattern [which] brings together certain relationships and events of historical life into a complex, which is conceived as an internally consistent system. Substantively, this construct in itself is like a *utopia* which has been arrived at by the analytical accentuation of certain elements of reality' (Method: 90, Weber's emphasis). There is, of course, an enormous literature concerned with the ideal-type.

always has had power over man, however limited and unstable this power is and always has been in the face of other forces of historical life. (IR: 324)[9]

In this instance, what Weber calls a 'genuine ethic of brotherliness'[10] (IR: 336) performs this dual function of being both a comparative theoretical tool and, also, a factor in the sociology of brotherliness itself in that it operates in everyday life as an ideal of goodness. However, it is certainly an odd kind of ideal-type in that, rather than being a theoretical construction 'prepared with a rational consistency which is rarely found in reality' (IR: 323), it is a combination of elements that tended to come together, according to Weber, at the beginning point of the historical life of this ethic. And the later social manifestations of brotherliness will become increasingly distant from this original ideal the more they are subject to the forces of rationalisation, either in terms of internal consistency or in terms of responding to the gathering rationalised forces of the social context.

Weber never explicates the precise nature of this model of brotherliness. However, based on his comments in the *Intermediary Reflection*, and through an examination of his religious sociology, it is possible to ascertain five important dimensions to this ideal-typical standard of historical measurement. Firstly, it is *universal* in scope – it applies to all human beings as sufferers. Secondly, it maintains a *personal* or *ethical* appreciation of the suffering of the other, emphasising the face-to-face nature of care. Thirdly, it is in *tension* with the orders of this world. As a consequence, fourthly, it rejects this world as imperfect, thus becoming to a great extent world-denying or *acosmic*.[11] Under this acosmic orientation, only the suffering of other human beings is deemed important in this world. Finally, as a consequence of these combined elements, it is *uncompromising* in its dealing with the world and refuses to accept any other value-position as valid or worthwhile. How Weber understands each of these dimensions will be elaborated as we move through this section of the chapter.

These dimensions of the ideal-typical model of brotherliness are identified by Weber in the early attempts of the main salvation religions to deal with human suffering. The major historical form of brotherliness at this stage is charismatic communism (to be discussed below) which stands closest to the ideal-type,

---

9   There is a seeming inconsistency between what is stated here in the *Intermediary Reflection* and the way Weber puts it in the methodological writings where the ideal-type is only a theoretical, analytic construction and should not be seen as itself having some historical force, especially in being 'ideal' in the sense of a value-judgement or ethically 'ideal' situation (Method: 91–2). Undoubtedly the notion of an ideal-type of brotherliness violates this methodological definition, but it is at least in keeping with the general aim of being a construction which aids our understanding of the empirical reality, and it also fully fulfils the *utopian* view of the ideal-type given by Weber in the preceding quotation from the methodological writings (in footnote 8).
10 '*der echten Brüderlichkeitsethik*' (Zw: 549).
11 See Bellah (1999) for an extended discussion of the meaning of 'acosmism'.

although it is not an exact fit in terms of the dimension of universality. The universal, personal, acosmic and uncompromising aspects of the ideal-type, along with a reference to the first communist communities, are explicitly expressed in the following quotation:

> The principle that constituted the communal relations among the salvation prophecies was the suffering common to all believers. And this was the case whether the suffering actually existed or was a constant threat, whether it was external or internal. The more the imperatives that issued from the ethic of reciprocity among neighbours were raised, the more rational the conception of salvation became, and the more it was sublimated into an ethic of absolute ends. Externally, such commands rose to a communism of loving brethren; internally they rose to the attitude of *caritas*, love for the sufferer *per se*, for one's neighbour, for man, and finally for the enemy … . In religions of salvation, the profound and quiet bliss of all heroes of acosmic benevolence has always been fused with a charitable realisation of the natural imperfections of all human doings, including one's own. The psychological tone as well as the rational, ethical interpretation of this inner attitude can vary widely. But its ethical demand has always lain in the direction of a universalist brotherhood [*Brüderlichkeit*[12]], which goes beyond all barriers of societal associations, often including one's own faith. (IR: 330)[13]

To the salvation religions, Weber argues, the brutal fact of unjustified suffering within this world marks it as an essentially irrational place. Attempts to solve and understand this problem of suffering have been the driving force behind the evolution of important aspects of all the major religions, including the development of an ethic of brotherly love (IEEWR: 272, 275; also ES: 518).

As the quotation above indicates, the origins of this religious love are to be found in the ancient neighbourly ethic common amongst, for example, hunters, villagers, and seafarers (IR: 329; also ES: 360, 632), which emphasised the giving

---

12 *Brüderlichkeit* or, more occasionally, *Brüderlichkeitsethik* are the terms Weber uses for this ethic of suffering. Gerth and Mills's usual translation is 'brotherliness', but sometimes they (and other translators) use the term 'brotherhood'. 'Brotherhood' is not as accurate and has other connotations. Weber's original German term has been included when more clarity is needed.

13 And one's family. The ethic of brotherliness created a community of believers who had to 'stand closer to the saviour, the prophet … the brother in the faith than to the natural relations and to the matrimonial community' (IR: 329; also ES: 580). Although not the dominant theme, Weber implies in his analysis of Chinese rationalisation (China: Ch. viii, 233, 236 especially) that the sib and 'magical garden' were never broken or challenged by a revolutionary salvation religion based on brotherliness. For this reason, Chinese cultural history was not subject to the same paradoxes of brotherliness as other cultures. This point becomes clarified if the explicit theme of brotherliness in the *Intermediary Reflection* is taken into account when *The Religion of China* is read. Although *The Religion of China* has been the subject of much scrutiny and critique, this point has been overlooked.

of aid and alms to those clearly in distress within the community.[14] From this basis the religious expressions of brotherliness first emerge, Weber asserts, when:

> The magical ties and exclusiveness of the sibs have been shattered, and within the new community the prophetic religion has developed a religious ethic of brotherliness [*Brüderlichkeitsethik*]. (IR: 329; also see ES: 361)

If the universal, personal love of fellow sufferers does become such an uncompromising ethic, then such a position places anyone pursuing these ideals in direct conflict and tension with the orders and value-spheres of the world, especially as the latter are rationalised according to their own inner logics, as we started to see in the last three chapters. Indeed, this is the very theme of the *Intermediary Reflection*, which we will explore more fully in the next chapter. But, for the sake of the argument at this stage, the relation between brotherliness and the value-spheres of modernity can be summarised in the following way: 'The tension between brotherly religion and the world has been most obvious in the economic sphere' (IR: 331); 'The *consistent* brotherly ethic of salvation religions has come into an equally sharp tension with the political orders of the world' (IR: 333, emphasis added); 'Above all there is tension between the ethic of brotherliness and the spheres of aesthetic and erotic life' (IR: 341); and there is an 'ultimate inward tension' between religion and intellectualism (IR: 352). All the forms of brotherliness will maintain tension with the erotic, aesthetic and intellectual spheres, but some will be able to overcome the tension with the economic and political orders of the world. It is this final point which will prove to be of crucial importance in differentiating types of brotherliness.

Within the origins of an ethic of brotherliness we see the dimensions emphasised by Weber in his ideal-typical model of that ethic. Yet from this common origin in religious attempts to solve the problem of 'theodicy' (IEEWR: 275), numerous historical forces have created a variety of empirical forms of brotherly love. Weber's work traces these historical trajectories, and, as mentioned, seems to concentrate on four main empirical forms of brotherliness – the types found in Puritanism, mysticism, organic social ethics, as well as early charismatic communities. Throughout Weber's work, we find a recurring demonstration of the inability of these empirical forms of brotherliness to measure up to the ideal-typical, 'genuine ethic' of brotherliness. Each of the four loses one or more of the crucial dimensions of the ideal-type – its universalism, ethical personalism, acosmism, tension with the world, and refusal to compromise. We can now examine each of these empirical variations, and its relation with the ideal-type of brotherly love, in turn. The first example, Puritan brotherliness, we have already briefly met as part of the fateful paradox of Calvinist theological consistency.

---

14 Weber provides an illustration of this emergence in his study of the Judaic tradition (AJ: 64, 67, 342–3).

Puritan Brotherliness

Puritan brotherly love is at variance with the ideal-typical form on four of the five scales of measurement. Weber particularly identifies two major trends which place it in direct contrast with the ideal-type of genuine brotherliness.

Firstly, the ideal of universalism stands in stark contrast to the idea of 'brotherhood' found in sects of religious virtuosi such as those found in early Protestantism (particularly in America). As 'The Protestant Sects and the Spirit of Capitalism' demonstrates, a much more limited form of brotherly love was developed within Protestantism when the idea of universal suffering was abandoned and boundaries for group membership were instead placed around proof of one's state of grace. This Protestant form of brotherliness might be termed 'sect brotherliness', as it is usually based on a requirement of care only for those 'brothers' in the faith (PS: 308, 318–19; India: 201–2) as against the universalism of the 'church' (IEEWR: 288; ES: 1204).

A qualification is needed here about Protestant exclusivity. Although the Protestant sects will put up certain barriers, there is also a universal aspect to Protestant brotherliness in the obvious sense that we are all God's children and that, beyond the American model at least,[15] Weber does say that systematic charities were organised for those not capable of work, like orphans and cripples (ES: 588). A universal aspect to the care of the suffering is thus evident in certain Puritan expressions. So, in terms of the ideal-type Protestantism is both exclusive and universal unevenly, with the major tendency moving against universality.

Second is the Puritan logic of abandonment of the personal, or ethical, aspect of the brotherly ethic of suffering. At stake here is what Weber precisely means by 'the personal'. This will turn out to be a vitally important point for all of our understanding of brotherliness and, also, for our understanding of Weber's depiction of modernity more generally.

In essence, 'personal' or 'human'[16] relations between people are regarded by Weber as the place where an ethical dimension is possible.

---

15   In *The Religion of India* Weber compares Jainism and the American Protestant sects precisely on this point. Weber writes: 'As with many American sects their economic power position depended also on the support of the individual by the parish; and when he changed place, he soon had personal contacts with his sect again. To be sure, in essence this solidarity was rather remote from the early Christian "brotherliness", and similar to the functional rationalism of Puritan welfare work, more in the nature of a discharge of good works than an expression of a religious "acosmic" love of which Jainism, indeed, knows nothing' (India: 201–2). The relevant point here concerns the discharge of good works of sect welfare in opposition to brotherliness of an earlier, more ideal kind.

16   It will be assumed that 'personal' and 'human' (as, for example, in 'man to man'/'person to person') are basically interchangeable on this point in Weber's writings. This assumption is supported when the specific quotations used here and in Chapter 7 are considered; and is supported by the various eminent translations of his work into English.

For every purely personal relationship of man to man, of whatever sort and even including complete enslavement, may be subjected to ethical requirements, and ethically regulated. This is true because the structures of these relationships depend upon the individual wills of the participants, leaving room in such relations for manifestations of the virtue of charity. (ES: 585)[17]

The contrast is with impersonal relations which are deprived of this ethical aspect, especially in the most rationalised economies. This quotation goes on to state:

> But this is not the situation in the realm of economically rationalised relationships, where personal control is exercised in inverse ratio to the degree of rational differentiation of the economic structure. There is no possibility, in practice or even in principle, of any *caritative* regulation of relationships arising from the holder of a savings and loan bank mortgage and the mortgagee who has obtained the loan from the bank, or between a holder of federal bond and a citizen taxpayer … . The growing impersonality of the economy on the basis of the association in the market place follows its own rules, disobedience to which entails economic failure and, in the long run, economic ruin. (ES: 585, emphasis added; see also ES: 636, 1186; IR: 331)

With this distinction between the personal and impersonal in mind we can better understand Weber's analysis of Puritan vocationalism as it examines how this religion encouraged its adherents to operate 'without regard to the person' – to relinquish, in effect, direct, personal love and care in the name of allegiance to God.

Puritan brotherly love became impersonal as it was subsumed into the everyday labour of the calling:

> *Brotherly love*, since it may only be practised for the Glory of God[18] and not in the service of the flesh, is expressed in the first place in the fulfilment of the daily tasks given by the *lex naturae*; and in the process this fulfilment assumes a peculiarly objective and *impersonal* character, that of service in the interest of the rational organisation of our social environment. (PE: 108–9, emphasis added)[19]

---

17 '*Jede rein persönliche Beziehung von Mensch zu Mensch, wie immer sie sei, einschließlich der völligsten Versklavung, kann ethisch reglementiert, an sie können ethische Postulate gestellt werden, da ihre Gestaltung von dem individuellen Willen der Beteiligten abhängt, also der Entfaltung karitativer Tugend Raum gibt*' (WG: 378–9).

18 To act only to promote the glory of God is thus constitutive of the Calvinist form of impersonal brotherly love. Another example of this point (which here concerns the sending of missions to the heathens) can be seen when Weber writes: 'they obviously originate in the ideas, running through the whole Puritan ethic, according to which the duty to love one's neighbour is satisfied by fulfilling God's commandments to increase His glory. The neighbour thereby receives all that is due him, and anything further is God's affair. Humanity in relation to one's neighbour has, so to speak, died out' (PE: 235 n6).

19 On Calvinist impersonality, also see ES: 1200; and China: 236, 241, 245.

For Weber, this impersonality is a logical consequence of the Puritan conceptualisation of predestination (as we have already briefly considered as part of the logic of paradox): God's plan cannot be known or doubted; those in need should not be helped as this would seem to question God's creation of the order of the world; those in need would seem to deserve their suffering since through labour there is always the opportunity to develop God's bounty; and to be in needful suffering and not labouring in the world would indicate damnation, which no action on this earth can, nor should try to, alter (see ES: 588 on begging and almsgiving).

If this is the case for those who were considered capable of labour, the same impersonal logic extends to those who could not work. Hence, the Puritan charitable institutions for cripples and orphans, mentioned above, were developed along the following lines:

> Care for the poor was oriented to the goal of discouraging the slothful ... charity itself became a rationalised 'enterprise', and its religious significance was therefore eliminated or even turned into the opposite significance. (ES: 589)

There is no longer any regard for the person and their suffering; rather such charity is aimed at promoting labour and the market.

In these ways brotherliness has become impersonal, and in one sense, loveless. And, as we have seen, Puritan brotherly love can even come to include a *hatred* of one's sinful[20] neighbour (PE: 122), when the ethical concern with the suffering of every person is so completely replaced by the elect's dedication to vocational labour and certainty of grace.

At least in the most extreme Protestant types, the impersonality of capitalism and the elect's impersonal denial of personal ethical relationships can come together without essential conflict and perhaps in fruitful harmony, as Weber's famous thesis on Protestantism and capitalism argues, and as the quotes just given strongly suggest. The world-denying acosmism of the early salvation religions is thus reversed. Labour in the vocational calling, in the very centre of the economy itself, becomes the absolute standard of moral worth. For the Calvinist:

> ... the wonderfully purposeful organisation and arrangement of this cosmos is, according both to the revelation of the Bible and to natural intuition, evidently designed by God to serve the utility of the human race. This makes labour in the service of impersonal social usefulness appear to promote the glory of God and hence to be willed by Him. (PE: 109)

Such certainty of activity in the world results, as we have noted, in 'the complete elimination of the theodicy problem and of all those questions about the meaning

---

20 Also, 'sin' for the Puritan must include idleness and waste, where God's prescription for mundane labour is ignored.

of the world and life, which have tortured others ...' (PE: 109; also IR: 359). The Protestant logic leads, then, to an impersonal brotherliness within the world, where suffering and the ethics of the personal are superseded because those who do not adopt the Puritan discipline of labour are beyond help.

This abandonment of both the universal and the personal in the drive to consistent 'loveless clarity' (as cited, IR: 359) is summarised in the following:

> As a religion of virtuosos, Puritanism renounced the universalism of love, and rationally routinised all work in this world into serving God's will and testing one's state of grace (IR: 332)

Impersonal and tending to exclusivity, Puritan brotherliness does escape the tensions with the economic and political worlds that other religions do not. In the injunction to vocational labour and the acceptance of 'the routinisation of the economic cosmos', the Puritans fulfilled their God-willed duty (IR: 332) in the economic sphere. There is no tension here – quite the opposite, according to Weber. Furthermore, the Puritan vocational logic means that this participation in the economy does not compromise this particular form of brotherly love. This same position with regard to tension and compromise is seen with politics. Puritanism interpreted God's will as allowing that His 'commandments should be imposed upon the creatural world by the means of this world, namely violence' (IR: 336), and this means that the state's 'consummated threat of violence, war' (IR: 335) can be reconciled with the Puritan ethic.

The Puritan brotherliness is, in this way, impersonal, mainly exclusive, world-affirming and without inherent tension in its dealing with the economic and political worlds. Yet it can maintain an uncompromised ethic in the very pursuit of these aspects of its highly consistent theology. In short, its internal logic pushes it to a position of extreme contrast with the ideal-type.

However, an important qualification has to be made at this point about this consistent Puritan form of brotherly love. In this extreme, rationalised model, Weber is offering us an ideal-typical account of Puritan brotherliness, which will be rarely found in the empirical reality. Some measure of personal charity and appreciation of suffering, of course, may well be exhibited in individual cases even beyond the sect, and these examples would then be in disagreement with the intellectualised logical extreme, especially of Calvinism. And such examples will be, in effect, enacting the personal dimension of the ideal-type of brotherliness against the ideal-type of impersonal Puritan brotherliness. Because the Puritan form is still part of the overall Christian understanding of theodicy, then to fail to live up to Puritan impersonality is to fall back on a less rationally consistent – and therefore personal – kind of brotherliness.

Mystic Brotherly Love

The second main form of empirical brotherliness examined by Weber is that of the mystic. Mystic forms of brotherly love maintain an acosmic, uncompromised universalism but, like the Puritan form, they tend towards the impersonal and can avoid tension with the economic and political world. Once again, intellectualised consistency is the reason for such impersonality and lack of tension.

At its most logically consistent, the acosmism found in this ethic of brotherliness leads to a complete rejection of this world including, therefore, a rejection of other human beings as important entities. This seems to be the basis of the problems, from an ideal-typical point of view, of mystic brotherliness. Mysticism logically exaggerates brotherliness to such an extent that the world is escaped or denied so that *anybody* who happens to cross one's path becomes the object of devotion and love (IR: 333, 336). 'The postulate of brotherly love' is therefore expanded to a 'completely unselective generosity' (ES: 589). Such love reaches a height of impersonality in that the actual person and their suffering are not of concern.

> ... the mystic's 'benevolence' ... does not at all enquire into the man to whom and for whom it sacrifices. Ultimately, mysticism is not interested in his person. Once and for all, the benevolent mystic gives his shirt when he is asked for his coat, by anybody who accidentally happens to come his way – and merely because he happens to come his way. Mysticism is a unique escape from this world in the form of an objectless devotion to anybody, not for the man's sake but purely for devotion's sake, or in Baudelaire's words, for the sake of the 'soul's sacred prostitution'. (IR: 333; see also ES: 589; and IEEWR: 291).

The motivating drive here is not *personal* brotherly love and the maintenance of the great problem of suffering but the salvation of the mystic. Mystic brotherly love involves, according to Weber, a search for *individual* salvation in the emotional state of love for love's sake. All people are treated equally as merely a means towards this end. The logical consistency of mystic brotherliness lies in the fact that the world is so thoroughly denied that there cannot be any attachment to *particular* suffering so that each person is only regarded as an 'anybody' and benevolence dispensed without individualised or personalised love. For this reason, from the viewpoint of an ethic of brotherliness that maintains some sense of the personal and the importance of the other and their suffering, it will be judged as essentially selfish. These points are reinforced in Weber's examination of the mystic brotherliness found in Buddhism.

According to Weber, Buddhism has a '*cool* temperance'[21] (India: 208; Weber's emphasis) that 'guarantees the internal detachment from all "thirst" for the world and men' (India: 208; also ES: 628). Here and here alone lies true salvation. An altruistic ethic of universal compassion is but a stage on the road to enlightenment:

---

21 'kühle *Temperierung*' (Hinduismus: 332).

> ... the specific form of Buddhistic "altruism", universal compassion, is merely one stage which sensitivity passes when seeing through the nonsense of the struggle for existence of all individuals in the wheel of life, a sign of progressive intellectual enlightenment, not, however, an expression of active brotherliness. In the rules for contemplation, compassion is expressly defined as being replaced, in the final state of mind, by the stoic equanimity of the knowing man. (India: 213)

Buddhist brotherliness reaches an extreme of impersonality in its detachment. In fact it is comparable to Puritanism in this regard:

> Buddhist *caritas* is characterised by the same impersonality and matter-of-factness as Jainism,[22] and in another manner, also that of Puritanism. The personal *certitudo salutis,* not the welfare of the neighbour is the issue. (India: 209)

Buddhism, in this way, represents for Weber the most prominent, consistent example of mystic, universal impersonality.[23]

Here an important distinction needs to be drawn within the ranks of acosmic brotherliness. In the *Intermediary Reflection,* Weber lists the Buddha along with Jesus and St Francis as a purveyor of brotherly religion (IR: 357). All three might be taken as examples of acosmic brotherliness (see ES: 630–33, 592 on Jesus; and ES: 540, 552 for St Francis), yet Buddhism is also stated to be a logical extreme of love's mystical escapism (ES: 627–8; IR: 339–40). Weber would appear to be distinguishing Buddhist mysticism from some Christian manifestations of acosmism. This is confirmed in the study of Buddhism where he states: 'The concept of neighbourly love, at least in the sense of the great *Christian* virtuosi of brotherliness is unknown' (India: 208, emphasis added). Both may be termed religions of acosmic brotherliness, but in their practice and belief they are qualitatively different.

The quotations given here suggest that Christian acosmic brotherliness is relatively 'warmer', more active and less distant than the Eastern forms, which are directly aligned with the ultimate coldness of Puritanism. Weber does not spell out this contrast further, but some additional points might be deduced.

---

22 As mentioned, Jainism shared many of the traits of exclusivity found in the Protestant sects (India: 201–2) and, Weber claims, 'is completely lacking the Christian conception of "neighbury love"', for the 'heart of Jainism is empty' (India: 201). Jainism thus seems even closer to the Puritan form than Buddhism in terms of these measures of sect exclusivity and impersonality.

23 However, it should be remembered that this extreme consistency might not be sustained in the empirical actuality. As with the consistent form of Puritan impersonal brotherliness, in keeping with his avowed methodology, Weber is giving an ideal-typical account of Buddhist brotherliness and its mystic impersonality. The personal might well be more apparent in specific empirical cases, and when this happens, it might be said, the ideal-type of brotherliness is being followed to some degree against the rationalised mystic form.

All consistent mystic acosmism, whether Eastern or Western (although Weber stresses the Eastern logics) will be subject to the judgement of impersonality. However, the great Christian virtuosi of brotherliness, although adopting an acosmistic position and indifference to the world (ES: 630–33), will not have travelled as far down the road of consistency to reach the point of pure *mystic* indifference. Hence, although Jesus (if we accept him as the first Christian virtuoso) and Buddhism both 'evoke the most radical demands for the ethic of brotherly love' (ES: 593), and although Jesus is said to adopt a 'mystically conditioned acosmism of love' (ES: 633), there are significant differences in terms of religious rationalisation. Jesus is characterised as a magician by Weber (ES: 630–31)[24] rather than a mystic; an important difference since the 'charisma of the pure 'mystic' [serves] only himself [while the] charisma of the genuine magician serves others' (IEEWR: 290). Further, Jesus' acosmic views are inconsistently mixed with contrasting Judaic attributes (ES: 633). This relative inconsistency is combined with a stress Weber puts on the *active* nature of Occidental acosmism, which is especially seen in the idea of ascetics being God's tools rather than as 'vessels of the divine' (IEEWR: 285). Being active in a world that is still denied, rather than following the path of contemplative withdrawal, perhaps allows this form of Christian brotherliness a more direct engagement with suffering. For these reasons, we can deduce how Christian acosmistic love can be contrasted to the Eastern variants. In this sense, the less intellectually consistent Christian virtuosi of brotherliness might be said to stand closer to the ideal-type than pure mysticism, in that their active, relatively 'warm' love approaches a personal concern with the sufferer. However, it has to be said that this form of brotherliness is hardly developed by Weber and this conclusion must remain speculative.

Mystic brotherliness also differs from the ideal-typical form in that its withdrawal from the world entails the elimination of tension with the economy and politics, whilst also maintaining, in agreement with the ideal-typical form, an uncompromised position in terms of its own theological consistency. For example, 'mysticism is the other consistent avenue [besides Puritanism] by which the tension between economics and religion has been escaped' (IR: 333). Since all the world is denied, there is no interest in the other, nor in any of the routines of economic life – the only interest is in salvation (as above, IR: 333; ES: 589). Similarly, with the political sphere, in its consistent acosmism mysticism simply 'withdraws from the pragma of violence which no political action can escape' (IR: 336; also ES: 594). Such consistent withdrawal allows mysticism an obvious way of dealing with the dominant spheres of the social world without tension,[25] or compromise.

---

24 Although this is just one element of Weber's depiction and is itself qualified (ES: 564).

25 Indeed, the tension it does feel with the world, particularly against art and eroticism, arises precisely because these value-spheres, with their similar withdrawal/separation from the world, are direct competitors with its 'bursting individuation' (IR: 348; also IR: 342–3, 348–9).

In sum, the most consistent mystic forms of brotherliness are universal, world-denying and uncompromised, but impersonal and without tension with the economic and political realms.

Organic Social Ethics

The third major historical expression of brotherliness that Weber discusses is a form of organic social ethics, which is universal, personal and full of compromises and tensions with the world. Unlike the consistent acosmic direction of mystical love, this organic brotherly ethic is *cosmic* in orientation:

> Organic social ethics, where religiously sub-structured, stands on the soil of 'brotherliness', but, in *contrast* to mystic and acosmic love, is dominated by a cosmic, rational demand for brotherliness. Its point of departure is the experience of the inequality of religious charisma. The very fact that the holy should be accessible only to some and not to all is unbearable to organic social ethics. (IR: 338, emphasis added)[26]

Though he makes brief mention of the Lutheran vocational life (discussed below), Weber's most sustained discussion is in relation to the medieval, hierarchical 'organic social ethic' associated with Aquinas (IR: 338–9; ES: 597–601).[27] Within these perspectives, a conservative, God-ordained social world is imagined and instantiated wherein an order of Catholic vocational life is set out on the acceptance of the *social* inequality between humans, but not the inequality of *suffering*. Such an order holds reality to be relatively rational despite its wickedness, since there are at least traces of the divine plan in the world. Herein lies its cosmic, that is, world-affirming, orientation (IR: 338–9). Perhaps the most important sociological reason for such affirmation of the world, and which ties into the universal nature of this type of brotherliness, is the 'democratic' impulse (IEEWR: 288) of the church that is so starkly opposed to the exclusiveness of the virtuosi sect (as above

---

26 Of all the secondary literature on Weber's religious works, it would seem that it is only that of Mitzman (1969: 197) which notes this important distinction between cosmic and acosmic brotherliness. At least in the English translations, such a distinction is not always easily detected in Weber's texts. For example, there is a misleading translation by Gerth and Mills of an important passage in *Introduction to the Economic Ethic of the World Religions*. Their version reads: 'The Buddhist monk, certain to enter Nirvana, seeks the sentiment of a cosmic love' (IEEWR: 278), when in fact the German provides a different interpretation based on the cosmic/acosmic distinction: '*Das* akosmistische *Liebesgefühl des seines Eingangs in Nirwana sicheren buddhistischen Mönches*' (Einleitung: 249, emphasis added).

27 The other organic social ethic, which is given much more substantial scrutiny by Weber than the Western medieval variant, is Hinduism. The karma/caste determination of the theodicy problem does not include an ethic of brotherliness, however, and so Hinduism will not be discussed further here.

PS: 308, 318–19; and PE: 201–2). Brotherliness exists, then, within the socially unequal order of the world and can be understood as universal in a double-sense: love should be extended to all sufferers equally – as brothers; and all should follow this ethic of brotherly love.

The possibility of this organic ethic rested on a certain period in the rationalisation of the Western economic and political spheres. In the medieval stage of Western social development, these value-spheres were not in the state of impersonality that they were to acquire in modernity. Weber therefore believes they were able to maintain a *personal* dimension to brotherliness:

> The medieval and Lutheran traditionalistic ethics of vocation actually rested on a general presupposition, one that is increasingly rare, which both share with the Confucian ethic: that power relationships in both the economic and political spheres have a purely personal character ... these relationships of domination had a character to which one may apply ethical requirements in the same way that one applies them to every other purely personal relationship. (ES: 600)[28]

Here Lutheran vocationalism is directly linked by Weber to the medieval organic form in being open to the ethics of the personal. In fact, at one stage, labour was specifically justified through brotherly love by Luther, because 'the division of labour forces every individual to work for others' (PE: 81). Weber describes this connection as 'highly naïve' (PE: 81), and suggests that the calling would come to be more fully justified by Luther as the only way to live acceptably in the eyes of God. A highly conservative, traditionalistic outlook is evident in this later approach of Luther: the individual should remain once and for all in the station and calling in which God had placed him, and should restrain his worldly activity within the limits imposed by his established station in life. While his economic traditionalism was originally the result of Paulinian indifference, it later became that of a more and more intense belief in divine providence, which identified absolute obedience to God's will, with absolute acceptance of things as they were (PE: 85). In other words, Luther initially understood vocational labour in terms of brotherly love specifically, but modified this position to a traditionalist acceptance of one's place in the world, which was, in this way, akin to the medieval organic form of vocational ethics in Medieval Catholicism. This later Lutheran understanding of the calling, even though the explicit ethic of brotherly love is no longer its justification, has the ethical possibilities of the personal available to it because of

---

28 It should be stressed that the ethical dimension of the personal can include much more than the ethic of brotherliness. This was the case in the patriarchal, patrimonial and feudal relations (ES: 1006, 1013, 1025–6, 1028–31, 1070, 1083, 1105; IR: 331) of the pre-modern West. Also, as mentioned, under Confucianism social/political personal and ethical relations were exclusively tied to the family, and so did not involve the brotherly ethic which went beyond the ties of the sib (as above, China: 236–7).

its traditionalist structure. It is here, in the personal relations of the labouring life itself, that the ethic of brotherliness can be pursued.

In this way, Weber suggests, prior to modernity, personal, ethical relations were possible in *vocational*[29] life, even if such societal order was highly unequal. Furthermore, although the form of brotherliness possible in such a social structure is logically undeveloped from the perspective of Calvinist and mystical consistency, it is precisely within this relative lack of intellectualisation that the ethic of the personal is preserved for Weber. Society and religion were thus uneasily allied as both were simultaneously underdeveloped from the viewpoints of modernity and theological rationalisation. Because of the pressures of history and rational theology, however, and the necessary conflict between this morality and social reality, such an ethic would be overwhelmed by the forces of the economy and politics, as well as by the logic of religious rationalisation in the shape of Puritanism.

This is how Weber explains the way the personal, universal ethic of brotherliness did once exist empirically. However, because the personal, universal relations in which *caritas* could be cultivated were part of vocational life, this period of the Christian Church entered into 'compromises and relativities' with the worldly spheres (IR: 338). Such a cosmic orientation, such a compromising integration with the economy, must be judged harshly 'as an accommodation to the privileged strata of this world' from the viewpoint of 'the radical mystical ethic of religious brotherliness' (IR: 338). The tension with this manifestation of brotherliness and the world is acute.

All these points – cosmic/acosmic, exclusive/universal, personal/impersonal, the tension with the world – are brought out in the following quotation where the contrasts between the cosmic brotherliness of organic ethics and exclusionary Puritanism on the one hand, and acosmic mystical brotherliness on the other, are made explicit:

> The organic pragmatism of salvation must consider the redemptory aristocracy of inner-worldly asceticism [as seen in Protestantism], with its rational depersonalisation of life orders, as the hardest form of lovelessness and lack of brotherliness. It must consider the redemptory pragmatism of mysticism as a sublimated and, in truth, unbrotherly indulgence of the mystic's own charisma. The mystic's unmethodical and planless acosmism of love is viewed as a mere selfish means in the search for the mystic's own salvation. Both inner-worldly asceticism and mysticism ultimately condemn the social world to absolute meaninglessness, or at least they hold that God's aims concerning the social world are utterly incomprehensible. The rationalism of organic doctrines of society cannot stand up under this idea; for it seeks to comprehend the world as an at least relatively rational cosmos in spite of all its wickedness. (IR: 338–9)

---

29 A Catholic not Protestant vocation. See the discussion in Chapter 3.

In sum, Weber seems to argue that the organic social ethics of Medieval Christianity (and Lutheranism) maintained a universal, ethical brotherliness, because an historical junction of social and ideational forms could allow the actual, if highly compromised, existence of such an ethic as part of the everyday, tension-filled, vocational world. Universal and tending to the impersonal, it had not yet developed in such a consistent way as to lose the ethical concern for the suffering of the other, nor had it yet been squashed under the weight of the autonomous cogs of the economic and political spheres.

Charismatic Brotherliness

A final form of empirical brotherliness mentioned by Weber is that of charismatic communism. Although this is the form of brotherliness closest to the ideal-type, it is the least discussed by Weber, mainly because it has no real historical significance for the problems of modernity. It is only obliquely referred to in the central arguments in the *Intermediary Reflection* and so should perhaps be seen as relatively less important than the other forms discussed.

As indicated, for Weber most religious ethics began with some form of brotherly love: 'caritas, brotherhood [*Brüderlichkeit*] and ethically imbued personal relations between master and servant … remain the foundation of every ecclesiastic ethic, from Islam and Judaism to Buddhism and Christianity …' (ES: 1188). That is, some similar, limited, *personal* ethical relations, in which caritas might be exhibited, can be seen to underlie all these religions, and Weber points to a common originating source – the ethic of neighbourliness. Further, in this move from the neighbourhood ethics to the brotherly love of salvation religions, a world-denying brotherhood is commonly found which lives by the ethic of brotherliness in terms of a 'charismatic communism' (ES: 1187; also ES: 581, 1119–20). In the quotation given from the *Intermediary Reflection* at the beginning of this chapter, Weber terms this early community a 'communism of loving brethren' (IR: 330). Although this might be seen in many religions, Weber particularly speaks of groups which came into being in the Middle East during the pre- and early Christian period. In the closing sections of *Ancient Judaism*, he comments on the Essenes, and suggests that although such groups lived with a personal ethic of brotherliness, were acosmic and in necessary tension with the rest of the world, they were exclusionary and were confronted by logics in the world which meant this ethic could only maintain a fleeting existence.

The Essenes, from the second century BC, rigorously segregated themselves from the less pure and shunned all economic possession beyond some bare necessities. 'Correspondingly they pushed the old social commandment of brotherliness to the length of an unworldly love communism of consumption' (AJ: 407). This ethic of the Essenes can be linked to original Christian practices in terms of a strict pacifism and love of enemies, and 'the communism of acosmic love' (AJ: 410).

Unlike the Medieval and Lutheran vocational ethics which entered into an ethically flawed relationship with the forces of the economy and politics, these early, founding religious communities cut themselves off from the impure, impersonal structures of society and tried to live out an uncompromising ethic of brotherliness. This separation from the larger society meant that they did not succumb to the social-economic compromises of the cosmic, organic ethic. Further, these social organisations offered another variant of mystical brotherliness in apparently still being able to maintain a personal ethic and were, consequently, not so 'selfishly' concerned with salvation as the world-denying flight of more developed mysticism. However, as was noted in Chapter 2, such charismatically inspired communities must fall under the paradox of charisma/routinisation. The routinisation of charisma inevitably follows the reign of the charismatic leader and brings charismatic communism back to the world it sought to exclude (as above, ES: Part 1, Ch. 111, v; also ES: 1121).

To be so radically world-denying (acosmic), and held together by charismatic religious authority, such 'anti-societies' could not long endure. This helps to explain their relatively minor historical importance. For Weber, they are a stage on the road to more significant forms of religious brotherliness.

In relation to the ideal-type, a certain aristocratic exclusivity of the brotherhood is apparent, especially in terms of purity/impurity, despite the fact that this particular pursuit of brotherliness was relatively untainted by economic social reality and did command 'a love of enemies' (AJ: 411). These early mystic communities were personal in their ethical relations, acosmic, in clear and uncompromised tension with the world they shunned, but lacked the universality of the ideal-typical brotherly ethic.

Summary

In order to understand Weber's notion of brotherliness, we have had to follow a trail of terms throughout his writings. Although this ethical theme is not a dominant topic in any of the major works beyond the *Intermediary Reflection*, a remarkably consistent account can be pieced together. A certain, if somewhat implied, ideal-typical brotherliness is offered by Weber as a kind of scale to measure the four main types of brotherliness that are present throughout his works: Puritanism, which is limited in scope and not based on a concept of fellow suffering; mystic brotherliness which addresses the suffering of others, but in an impersonal manner (as seen in Buddhism); cosmic brotherliness (as found in medieval Christianity) which, unlike the first two, compromises itself with the structures of this world whilst seeking a personal concern for all sufferers; and the charismatic communities which displayed all the traits of the ideal-type except a clear universalism. Only the cosmic, medieval type attempted historically to bend the world (especially the economic and political spheres) towards an ethic of brotherliness, entangling itself in power interests and this-worldly compromises as a result (IR: 336–7). Neither the mystic, Puritan nor charismatic community attempted to transform the world in alignment with such an ethic; instead they either used the economic/political orders, or escaped them.

All four types can be seen, then, to fall short of the 'pure' ethic outlined in Weber's idea-typical brotherliness, with the Puritan form being the most distant from the ideal-type and the charismatic the closest. The types of brotherliness might be schematised in the following way to reveal their elemental structure.

Table 6.1 Types of brotherliness in Weber's *Sociology of Religion*

Type of Brotherliness	Universal	Personal/ ethical	Acosmic/ world-denying	Tension with the world (economic and political spheres)	Compromises with the world
Ideal-type	Yes	Yes	Yes	Yes	No
Puritan	No (and yes on a more minor level)	No	No	No	No
Mystic (e.g., Buddhist)	Yes	No	Yes	No	No
Organic Christian (Medieval Catholic, Lutheran)	Yes	Yes	No	Yes	Yes
Charismatic communities (e.g. the Essenes)	No	Yes	Yes	Yes	No

Weber consistently uses these explanatory parameters in all of his widely scattered commentaries on brotherliness. The obvious qualification must be made, however, that such a schema loses many of the important differences that exist within each simplified category, especially the differences in: Christian and Eastern mysticism; the Puritan and mystic resolutions to tensions with the world; and, the huge variety of Puritan doctrines and practices.

Conclusion

What conclusions can we draw from this survey of the forms of brotherly love, especially as we move to consider the place of this ethic in modernity? Four broad concluding points might be identified as emerging from Weber's sociology of religious brotherliness.

Firstly, as outlined in a previous chapter, brotherliness is marked by the fundamental paradox of meaning. As the Puritan and mystic cases in particular show, the more that brotherliness is consistently developed the more the ideal-typical form is diminished.

Secondly, an understanding of the ideal-type of brotherliness is strengthened when the arguments on the forms of brotherly love in the *Intermediary Reflection* are considered. Weber will often compare different forms with each other – the mystic versus the organic, the mystic and the Puritan, and the originating charismatic communities against all the other forms. By adopting these different religious perspectives, Weber is continually pointing to the 'genuine' ideal-typical form in the way each of the empirical/historical forms will possess certain elements that can be used to critically judge other exemplifications. When we tease out what these elements are we can build up a picture of the ideal-type of genuine brotherliness. So, the pure mystic is able to criticise the compromises with the world that come with the organic medieval form, and impersonal indifference is judged harshly from the communist and organic perspectives. However, in contrast, it is not the case that the elements of worldly compromise and impersonal love are used as standards of judgement. The fact that there is this selection of positive values that can be extracted from the pattern of empirical brotherliness indicates the presence of the ideal standard for Weber. What also becomes increasingly apparent is the way all the empirical examples must fail this ideal-typical standard in some way. It is an impossible ideal to put into historical practice, so that when one element is emphasised another aspect is necessarily compromised.

Thirdly, in the West, it has to be reiterated how the Protestant, impersonal, rationalised form of brotherliness fits and enhances the economic forces of developing capitalism. The actual ethical attributes of the Protestant Ethic thesis become much clearer when the concept of brotherliness has itself been clarified.

Finally, perhaps the most important aspect of the paradox of brotherliness is that with increasing intellectualism and rational consistency the personal dimension of the ideal-type of brotherliness is increasingly overtaken by the impersonal. The driving force here is the ideal interest in death and salvation and as this becomes more rationalised in the Puritan and mystic forms then the response to the problem of theodicy is altered accordingly.

This last point is particularly noteworthy because, as we will see in the next chapter, the kind of relation between the ideal interests in salvation and suffering that is on exhibition here in Weber's accounts of religion will also be part of the fate of brotherliness in modernity.

Chapter 7
Brotherliness and Modernity

Introduction

The *Intermediary Reflection* argues that brotherliness is opposed to all the value-spheres of modernity – in fact this is the major theme of this pivotal and famous text. This adds to Weber's theorisation of the overall meaninglessness of the modern world, but more specifically provides an account of the fate of theodicy and its ethic. With the understanding of paradox and the forms of brotherliness behind us we are now in a position to consider this fate.

A vital aspect of the fate of brotherliness for Weber is the rise of impersonality in the modern world. 'Impersonality' is one of those themes which has had a strong presence in many interpretations of Weber (e.g., Hennis, 1988; Gane, 2002); and it is a concept that, in addition to its presence in the *Intermediary Reflection* and the Vocation lectures, flows through the studies in *Economy and Society* on law, bureaucracy, legitimation and the economy. It is the key element in Weber's understanding of modernity in terms of formal, legal legitimation (as opposed to charisma and tradition):

> The following characteristic must be considered decisive for our terminology: in legal authority, submission does not rest upon the belief and devotion to charismatically gifted persons, like prophets and heroes, or upon sacred tradition, or upon piety toward a personal lord and master who is defined by an ordered tradition, or upon piety toward the possible incumbents of office fiefs and office prebends who are legitimised in their own right through privilege and conferment. Rather, submission under legal authority is based upon an *impersonal* bond to the generally defined and functional 'duty of office'. (IEEWR: 299, Weber's emphasis)

The full understanding of impersonality can only come about, however, when its contrasting position – the personal – has been more properly theorised. Brotherliness is not the only part of the 'personal', but it does have an importance for Weber as, in fact, the central moral dimension of Christianity that the impersonal will tend to exclude. To complete our understanding of Weber's religious perspective on modernity, then, these elements of the personal/impersonal, brotherliness and the value-spheres will need to be ordered into a theoretical whole. If we interpret this task in terms of ideal interests then the job is to make sense of the way that the ideal interest in suffering works in modernity, and in this process the relation between this ideal interest and the ideal interest in life and death will, it is hoped, start to emerge more clearly.

The chapter will be divided into two sections. With impersonality as a key theme, the first section will consider the fate of brotherliness in detail by, once again, taking up the value-spheres of modernity as they are proffered in the *Intermediary Reflection*:[1] the explicit way that each value-sphere opposes brotherliness and foregoes the problem of suffering will be stated as part of Weber's understanding of how ideal interests constitute modernity. It will also emerge, as part of Weber's argument here, that the ethic of brotherliness will have to be considered as an ongoing presence in modernity, despite its systematic exclusion from all the value-spheres. Weber understands this ethic as having a continuing effect beyond its religious manifestation in the history of the West because, from the judgement emanating from the ideal form of brotherliness, modern culture is imbued with a sense of its own guilt.

The second, briefer section of this chapter will take stock of Weber's overarching argument about meaning and modernity. Two points will be taken up as we try to come to terms with the argument as a whole. Firstly, the importance of the way subjectivity and subjective experience are constitutive of modernity's self-understanding – from within the value-spheres – will emerge from Weber's perspective of meaning. And, secondly, what arises from the argument so far on meaning in modernity is that the very pursuit of meaning in terms of life, death and salvation will not only paradoxically result in meaning within meaninglessness, but it will result in the denial and exclusion of brotherliness itself. That is, following the specific ideal interest in the meaning of life and death will lead to the loss, or lessening, of the content of the other ideal interest in the West (suffering and its ethic) – a final paradox will be seen to be at work between the very poles of Western meaning themselves.

The Value-Spheres and Brotherliness

The Economic Sphere[2]

Two aspects might be stressed with regard to the relation between brotherliness and the economic value-sphere: firstly, the link between internal, economic

---

1 In this chapter the order of the value-spheres follows the one that Weber sets out in the *Intermediary Reflection*.

2 Within the economic and political value-spheres the place of impersonality is fairly straightforward on the whole, and has often been stated in the commentaries. In consequence, much of what follows on these two spheres will be reiterating what others have said. Also, it should be noted that, of course, the overall force of impersonality in modernity mostly emanates from these spheres – it is in economic and political/legal experience that unbrotherly impersonality will have its greatest impact.

rationalisation and impersonality; and, secondly, the link between this internal development and Puritan brotherliness.

Firstly, the tension between brotherly religion and the economic world increases with the development of capitalism. This is because, as we have noted, the economy of capitalism is marked by impersonality in an extreme form, in opposition to the personal dimension possible in medieval vocational life. The economic value-sphere in modernity is thus defined by its fated hostility to brotherliness.

> A rational economy is a functional organisation oriented to money-prices which originate in the interest-struggles of men in the *market*. Calculation is not possible without estimation in money prices and hence without market struggles. Money is the most abstract and 'impersonal' element that exists in human life. The more the world of the modern capitalist economy follows its own immanent laws, the less accessible it is to any imaginable relationship with a religious ethic of brotherliness. The more rational, and thus impersonal, capitalism becomes, the more is this the case. In the past it was possible to regulate ethically the personal relations between master and slave precisely because they were personal relations. But it is not possible to regulate – at least not in the same sense or with the same success – the relations between the shifting holders of mortgages and the shifting debtors of the banks that issue these mortgages: for in this case, no personal bonds of any sort exist. (IR: 331, Weber's emphasis)

This is the strongest, clearest point about this value-sphere in the *Intermediary Reflection*: capitalism becomes increasingly 'less accessible' to brotherliness as impersonality is strengthened in capitalism's own development. This economic rationalisation is bound into a complexity of reinforcing aspects, so it is in this sense that Weber emphasises how modern capitalism is founded on the rational, formal calculation of labour, book-keeping, technology, law and administration (AI: 21–6). The success of capitalism, and its ongoing expansion, relies on this process of rationalisation which must increasingly and systematically favour an impersonal worldview. Ethical personal relations, *Mensch zu Mensch*, will of course occur in the practical reality of economic life, but the ideal-type of capitalism will necessarily be formed without such an ethic and with the problem of theodicy absent from its calculations.

Secondly, the links between capitalism and Protestantism are given an added element with the impersonal/brotherliness relationship found in the rationalised economy.[3] The *Intermediary Reflection* states that the tension between religion and the economy is only consistently resolved by mystic indifference and Protestantism. The Protestant resolution is partly possible because of the 'standpoint of unbrotherliness' (IR: 333) and the consistent Protestant renunciation

---

3 Again it should be remembered that the *Intermediary Reflection* is part of Weber's sociology of religion and placed in the same volume as *The Protestant Ethic and the Spirit of Capitalism*.

of 'the universalism of love' (IR: 332). Although the logic of rationalisation in the economy is the dominant force for impersonality, the religious heritage of capitalism that is proffered in *The Protestant Ethic and the Spirit of Capitalism* also contains the Puritan form of brotherliness (outlined in the Chapter 6), and this impersonal ethic might be considered as having a reinforcing affinity, and even to be part of, the capitalist ethos itself. Weber does not quite say this, but if the vocational spirit is still a haunting presence in current economic life, then the vocational view of suffering and brotherly love might also be allowed a role in the impersonality of capitalism. That is, Protestant meaning extends into modernity, beyond its religious expression, in the form of impersonal unbrotherliness found in capitalism.[4] Indeed, this point will be developed below to show a more general paradoxical tension between the meaning of the value-spheres and the ethic of brotherliness.

The Political Sphere

The political sphere presents a slightly more complex relation to brotherliness than the economic. Weber deals in two areas here: firstly, the reasons of state, i.e., power, but especially violence; and, secondly, bureaucracy.

So, firstly, if the state is by definition the bearer of legitimate, inescapable violence then the political sphere must stand in clear tension with an ethic of brotherly love (IR: 334). This must be the case since, on an obvious level, the state, through violence, is the purveyor of the very suffering that brotherliness seeks to alleviate through personal love. However, it has to be remembered as previously noted, that the legitimate control of violence also allows a form of meaning in the political sphere that rivals religion: war (IR: 335–6). In war death has meaning and there is a form of brotherly love that binds the warrior community together in the face of such violent suffering. Nevertheless, from the perspective of *religious* brotherliness such meaning in war must be deemed unethical:

> The brotherliness of a group of men bound together in war must appear devalued in such brotherly religions. It must be seen as a mere reflection of the technically sophisticated brutality of the struggle. And the inner-worldly consecration of death in war must appear as a glorification of fratricide. (IR: 336)

---

4 Weber comes very close to saying exactly this: 'Today, however, the *homo politicus* as well as the *homo oeconomicus* performs his duty best when he acts without regard for the person in question, *sine ira et studio*, without hate and without love, without personal predilection and therefore without grace, but sheerly in accordance with the impersonal duty imposed by his calling, and not as a result of any concrete personal relationship' (ES: 600).

If the state must always stand in tension with brotherliness in terms of this defining issue of violence,[5] Weber considers that the necessity of bureaucracy in the modern state occasions an even greater threat to the brotherly ethic. In this second area of tension between politics and brotherliness, impersonality is again the key.

The rationalised fulfilment of the economy in capitalism is clearly the greatest source of unethical impersonality. Politics, however, is not far behind. In the political sphere:

> The bureaucratic state apparatus, and the rational *homo politicus* integrated into the state, manage affairs, including the punishment of evil, when they discharge business in the most ideal sense, according to the rational rules of the state order. In this, the political man acts just like the economic man, in a matter-of-fact manner, 'without regard to the person', *sine ira et studio,* without hate and therefore without love. By virtue of depersonalisation, the bureaucratic state, in important points is less accessible to substantive moralisation than were the patriarchal orders of the past ... (IR: 334; also ES: 600–601, 975)

Again, the explicit opposition between the modern political sphere and brotherliness is clearly articulated, with the state here understood in terms of bureaucratic impersonality.

A qualification is needed at this point. Even if Weber does see the bureaucratic structure as so dominating that the formal, impersonal calculation of the modern state has to be seen as intractably opposed to the ethic of brotherliness, 'Politics as a Vocation' does point to seemingly countervailing, irrational elements in the political value-sphere with its emphasis on the passion of the 'cause' and the 'personal' character of the politician (PV: 95). Such emotional factors are in conflict with the impersonal forces of the modern state, and Weber emphasises the importance of such opposition. Yet, however much these irrational aspects of modern politics might be contrasted with the unfeeling impersonality of bureaucracy, they cannot be equated with the personal love of the brotherly ethic.[6] In this sense they do not overcome the *ethical* problem that resides in the rule of impersonality over the personal – they are not concerned with the problem of theodicy.

In order to make sense of the way the irrational and impersonal exist in Weber's account of modern politics, it might be added that, as was the case with the economic sphere, the Puritan origins of vocational meaning might again be regarded as providing some measure of antipathy to brotherliness. That is, in so far as these irrational elements are part of the *vocation* of politics, they will stand in some measure against the ethic of brotherly love. The calling to the mundane work

---

5   In common with the economic sphere, only Puritanism and mysticism can overcome this tension, as witnessed in Chapter 6.

6   Even if the content of the cause aims at alleviating suffering and includes some motivation derived from ideals of brotherly love. We will return to this possibility below.

of politics, even including these emotional components associated with the task of the cause, might still be regarded as bearing the trace of Puritan unbrotherliness.[7]

In the end, the presence of these pieces of vocational irrationality does not in any way lessen the *unethical* impersonality of modern politics. Also, even though the expansion and importance of the modern state does lead to the development of political, vocational meaning in modernity, much more emphatically, from the perspective of religious brotherliness, it also leads to the strengthening of this immense force of rationalised impersonality that accompanies the necessity of increasing bureaucracy. It is the rational growth of the state that is decisive for Weber on this point:

> The more matter-of-fact and calculating politics is, and the freer of passionate feelings, of wrath, and of love it becomes, the more it must appear to an ethic of brotherliness to be estranged from brotherliness. (IR: 334–5)

The Aesthetic Sphere

We have seen how the irrational value-spheres of eroticism and aestheticism provide a kind of salvation in modernity in the sense of a 'salvation from' the rationalised spheres of the economy, politics and science. It is here that Weber's sociology of meaning understands the tremendous status that these separated value-spheres have in a time that is dominated by routinised, formal, instrumental impersonality. However, Weber will stress that these irrational spheres are still hostile to brotherliness, even if they avoid the paradox of rationalised meaning once the polytheistic believer steps within these sheltered and dependent places of worship. As quoted already, Weber states: 'Above all, there is tension between the ethic of religious brotherliness and the spheres of aesthetic and erotic life' (IR: 341). So, let us reconsider the values of these spheres from the perspective of suffering and its ethic.

Firstly, with the aesthetic sphere's values of taste, the creative subject and form there is the formation of a separate cosmos that competes with religion in terms of salvation, and such salvation is marked by an absence of ethical love:

> With this claim to a redemptory function, art begins to compete directly with salvation religion. Every rational religious ethic must turn against this innerworldly, irrational salvation. For in religion's eyes, such salvation is a realm of irresponsible indulgence and secret lovelessness. (IR: 342)

Each of the aesthetic values excludes brotherliness from the realm of art. Such is the case when the aesthetic sphere provides a new standard of judgement in modernity with its valorisation of 'taste'. Aesthetic 'taste' is anti-ethical and necessarily opposed by religious brotherliness:

---

7 See footnote 4 above for a confirming quotation from *Economy and Society*.

> In contrast with this ethical attitude, the escape from the necessity of taking a stand on rational, ethical grounds by resorting to aesthetic evaluations may very well be regarded by salvation religion as a very base form of unbrotherliness. (IR: 342; also ES: 608)

A similar exclusion of brotherliness can be witnessed with the value of artistic 'unappealable subjectivity' (ES: 608). Indeed, an ethic like brotherly love is a threat to the very pursuit of the artistic self of creativity and reception, and blocks a 'return to one's own nature' (SV: 142) and 'experience as such' (as quoted, SV: 143). Brotherliness is precisely the kind of 'ethical norm' that for the 'creative artist' will 'easily appear as a coercion of their genuine creativeness and innermost selves' (as quoted, IR: 342).

These values of taste and subjectivity are combined when Weber states that ethical judgement will be opposed 'partly from subjectivist needs and partly from the fear of appearing narrow-minded in a traditionalist and Philistine way' (IR: 342; also ES: 608). The aesthetic subject would necessarily be antagonistic to the ethic of brotherliness because of the restraint on the inner-most self, but also because brotherly love is indeed tied to the old-fashioned and traditional, so that such an ancient, religiously-informed ideal must be regarded as completely out-of-touch with the modern pursuit of taste and its obligatory addiction to the new and innovative.

Lastly, in addition to taste and subjectivity, Weber mentions the pursuit of form as part of the separate value structure of the aesthetic. As mentioned, form is the source of great tension between art and religion, even to the extent of 'prohibition in devout Jewish and Puritan circles of uninhibited surrender to the distinctive form-producing values of art' (ES: 610). The specific religious content of the ethic of suffering must be extraneous to the logic of form within the aesthetic sphere:

> On the part of art, however, the naive relation to the religious ethic of brotherliness can remain unbroken or can be repeatedly restored as long and as often as the conscious interest of the recipient of art is naively attached to the content and not to the form as such. (IR: 341)

If form, or style, is valued over content, as is the case in the aesthetic value-sphere, then clearly the actual ethic concerned with suffering in the world must be at least subordinate to this empty, shifting category.[8] Indeed, from the perspective of the aesthetic sphere, such an ethic must serve as an inhibitor to the development of form in the same way it does to creative subjectivity.

Taste, subjectivity and form – the values of the aesthetic sphere – are followed to gain salvation from the rationalised world, and in so doing they must consistently

---

8 Suffering can, of course, be the content of specific works of art, but it cannot be the basis of one of the values of art itself. This is the problem that fundamentally besets Adorno's aesthetic theory.

exclude brotherliness and the problem of suffering. The inner cosmos of aesthetic values only works if such ethical content is not determinate.

Some consideration needs now to be given to how the aesthetic sphere gains some measure of salvation from the *impersonal* side of the rationalised order. Weber does not directly comment on this aspect of the salvation from rationalisation, but there are hints and fairly easy lines of argument that continue on from what is explicitly said. Simply, the irrational spheres, as reactive formations to the rationalised world, can be assumed to offer salvation from the formal, calculative treatment of persons that exists as part of the fateful impersonality of the economic and political/legal spheres of modernity (and to a lesser degree within the impersonal order of science). Of course, the answer here cannot be the human ethical relationship of brotherliness, as we have seen, because this would be a fetter to the pursuit of aesthetic values. In fact the basis of the irrational in the subject – 'their innermost selves' – serves as a kind of antidote to impersonality through its emphasis on passionate originality and individual difference (as exhibited in the artwork) as against the unemotional indifference of the impersonal. The 'I' is validated above all else in the aesthetic sphere because of the differences between each 'I' that art can reveal and celebrate – such difference stands as a counterpoint to the impersonal, impartial treatment of all as formally the same that marks the development of the most rationalised value-spheres. So, as part of the salvation from the rationalised orders of the world, some escape from impersonality is in evidence in the emotional internal subjectivity of the artist and aesthetically attuned.

However, although some measure of the personal has to be retrieved for this salvation from impersonal rationalisation to succeed, impersonality is still, in the end, the determining presence for art in modernity. The aesthetic sphere, in both its social 'community' and its subjectivity, is determined by impersonality in two senses. Firstly, one of the paradoxes of aesthetic meaning already described also applies when brotherliness and impersonality are considered. Since the content and status of aesthetic values are reactions to, and an escape from, the impersonal, modern cosmos of rationalised society and nature, the aesthetic sphere can only function as an option in the polytheism of modernity, where the gods of impersonality must be honoured. The dominant presence of impersonality in the modern world is, consequently, not only untouched by the aesthetic alternative, the aesthetic sphere in fact depends upon the ongoing strength of impersonal rationalisation for its very existence – it needs the rational, impersonal spheres to react against. Secondly, impersonality is not just a presence as contrast and reaction; its very content is still present in the aesthetic sphere because the ethical/personal is rejected. That is, the growth of impersonality, as part of the logic of paradox, has the all-important ethical consequence for Weber of increasingly excluding a place for the personal ethic of brotherliness. The aesthetic values, however much they might seem to be able to avoid the impersonal, do not, as we have seen, recover the personal as ethical. In this 'lovelessness' they sustain and confirm the impersonality of modernity in the crucial sense that, for Weber, suffering – the problem of theodicy – is absent, or has a presence only as the subject matter for art.

The Erotic Sphere

A somewhat similar story to that of the sphere of art takes place with the erotic sphere, but with some key variations.

As a kind of salvation from the dominant rational value-spheres, the erotic sphere is an inner cosmos of values which is seemingly a place of the personal and of love; and as part of this salvation there is an undoubted escape from the impersonal aspect of the rationalised world. However, despite this appearance of convergence with personal brotherly love, the value-sphere of the erotic is in utter contrast to the ethic of brotherliness. Again, we will need to tie together some of Weber's various related but scattered points on these topics, and add some additional argument not explicitly provided by Weber.

As has been discussed, the erotic gains its great status in modernity through being valued as 'natural' and 'religious'. So let us consider each of these values in turn from the perspective of brotherliness.

It is through love that the natural/life can be retrieved from the cold, unemotional rational order and its routines, and especially from the disenchanted meaninglessness of the unethical universe of the scientific view of nature. Recall that in 'Science as a Vocation' it is precisely the intellectualised rational path of modern science that provokes such a fervent irrational reaction:

> And today? 'Science as the way to nature' would sound like blasphemy to youth. Today, youth proclaims the opposite: redemption from the intellectualism of science in order to return to one's own nature and therewith to nature in general.
> (as quoted in SV: 143)

The irrational sphere of the erotic is the prime site for such redemption and recovery of the natural. Life is regained and the 'death' – 'the cold skeleton hands' – of rationalised nature escaped.

But how is this value of life and nature regarded from the viewpoint of the ethic of brotherliness? Essentially, this sense of the natural, which stands against the disenchanted, meaningless nature of science, exhibits two qualities which work to exclude brotherliness. Firstly, the ideal interest that is being addressed is that of death and its meaning, with the theodicy question and the fact of suffering in the world notably absent. Secondly, this new nature found in this irrational salvation from 'death' is gained through the specific individual – 'one's own nature' – in the sense that inner subjectivity becomes the basis for 'nature in general'. So, as with the aesthetic sphere, subjectivity and the experience of the subject are constitutive of the natural value of the erotic sphere. Also, as with aesthetic subjectivity, the ethical concern with the other can be considered as, at least, in conflict with this pursuit of the natural, irrational experience of the self; and it might be seen, more strongly, as a restraint on such subjectivity. The added value of life/nature to sexual relations is, therefore, on both these counts, antipathetic to brotherliness.

At this stage it might be said that surely this 'love' must entail more than subjective experience and include the personal love of another. Indeed, this is how the inner cosmos of erotic meaning understands itself, and this leads to consideration of the second value of the erotic sphere: religiosity.

If rationalisation has been partly overcome in this first way by subjective nature, it has been achieved because the lover's self-conscious understanding is one of a personal relation of love of the other against the unemotional rational social order, not as individualised, subjective experience. The personal side of love is the key to salvation, and this personal love is given value because it is understood in religious terms. To again revisit a quotation from the *Intermediary Reflection*:

> Under these conditions, the erotic relation seems to offer the unsurpassable peak of the fulfilment of the request for love in the direct fusion of the souls of one to the other. This boundless giving of oneself is as radical as possible in its opposition to all functionality, rationality, and generality. It is displayed here as the unique meaning which one creature in his irrationality has for another, and only for this specific other. However, from the point of view of eroticism, this meaning, and with it the value-content of the relation itself, rests upon the possibility of a communion which is felt as a complete unification, as a fading of the 'thou'. It is so overpowering that it is interpreted 'symbolically': as a sacrament. (IR: 347)

The stress here is on how this love is only for the particular, 'specific other', and erotic love is thus able to gain this religious value of emotional meaning in modernity through the personal, irrational losing of oneself in the other – 'the direct fusing of the souls one to the other'.

The religious value is added to in the way this personal, ecstatic love is regarded as ethical – as goodness itself:

> The euphoria of the happy lover is felt to be 'goodness'; it has the friendly urge to poeticise all the world with happy features or to bewitch all the world in a naive enthusiasm for the diffusion of happiness. (IR: 348)

There is a return to a kind of enchanted, natural goodness which stems from the joy of personal love.

So, as we have seen when this religious value of the erotic sphere was considered previously, erotic love gains its tremendous status through the recovery of so much that seemed to have been lost when the logic of modern meaninglessness forced religion into the irrational beyond the value-sphere structure of modernity – this intensely emotional relation between the lovers is felt as a communion, a sacrament that is good and gives the world meaning. This is clearly an essential part of the redemptive power and appeal of the inner cosmos of the erotic. What flows from this, for the purposes of the present argument, is that there is salvation from rationalisation through a love that is personal, ethical and with the qualities of religion, so there would seem, therefore, to be some level of convergence with brotherly love.

However, for Weber, the opposite is the case: 'A principled ethic of religious brotherhood (*Brüderlichkeitsethik*) is radically and antagonistically opposed to all this'. (IR: 347) Primarily, this is because:

> From the point of view of any religious ethic of brotherhood [*Brüderlichkeitsethik*], the erotic relation must remain attached, in a certain sophisticated measure, to brutality. The more sublimated it is, the more brutal. Unavoidably, it is considered to be a relation of conflict. This conflict is not only, or even predominantly, jealousy and the will to possession, excluding third ones. It is far more the most intimate coercion of the soul of the less brutal partner. This coercion exists because it is never noticed by the partners themselves. Pretending to be the most humane devotion [*menschlichste Hingabe*][9], it is a sophisticated enjoyment of oneself in the other. (IR: 348)[10]

Three points arise here. Firstly, with its jealous exclusion of third parties, this love is utterly exclusive and, consequently, distantly removed from the *universal* ideal of brotherliness. Secondly, erotic love is concerned with the gratification of the self, not the suffering of the other, from the viewpoint of the brotherly ethic. Despite all its intellectualised self-consciousness, the irrational basis of erotic love is, primarily, just sexual satisfaction. Lastly, even more unethically from the perspective of religious brotherliness, erotic love is in fact a cause of suffering in that it involves an element of coercion and even brutality. In the end, although there is the self-belief that this is the most ethical, human love – 'pretending to be the most human/e devotion' – erotic love is exclusive, selfish and brutal.

Indeed, Weber extends this point on exclusivity and selfishness when he stresses the experience of the lover and compares modern erotic love to the selfish love of mystic salvation. Weber says:

---

9   Perhaps what should be given more stress here is the way *menschlich*/human denotes an ethical relation for Weber. 'Humane', as the Gerth and Mills's translation of *menschlichste*, partly loses this meaning.

10   This quotation goes onto say: 'No consummated erotic communion will know itself to be founded in any way other than through a mysterious *destination* for one another: *fate*, in this highest sense of the word. Thereby, it will know itself to be 'legitimised' (in an entirely amoral sense [*in einem gänzlich unethischen Sinn*])' (IR: 348). The fateful nature of erotic love, where the lovers feel that is a matter of destiny not choice, is an indication for Weber that this love is not an ethical one (note also that the translation of *unethischen* as 'amoral' seems too weak and loses the connections that the notion of the ethical has to Weber's understanding of brotherliness). We will need to return to this idea of the fate of erotic love.

> This consciousness of the lover rests upon the ineffaceability and inexhaustibleness of his own experience. The experience is by no means communicable and in this respect it is equivalent to the 'having' of the mystic. This is not only due to the intensity of the lover's experience, but to the immediacy of the possessed reality. Knowing 'life itself' joined to him, the lover stands opposite what is for him the objectless experiences of the mystic, as if he were facing the fading light of an unreal sphere. (IR: 347)

The lover is unlike the mystic in joining him/herself to 'life itself' as opposed to the life-emptying experience of the mystic. But the love of the other in the erotic sphere is, akin to mystic brotherliness, for the salvation experience of the lover. As well, the emphasis on 'experience', as in the aesthetic sphere, indicates that this sense of the personal is purely subjective and not concerned with the other in an ethical, personal relation. The fact that this experience is unable to be communicated is a further indication here of this essentially unbrotherly love, i.e., that this irrational experience of sexual gratification, as the basis of erotic love, is tied necessarily and only to the individual subject and, in fact, this experience is not even able to be communicated to the other. In other words, the talk of love, from the perspective of brotherliness, disguises the fact that the irrational experience of the erotic is for the self and nothing to do with the relation of the other in terms of what can be, and is, communicated between the lovers. This point is clarified when the selfish nature of this love is bluntly stressed by Weber. In contrast to the ideal expressed in Tolstoy, Weber states:

> The most sublimated eroticism is the counter-pole of all religiously oriented brotherliness, in these aspects: it must necessarily be exclusive in its inner core; it must be subjective in the highest imaginable sense; and it must be absolutely incommunicable. (IR: 349)

Here erotic love, in utter contrast to brotherliness, is understood to be necessarily and primarily concerned with the exclusive subject; in fact it is 'subjective in the highest imaginable sense'. Simply, it stands as the opposite to a universal, ethical relation of love of the other person. Finally, for the religious ethic of brotherliness, it is not a personal love at all.

The religious valuing of erotic love is fundamental to the working of the inner cosmos of the erotic sphere in modernity: from within this cosmos of values – and, even from within the more general worldview of the value-spheres of modernity as a whole – such religiosity is possible and necessary. But, from the standpoint of religious brotherly love standing outside the value-sphere structure of modernity, and 'never noticed by the partners themselves' within the erotic sphere, such love is just subjective and unethical.

At this stage a contrast between the aesthetic and erotic values can be made. The two values of the erotic sphere – the sense of life/nature and religiosity – are both clearly the recovery of lost meaning within meaninglessness. Unlike the values of the aesthetic sphere they hark back to the meaningful past and retrieve a semblance of the meaningful cosmos within the inner cosmos of the erotic sphere: a natural order is intellectually recreated with a seeming place for the ethical. This is how the erotic works as salvation from rationalised senselessness. But the *Intermediary Reflection* wants to show both how this salvation does work and how it is also in direct opposition to the religious perspective of brotherly love. As we have just seen, the ethical, religious, natural love within the erotic value-sphere is, from the standpoint of brotherliness, a pretence for unethical, selfish subjectivity which is unable to be known by the lovers within the value-sphere. Wrapped in this disguise of the natural and religiosity, the erotic sphere can therefore be seen to work in a somewhat different way from the aesthetic sphere, where the value of irrational, subjective experience is undisguised and blatantly promoted.

If this is the way the erotic values fail the test of personal brotherly love, it has to be added that, like the aesthetic sphere's relation to impersonality, the erotic does avoid the impersonality of the rationalised world, and this is a vital part of what constitutes salvation from rationalisation. This is done in two ways. Firstly, and most obviously, the emotionless side to impersonality is going to be countered by sexual love which Weber describes as 'the greatest irrational force of life' (IR: 343); and, secondly, the values of life (the natural) and religiosity are clearly created, to some degree, as salvations from the more obvious anti-personal qualities of 'impersonality'. That is, at both the level of self-conscious understanding of itself as personal, ethical love and also at the level of its actual basic selfish subjectivity, the impersonal is opposed.

However, even if impersonality is avoided by the values of the erotic sphere, like the aesthetic values, erotic love in fact sustains the logic of impersonality in a double sense. Firstly, as with art, the erotic sphere is only an irrational, dependent alternative within the dominant intellectualised and impersonal culture of our times; and, secondly, again like the aesthetic value-sphere, the 'personal' that is invoked is completely subjective and is not concerned with the ethical relation between persons, despite the label of 'love' that is attached to the erotic experience – a label that must be considered misleading from the viewpoint of brotherly love. In other words, if the problem with the impersonality of the modern world, from the perspective of brotherliness, is its unethical disregard for suffering, then even if this erotic 'personal' subjectivity might well be a salvation from impersonality, it does not address the ethical problem of impersonality which is in fact sustained at the very core of selfish erotic 'love'. In sum, the erotic, personal solution to impersonality reproduces the unbrotherliness of impersonality.

Before leaving the erotic sphere mention must be made of the way Weber does accord *conjugal* love a possible ethical dimension, if, perhaps, not one of brotherliness. Weber discusses the way religion deals with the erotic through the legitimising means of marriage, and moves on to the strict Protestant form of a rationally regulated marriage with its extreme condemnation of passionate eroticism as 'residues of the Fall' (IR: 349). But then, within the Protestant range of beliefs, Weber allows for an ethical marriage, where love is contrasted to the 'purely erotic sphere'.

> The ethic of the Quakers (as it is displayed in William Penn's letters to his wife) may well have achieved a genuinely humane interpretation [*zu einer echt menschlichen Interpretation*] of the inner and religious values of marriage. In this respect the Quaker ethic went beyond the rather gross Lutheran interpretation of the meaning of marriage.
>
> From a purely inner-worldly point of view, only the linkage of marriage with the thought of ethical responsibility for one another [*ethischer Verantwortlichkeit für einander*] – hence a category heterogeneous to the purely erotic sphere – can carry the sentiment that something unique and supreme might be embodied in marriage; that it might be the transformation of the feeling of a love which is conscious of responsibility throughout all the nuances of the organic life process, 'up to the pianissimo of old age', and a mutual granting of oneself to another and the becoming indebted to each other (in Goethe's sense). Rarely does life grant such value in pure form. He to whom it is given may speak of fate's fortune and grace – not of his own 'merit'. (IR: 350)

Ethical and human (*menschlich*), a personal love is gained in these rare marriages that is opposed to the purported personal love of the erotic. The impersonal might, in this way, be avoided in this less harsh Protestant environment. Weber is not entirely explicit, but although this love is personal and ethical and so approaches the ideal of brotherliness, it is not universal brotherly love in, at least, the obvious sense that it applies only to husband and wife. However, the brotherliness ideal is clearly at work in terms of providing a perspective that allows the sharp comparison between erotic love and the ethical, conjugal love exhibited by William Penn and his wife.

The Intellectual Sphere/Cultural Values[11]

The paradox of meaning – the plunge into senselessness – by the Western tradition of reason carries with it the denial of a place for brotherliness within the intellectual sphere. This happens in two senses: firstly, in the rational understanding of nature itself; and, secondly, within the social community of scientists.[12] Note that the account of the intellectual sphere is rather thin and ambiguous in the *Intermediary*

---

11 Just a reminder that the *Intermediary Reflection* in German does not have the clear headings added into the English translations. This really only becomes a problem with the intellectual sphere which, unlike the other value-spheres, is not clearly delineated in Weber's text. A variety of arguments are brought together in this section of the work.

12 It should be added that, as with the economic and political value-spheres, the Protestant heritage of vocation in the scientific/intellectual sphere adds another factor in favour of unbrotherly impersonality.

Reflection, so we will have to use some other texts and additional argument to fill out the relevant points.

Firstly, we need to return to the point that the meaningful cosmos, in which the ethical once had a place, has been systematically dismantled by disenchanting science (IR: 350–51), so that, as part of the paradox of meaning in the West, what is studied by science itself must lose a place for the ethical.

> Ethical religiosity has appealed to rational knowledge, which has followed its own autonomous and inner-worldly norms. It has fashioned a cosmos of truths which no longer had anything to do with the systematic postulates of a rational religious ethic; with the result that the world as a cosmos must satisfy the demands of a religious ethic or evince some 'meaning'. On the contrary, rational knowledge has had to reject this claim in principle. The cosmos of natural causality and the postulated cosmos of ethical, compensatory causality have stood in irreconcilable opposition. (IR: 355)

It follows that the gathering meaninglessness of science (and Protestant religion) – the disenchantment of the world – will finally deny any cosmic place for the ethic of brotherliness. The logic of disenchantment constitutes the fundamental aspect of the rationalisation of the intellectual/scientific sphere for Weber; and thoroughgoing disenchantment disallows the personal ethical relation any sense of being part of the God-given order of the world – as it once did have. The medieval worldview, in which such a cosmic form of brotherliness might be allowed, will be dismissed by science (as well as by consistent Protestantism). To put this more generally, when the meaningful world becomes meaningless nature then the idea that there is a place in the cosmic whole for ethics becomes simply irrational.

In the *Intermediary Reflection* Weber does not accord 'impersonality' to the intellectual sphere, but in other places he does and there is a strong sense that the natural world itself can be seen as becoming impersonal in its loss of ethical meaning. It is in this sense that we read in *The Religion of India* about the 'pure factual rationalism of the West, which practically tries to discover the impersonal laws of the world' (India: 342: also IEEWR: 281).[13] Yet what does 'impersonal' mean here? Again we will have to extend Weber's explicitly stated arguments to fill out this claim, and it can be discerned that three senses of the impersonal present themselves when the scientific 'laws of the world' are considered.

Firstly, the loss of the ethical cosmos with the advance of disenchanting science means that nature in this rational guise has become cold and indifferent to suffering, so that there is a parallel with the impersonal social order of capitalism and bureaucracy in the natural order itself. In fact it is necessarily a stronger kind of impersonality emanating from science in that the laws of nature allow no possibility of some concessional place for the personal/ethical within the vast,

---

13 This process happens in religious intellectual rationalisation as well, for example, in India (IEEWR: 282); but Western science is the extreme development of this trend.

unfeeling structure of the universe; whereas, in contrast, the ideal-typical rules of impersonal relations in the economic and political spheres can, exceptionally, be broken and allow the ethical/personal a space in the social structure of the world. The laws of nature, then, provide an ethically brutal complement to the economy and the state, so that the whole world – natural and social – takes on the garb of impersonality, to varying degrees.

The second point to be made about impersonality in the intellectual sphere is that scientific laws of the world do not just establish a dominant unethical, indifferent impersonal nature, but they are ideal-typically legitimated by rational values and methods that are also, necessarily, unemotional[14] and without regard to persons. Suffering and brotherliness cannot be part of scientific procedure and discussion – it would be irrational to follow such an ethical concern. Impersonality then must be part of the scientific legitimation of the laws of nature within the intellectual sphere.

Thirdly, this last point on legitimation might be extended in the sense that part of the makeup of the impersonality of the rational spheres of the economy and politics is the basic assumption of rational legitimation as opposed to tradition and charisma (where the personal/ethical had a possible place), and such legitimation is dependent on the ultimate model of rationality provided by science. In other words, if economic and political impersonality is part of the overall rationalisation of the West, particularly in the form of the rise of rational legitimation, then science is in fact tied to such impersonality that lies beyond the intellectual sphere itself. The impersonality of the laws and methods of science, which arise from the intellectual sphere, are thus implicitly present in the impersonality of the other rationalised spheres: rational legitimation depends upon it. In this way the intellectual sphere might be considered to be part of the overall formation of modern impersonality.

If this is how the natural laws and rational methods of science might be considered in opposition to brotherliness, Weber goes onto to discuss another way that the values of the intellectual sphere work against the ethic of brotherly love. This is the second argument in the *Intermediary Reflection* about science and brotherliness and, as opposed to the laws of nature and their rational legitimation, concerns the way intellectuals form 'an unbrotherly aristocracy'. There are two movements in Weber's argument here. Firstly, he is concerned with a purely intellectual aristocracy of mind; but, secondly, he goes beyond the purely intellectual and links the value-spheres of science and art with his notions of 'cultural values' and the *Kulturmensch*. This association between art and science is in fact Weber's major, explicit argument on the intellectual sphere in the *Intermediary Reflection*. In these specific arguments 'impersonality', it should be noted, is not such a key factor.

---

14 Although emotion is, of course, present in the intellectual sphere when science is considered as a vocation.

In the first part of this argument the intellectual sphere is, sociologically, marked by an 'unbrotherly aristocracy' because of the inevitable intellectual pursuit of the cultural value of mind (IR: 354).

> Science has created this cosmos of natural causality and has seemed unable to answer with certainty the question of its own ultimate presuppositions. Nevertheless science, in the name of 'intellectual integrity', has come forward with the claim of representing the only possible form of a reasoned view of the world. The intellect, like all culture values, has created an aristocracy based on the possession of rational culture and independent of all personal ethical qualities of man. The aristocracy of intellect is hence an unbrotherly aristocracy. Worldly man has regarded this possession of culture as the highest good. In addition to the burden of ethical guilt, however, something has adhered to this cultural value which was bound to depreciate it with still greater finality, namely, senselessness – if this cultural value is to be judged in terms of its own standards. (IR: 355)

We have already seen how the paradox of meaning in science contains the inability of science to answer the questions of its own value, which it must assume. What is being proclaimed is a monopoly on 'a reasoned view of the world' based on intellectual, cultural values, which are regarded 'as the highest good', but which are necessarily in opposition to brotherliness because they are 'independent of all personal ethical qualities of man'. To pursue and exhibit these values of mind is to differentiate oneself from the uncultivated intellect and to promote a hierarchy – an aristocracy – of achievement that is (and here again we must extend Weber's stated argument), at best, indifferent to suffering and its ethic. Indeed, such an intellectual perspective may well regard the ethical imperatives of brotherliness as a restriction on the attainment of these values. However, of course, from the perspective of the religious ethic of brotherliness, the pursuit of the values of mind – however high the level of achievement in the intellectual hierarchy – is both senseless and unethical.

In the second stage of this argument, beyond just a consideration of the intellectual sphere, Weber ties this value of 'mind' to the value of 'taste', to form the couplet of cultural values. In doing so he therefore forms an alliance between the intellectual and aesthetic spheres[15] that we have met already when the paradox of the endlessness of cultural values was discussed. There are two points that flow from this association of the aesthetic and scientific in terms of brotherliness. Firstly, Weber links the intellectual valorisation of mind with the aesthetic pursuit of taste in terms of their ethical worth, and the basic unethical nature of taste had already been stressed in the *Intermediary Reflection*. Then, secondly, it points to

---

15 This bringing together of these rational and irrational spheres in the *Intermediary Reflection* goes some way towards explaining the difficulty of understanding the structure of Weber's argument at this point in the text.

the unethical ideal of the cultivated individual or 'man of culture' (*Kulturmensch*)[16] (IR: 356, also SV: 140) who endlessly pursues both these values and so proves:

> ... to be bound to the charisma of the mind or of taste. Their cultivation has seemed inevitably to presuppose modes of existence which run counter to the demand for brotherliness. (IR: 354)

Within the value-sphere structure model of modernity Weber argues that the rational values of science/the intellectual (mind) and the irrational values of art (taste) can and do combine, and when they do it is possible to gain status of charismatic heights. That is, such cultivation comes from worshipping the dual gods of art and science in the modern polytheism and the resultant *Kulturmensch* will surely have achieved much in terms of the standards of the modern world. However, Weber reminds us again, to gain a place in this modern aristocracy of culture comes at the price of both senselessness and unbrotherliness – from the perspective of the religious ethic of brotherly love.

In short, in terms of the scientific laws of nature, the intellectual sphere has undone the ethical cosmos and replaced it with natural laws that themselves can be regarded as impersonal; also, this scientific achievement is plainly a lynchpin of the overall rationalisation of the west; and, more specifically, it is fundamental to rational legitimation upon which the impersonality of the economy and the state relies. In addition to this basic hostility to the brotherly ethic, intellectual values form an aristocracy of mind within the intellectual sphere, and a further social hierarchy in combination with the values of taste. The cultivation of these cultural values is necessarily unethical but represents a point of highest achievement for the worldly denizens of the spheres of modernity.

Guilt[17]

There is, however, another side to this fated relationship between the value-spheres and brotherliness. Simply, there is more to an understanding of brotherliness and modernity than the fact that the value-spheres are hostile to this ethic: brotherly love has a judgmental presence even within the antagonistic culture of the modern world. Weber takes up this point as part of his account of the intellectual sphere and cultural values in the *Intermediary Reflection*.

---

16 'Culture' ('*Kultur*') here denotes high, elitist culture, as opposed to the universal human culture of meaning that was mentioned in the introductory chapter and which is the way Weber uses the term in his Methodological writings.

17 Of course, this theme of guilt in the *Intermediary Reflection* has often been mentioned in the commentaries. But without a fuller understanding of brotherliness – a term which must always be part of such commentary, even in passing – what guilt entails for Weber will be difficult to envisage.

So far, what we have found is that all the spheres of modernity will follow their own values in opposition to brotherliness; and all these spheres will be determined, to varying degrees and in different ways, by impersonality. However, the additional factor that now has to be taken into account is that this understanding of the values of the age in fact assumes that the 'genuine' ideal-type of brotherliness is a presence in modernity as the ethical contrast to the polytheistic values of the spheres. The western religious heritage of theodicy, despite its Puritan dissolution as a problem, is sustained beyond its religious formation as a kind of ethical judgement on modernity. One way that Weber indicates this presence is his allusion to the 'guilt' of the age. As the values of mind and taste achieve their status in modernity, the religious, ethical heritage is not able to be just surpassed as might be supposed from a modernist, Enlightenment perspective. Rather, to build on earlier quotations where modern values are said to carry this 'burden of ethical guilt' (IR: 355), Weber says:

> Thereupon the ethical rejection of the empirical world could be further intensified. For at this point onto the religious horizon could enter a train of thoughts of far greater significance than were the imperfection and futility of worldly things, because these ideas were fit to indict precisely the 'cultural values' which usually rank highest.
>
> These values have borne the stigma of a deadly sin, of an unavoidable and specific burden of guilt. They have proved to be bound to the charisma of the mind or of taste. Their cultivation has seemed inevitably to presuppose modes of existence which run counter to *the demand for brotherliness* and which could only be adapted to this demand by self-deception. The barriers of education and of aesthetic cultivation are the most intimate and the most insuperable of all status differences. Religious guilt could now appear not only as an occasional concomitant, but as an integral part of all culture, of all conduct in a civilised world, and finally, of all structured life in general. And thereby the ultimate values which this world offered have seemed burdened with the greatest guilt. (IR: 354, emphasis added)

Yet, as this quotation indicates, it is not just the cultural values of mind and taste that are fated to carry this burden of guilt; in fact all modern culture and 'structured life in general' are subject to this judgement that is maintained from the religious heritage of the West. By revisiting arguments he had already presented in the *Intermediary Reflection* on the nature of the value-spheres, Weber briefly captures how each of the spheres is subject to such ethical assessment (IR: 355 for all the following quotations): with politics the inherent violence and brutal force of the state signifies the 'absence of love'; and such 'absence of love' is again significant in the 'routinised economic cosmos' especially as the economy develops to the 'rationally highest form of the provision of material goods'; with erotic love there is the 'veiled and sublimated brutality' that is 'hostile to brotherliness'; and with science there is the 'irreconcilable opposition' between the rational laws of natural causality and the cosmos of ethical, compensatory causality'. Only the aesthetic sphere is not directly referenced here, but there is no doubt that this realm of unbrotherly taste is subject to the same ethical critique as those that are listed.

Weber is able to sum up the guilt of the age with the statement 'All forms of activity in the structured world have appeared to be entangled in the same guilt' (IR: 355). This is part of the fate of our times. Indeed, the *Intermediary Reflection* is itself written from precisely this religious perspective in its account of modernity: brotherliness is assumed as an ideal against which the value-spheres must be judged.

So here is another twist to the paradoxical tale of brotherliness. It will be excluded by all the value-spheres but it is not entirely lost from modernity. The religious determination of the modern world is such that a fragment of brotherliness remains as the ethical judgment of the times. It is diminished in that it cannot take religious form[18] but it is also thereby purified and finds the modern value-spheres guilty in terms of its own absolute standards.

Consequences

Subjectivity and Meaning

After this discussion of the fate of brotherliness in terms of each of the value-spheres two more general points can be made. Firstly, the place of subjectivity in Weber might be clarified.

The individual subject, or subjectivity – the centre-piece of so much modernist understanding and indeed the centre-piece of much understanding of Weber (e.g., Scaff, 1991; Brubaker, 1984) – is understood by Weber to be at work in the value-spheres but it is not part of his own theory of modernity, except in the way subjectivity is to be explained by the overarching perspective of meaning and ideal interests. As we have seen in the irrational spheres, the values of the internal cosmos cluster around the individual subject and inner subjectivity, even if coated over by other values in the case of erotic love. However such subjectivity is part of the internal dimension of the value-sphere structure of the modern world which has to be left if the perspective of meaning is to be made available. Weber in fact explicitly understands the claims of subjectivity in terms of his sociology of religion, that is, as he puts it in 'Science as a Vocation', the inner subject as the site of experience is the basis of the salvation offered by the irrational spheres.

Comparison might be made here between the subjectivity of the irrational spheres, and Weber's treatment of the political sphere. In 'Politics as a Vocation' Weber does not take up some political position, nor does he talk in terms of the

---

18 Except as part of some religious belief, of course. However, such religion lies outside the value-sphere structure of modernity and is no longer of theoretical concern to Weber.

standard Enlightenment values of liberty and equality. Rather, from the perspective of meaning, he uses the concepts of the 'cause' and vocation. Similarly, with the irrational spheres, Weber does not use an outlook reliant on modern subjectivity, but, instead, looks to how this fundamental premise of modernity must itself be theorised in terms of meaning.[19]

Brotherliness and the Paradox of Meaning

If subjectivity can be accorded this broader understanding, a second more general point can also be made about brotherliness and meaning.

We are now in a position to consider brotherliness and its antagonism to the value-spheres in a somewhat wider context of meaning and modernity. If the Western tradition of meaning gives suffering and death the emphasis we have seen, these twin poles of meaning in the more general sense have themselves an inner relationship of paradox, which has been hinted at in the preceding arguments.

In all the value-spheres Weber has shown how the ideal interest in giving meaning to life and death is still at work within the overall meaninglessness; and how there is paradox present, in varying ways and degrees, even at this level of meaning. From the tight knot of arguments in the *Intermediary Reflection*, we can see how this thread of meaning as paradox is bound together with brotherliness in a further relation of paradox: the pursuit of the meaning of life and death in each value-sphere will fatefully lose the ethic of brotherliness. In other words, the impersonal or unethical is reached as part of the pursuit of one pole of meaning (life/death) and, partly by this very process, the other pole of meaning (suffering/ brotherliness) is lost. Ideal interests then shape the value-sphere structure of modernity through the domination of the meaning of life/death, and the diminution, or loss, of the ethic of suffering.

The discussion of the irrational spheres in the *Intermediary Reflection* demonstrates this relationship. Weber shows how both the aesthetic and erotic spheres develop as forms of salvation from the ersatz death emanating from the rationalised spheres, and how this very development excludes the problem of suffering and the ethic of brotherliness; both parts of the overall question of meaning are brought together as part of the same, if complex, theory in the *Intermediary Reflection*. Weber's argument here is that the religion-rivalling inner cosmos of values that marks each of the irrational spheres provides a new form of 'life' over life-denying rationalised routine and impersonality; or, to phrase it slightly differently, in the irrational spheres the passionate subjective experience of art and the erotic give meaning within meaninglessness. Yet we have just seen how Weber is also saying that this irrational salvation from death is the antithesis of

---

19 The obvious qualification must be made here that 'inner subjectivity' is itself part of religious experience, for example, as Hegel will emphasise in his account of the Christian West. In such cases subjectivity is part of the overall determination of religious meaning, as opposed to the role of the subject in the value-spheres of meaningless modernity.

brotherliness. Crucially, suffering is absent as a defining problem. In the aesthetic sphere contentless form, unethical taste, and inner subjectivity must exclude theodicy as stifling. In a parallel fashion, the erotic sphere's valuing of the natural is predicated on an inner subjectivity that must be hostile to brotherliness; and the coating of sex with goodness and religiosity, that also forms the value-sphere of the erotic, covers over the brutal subjectivity that works completely against personal ethical love and its foundation in the fact of suffering. For Weber, then, the very makeup of the irrational spheres shows how part of the logic of paradox in modernity is that the pursuit of meaning in terms of death will lose the meaning of suffering. Within the overall meaninglessness, ideal interests will partly form the value-sphere structure of modernity in terms of this inner paradox between the two poles of the Western tradition of meaning.

The irrational spheres have this double movement in the argument of the *Intermediary Reflection* – of salvation from 'death' and as the antithesis to brotherliness. However, the discussion of the rationalised spheres in the *Intermediary Reflection*, although it still includes both poles of the problem of meaning, overwhelmingly favours the argument on impersonality and the loss of brotherliness, especially in the economic and political spheres, and it does not include the notion of vocation at all. In order to understand this paradox between the meaning of death and the ethic of suffering in the rationalised spheres, which has been briefly put already, we need to extend our understanding to texts beyond the *Intermediary Reflection* – back to *The Protestant Ethic and the Spirit of Capitalism* and the Vocation lectures, in fact. In these texts, as we have seen, the dominant argument (at least in terms of meaning) is about the vocational meaning of life/death, and suffering and brotherliness have a much more minor presence. Each of the rationalised spheres[20] will be briefly examined in turn.

In the economic sphere the haunting presence of Protestant vocation allows some meaning in modernity, and to follow this vocation, in whatever way, must entail that the money-making values of the capitalist market are followed. As discussed, impersonality is a necessary component of this highly rationalised economy, so that, to add the *Intermediary Reflection* and *The Protestant Ethic and the Spirit of Capitalism* together here, the spirit of capitalism allows the semblance of meaning as vocation, as it must also exclude the ethic of brotherliness and the problem of suffering. To gain this part of meaning (life/death) is to lose the meaning of theodicy. That this is the fate of the economic sphere is not surprising given that the form of Puritan brotherliness was – as part of Puritan vocational meaning – in such opposition to the brotherly ideal of love.

---

20 It has to be noted that these rationalised spheres have their own inner logics of rationalisation that are not about meaning, or not directly so (for example, becoming more efficient, calculable, formal); and there has been much commentary devoted to the explication of such rationalisation. This is in contrast with the irrational spheres which, for the purposes of Weber's argument in the *Intermediary Reflection*, are almost wholly explained as expressions of ideal interests – salvation is the basis of their formation.

The political sphere is slightly more complex.[21] When politics is understood as a vocation by Weber this paradox between the poles of meaning is again apparent, but how does this political example of meaning within meaninglessness seen in 'Politics as a Vocation' relate to the ideal interest of suffering and brotherliness taken up in the *Intermediary Reflection*? On a general level there are three factors that make up politics as a vocation: the Puritan tradition of labour in the mundane world; the added value of the cause; and the set of paradoxes that inevitably awaits the realisation of the cause and which the politician has to accept as the fate of politics. With this combination of factors in place the ideal interest in meaningful life and death might be partially, if paradoxically, met. Yet, as this vocational meaning is pursued, the ethic of brotherliness and the problem of theodicy are necessarily lost by the first and third of these factors, and almost always lost by the second.

The lingering traces of the Puritan tradition of labour – the first element – provides a way of acting in the world that has its origins in an obsessive concern with salvation, and where the problem of suffering had been dissolved with most unbrotherly results. The theological content might well be long gone but, in so far as the calling in politics is still extant, then satisfying the ideal interests in life/death – however slight that satisfaction might be in modernity – will be at the expense of the ideal interest in suffering and its ethic. The third factor more directly opposes brotherliness with the inherent paradoxes occasioned by the violence of the state and the impersonality of bureaucracy. If these paradoxes must be factored into the vocational pursuit or meaning in politics, then brotherliness, for reasons just elaborated, must be shut out. Therefore, on the basis of these two constituent ingredients of politics as a vocation the paradox between the poles of meaning – life/death and suffering – will be played out in the political value-sphere. But the second element – the cause – provides an extra dimension.

The political cause will generally not be concerned with brotherliness and its content will usually be indifferent to suffering. This cannot, however, be the whole

---

21 An additional aspect of this complexity occurs with war – an element that must always be present when the question of politics and meaning is being considered. As mentioned, under the determination of the 'reasons of state' – power and, especially, violence – war does provide both a meaning for death and, also, a form of brotherliness in the face of such obvious suffering. In this provision of meeting both ideal interests war stands out as unique amidst the meaninglessness of modern culture. The essential paradox of meaning within the value-spheres, where to gain some measure of the meaning of death must come at the cost of the meaning of suffering, is therefore not present in the special case of war. However, even given this exceptional inclusion of a form of brotherliness alongside a meaning to death, the *religious* brotherly ethic must, as noted, stand outside this kind of meaningful brutality and condemn it (IR: 335–6). To gain such meaning in war, therefore, comes with the loss of the ideal of religious brotherly love, so that we might conclude that a variant of the paradox of meaning within meaningless modernity is still apparent here; although it is not the more common type of paradox where the ideal interest in the meaning of life and death subordinates suffering to the point where ethical love is absent.

story. Here we must add to Weber's account and include the obvious possibility that the brotherly ethic and the fact of suffering in the world might well form the motivating vocational cause for work in the political sphere.[22] If such is the case then this cause is subject to the paradoxes that await all political causes as part of the vocation of politics; but there is an additional burden that faces the cause that contains some measure of the brotherly ethic – the brutality of state violence and the impersonality of modern state bureaucracy must be especially threatening.[23] So, even if brotherly love does find its way into the pursuit of vocational political meaning it will be lost or lessened more than any other cause. An additional layer of paradox might therefore be seen to be present if the content of brotherliness does, in fact, claim a place in the political sphere in this way.

However, this layer of paradox has still another aspect to add to this already complex picture. It is not just the case that the pole of suffering and brotherliness will be more easily lost or lessened than other causes if taken up as part of the other pole of meaning (that is, as part of the cause in the pursuit of politics as a vocation), but, conversely, the pole of vocational meaning itself will also be under greater threat if the brotherly ethic is part of its content. This is so because the politician is more likely to lose this side of meaning – the sense of vocation – due to the overwhelming difficulties of pursuing the brotherly ethic within the political sphere. In other words, the vocation for politics, in Weber's view, must contain the self-understanding of the paradoxical fate that awaits any cause and which is a constant and often overwhelming threat to vocational meaning; but this threat must be greatly increased if some part of the brotherly ethic is present because the forces that stand in the way of the realisation of all causes are intrinsically in opposition to brotherlinesss in particular. Both poles of meaning are therefore subject to paradoxical loss in this instance. In this way, perhaps, it becomes clearer why politics is so inimical to suffering and brotherliness, as Weber had stressed in the *Intermediary Reflection*.

Consequently, in politics there is an intricate pattern at work that ties the two poles of meaning together, but a paradox is in evidence throughout – the pursuit

---

22 'Genuine' brotherliness could not countenance the compromises which any engagement with the political world necessitates, so here only heavily qualified, partial versions of the ideal-type of brotherly love are being considered which might also, perhaps, be mixed with other motivating values.

23 This paradox goes to the heart of the welfare state as a means of not just overcoming inequality but relieving suffering. Suffering might well be lessened so that the political cause behind state welfare has, in part, succeeded in following the ethic of brotherliness; but the cost will almost certainly be an increase in bureaucratic impersonality as a necessary consequence of the rationalised administration that such welfare demands. From the perspective of the religiously-derived ideal of brotherliness, the personal love of the sufferer will almost certainly and necessarily be absent. So here, with brotherliness and impersonality, we find a particular example of the familiar paradox of bureaucracy where the bureaucratic means undermines or determines the political ends.

of meaning both in war and the vocation (whatever the content of the cause) must result in the loss or diminution of brotherliness.

'Science as a Vocation' reveals how the intellectual/scientific sphere also contains three elements that contribute to the pursuit of the life/death pole of meaning: the Puritan heritage of vocational labour in the mundane world; the internal, objective, rationalised values of this scientific labour, i.e., logic and rules of evidence; and the irrational assumption that the results of intellectual labour must be worth knowing – that they have some meaning. Now the first two elements – vocation and objective rational values – clearly work against an ethic of personal brotherly love. The third aspect – the irrational assumptions – might be regarded as playing a similar role to the cause in politics in that the alleviation of suffering could be what is assumed to be the point of the intellectual endeavour, as is the case with medical research. However, two qualifying comments can be made on this possible sympathetic role of brotherliness in the pursuit of science as a vocation. Firstly, as discussed, Weber explicitly draws attention to the way the rationalised, technical values of the intellectual value-sphere will lead away from this ethic in the case of the medical treatment of certain kinds of suffering; and they will in fact lead towards the maintenance of life and the postponement of death – such values will favour the life/death pole of meaning. Secondly, within the vast, specialised realm of intellectual reason in modernity the place of brotherliness as a motivating assumption will be slight, and, in fact, much slighter than in politics.

Therefore, the rational and irrational spheres, in their different ways, all follow this same logic of paradox that exists between the very poles of Western meaning itself. This extra paradox brings the way meaning works in modernity into even clearer focus.

Conclusion

Brotherliness is the ethic to which Weber repeatedly returns throughout his empirical work and the Vocation lectures, and it is the key term in the *Intermediary Reflection*. In order to understand the meaning of this ethic precisely we had to trace its path throughout Weber's works in the previous chapter and only then could its crucial role in Weber's value-sphere structure of modernity be more clearly understood.

Now if we combine the arguments of all the chapters on paradox and brotherliness we get a core conclusion: modernity is meaningless in terms of the meaning given to death and suffering by the West's religious history, but this religious history of meaning is still sustained not only within and between the value-spheres, but also in the way the values of these spheres are ethically judged. The content of this meaning within modernity lies in: the vocational nature of the rationalised spheres; the 'salvation' from the rationalised spheres through the inner cosmos value structure of the irrational spheres; and the ethic of brotherliness that, despite being systematically excluded by the impersonal forces at work in and between the value-spheres, remains as a source of guilt for modern culture generally.

For Weber these are fateful circumstances. Not only is a return to religion as meaning not part of this logic of modernity, but the religious remnants that still shape modernity are just as fatefully inescapable. Meaning within meaninglessness is just as much a necessary part of our historical fate as meaninglessness itself. This is how the value-sphere structure of modernity works for Weber in terms of the universal condition of human ideal interests, and how the *Intermediary Reflection*, as the final, dense articulation of these spheres, works as part of Weber's sociology of religion.

This overall theory of meaning only became clearly apparent after the knots of arguments in Weber's texts were unpicked and the various strands examined and compared. Remarkably, a coherent theory did in fact emerge and, perhaps ever more remarkably, Weber can be seen to have been able to sustain the perspective of his sociology of religion throughout, and was not drawn into debates, the use of terms and the assumption of values that are the substance of the secular, modern worldview. Modernity is able to be understood in terms of the value-sphere theory precisely because the perspective of religious understanding – from within the sociology of religion – was not left behind. The result is that Weber presents us with a view of modern life that is based on ideas of vocation, salvation, fate, brotherly love, death and suffering – he shows us how modernity works as meaning.

With this account of meaning and modernity in place we are in a position to consider some of Weber's most debated terms and ideas. Especially, we can return to the Vocation lectures and examine Weber's prescriptions for this life of meaning within meaninglessness.

PART III
Implications

Chapter 8
Prescriptions

Introduction

When we go back to what Weber said about Tolstoy's questions – what shall we do? How should we live in the world? – the paradox of modern meaning becomes apparent. Such questions are now meaningless, chiefly because death has lost its religious understanding, but the questions of meaning themselves must still be asked; and it is in the value-spheres that – paradoxically – they can still be answered. The whole theory of meaning that has been teased out of Weber's extensive writings shows how this 'meaning within meaninglessness' works. Yet there is a further step that can now be taken – we can consider Weber's own prescriptions for what one should do in the modern world from the perspective of his theory of meaning. The most obvious place to find such views is in the Vocation lectures, and with some consideration needed for the end of *The Protestant Ethic and the Spirit of Capitalism*.

As usual, the prescriptive passages of these texts, with their prophetic advice and warnings, have been subjected to extensive examination and interpretation. However, armed with a more articulated theory of meaning, we might be better served to enter into the sense of these difficult, contentious statements.

This chapter has two sections of unequal length. Firstly, the bulk of what follows will be devoted to an explanation of the answers that Weber in fact gives to Tolstoy's questions, and this section will also have to include the secondary literature that has specifically considered these ideas of Weber in relation to brotherliness. In the smaller second part to the chapter, an apparent contradiction will be confronted and partly explained through an engagement with the ancient Greek references that are laced through Weber's arguments, especially as they are found in the final stages of 'Science as a Vocation'. The section concludes with a brief argument concerning the metaphor of the 'iron cage'.

The Advocacy of Vocation

Against so much of the interpretative tradition that has sought to bring Weber's remarks on what one should do in the world into some wider philosophy (especially some variant of existentialism), we will stick with our guiding premise of understanding Weber within his own terms. It has to be stressed again that the Vocation lectures should primarily be seen as *just* that – they are concerned with how and why a vocation should be followed in modern times. For Weber it is the question of meaning in modernity that is at stake and his larger sociology of religion is needed as the context in which the often brief and enigmatic expressions of the Vocation lectures can be understood.

Almost at the end of 'Science as a Vocation', as the second last sentence, Weber writes:

> We will set to work and meet the 'demands of the day' in human relations as well as in our vocation. (SV: 156)[1]

It is just these two areas with which he is concerned. The human (*menschlich*) side will be shown immediately below to be concerned with brotherliness, but what can be said about the more obviously and directly stated 'vocation'?

What it takes to follow the vocations of science and politics has been detailed in previous chapters;[2] and we can also see why Weber is prescribing vocation in modernity – there is an assumed imperative that these vocations should be followed if they can be. Simply, it does offer some semblance of meaning within the overall disenchanted senselessness of modernity. As meaning-seeking *Kulturmenschen* this is something that is profoundly desired even if the larger questions of existence can no longer be articulated in the terminology of the intellectual value-sphere because, as Weber shows, such meaning is necessarily absent from science/intellectualised reason, if also assumed by such reason.

'Politics as a Vocation' and 'Science as a Vocation' can both be read as providing a depiction of the paradoxical fate of meaning in modernity; and they both can be seen to be advocating the pursuit of such paradoxical meaning – a task which takes great resolve precisely because of the paradoxes involved.[3] So, for Weber, not to be able to take the vocational path in politics means that:

> ... they have not measured up to their own doings. They have not measured up to the world as it really is ... (PV: 128)

Similarly, towards the end of 'Science as a Vocation', he addresses those who cannot face the vocational task of science in a disenchanted world – 'the demands of the day' – as someone who (in now outdated, masculinist terms) 'cannot bear the fate of the times like a man ...' (SV: 155).[4]

---

1 '... *an unsere Arbeit gehen und der "Forderung des Tages" gerecht werden – menschlich sowohl wie beruflich*' (WB: 111). The 'demands of the day' (a quotation from Goethe) are, mostly, the greater disenchanted senselessness that Weber lays out in 'Science as a Vocation'. We will consider this again below as part of a discussion on 'fate'.

2 And, as usual, has been the subject of a great deal of discussion in the secondary literature.

3 And partly because of the times, as well as the sheer baseness and stupidity of the world (PV: 128).

4 '*Wer dies Schicksal der Zeit nicht männlich ertragen kann*' (WB: 110).

Weber only discusses in detail the vocational life of the elected politician and the scientist/intellectual. However, this cannot be the whole story, since a sense of the vocation can clearly arise in a huge range of occupations which, it can be safely assumed, are also to be advocated as part of Weber's overall sociology of meaning. Weber himself said that, within the sphere of politics, vocational possibilities were there for journalists and even bureaucrats; and the pure economic value-sphere itself might still offer the opportunity for a calling that rises above the mere whiff of vocational meaning that resides in capitalism as its all-pervasive spirit. Based on what Weber does say in relation to science and politics, some speculative points might be made to try to make sense of this more generalised prescription of vocation in modernity.

The theory of meaning that we have been able to distil from Weber's works has shown that the Protestant legacy of vocational meaning has two basic factors: the mundane routines of labour which have been made part of our cultural fate because of the ongoing fact of capitalism; and the extra value/meaning that can be added onto this Protestant labour from within the specific histories of each value-sphere in the terms of the task, for example, with the 'cause' in politics, and the history of Western cosmic meaning which lies behind contemporary intellectual labour. This basic two-part template might be applied to a range of occupations that have been followed as a calling – even in art.

The aesthetic value-sphere is undoubtedly a place where the pronouncement of the calling is extremely common. In fact, Weber does make some brief allusions to the artistic vocation: at the end of *The Protestant Ethic and the Spirit of Capitalism* he mentions the calling as applying to 'the highest spiritual and *cultural* values' (PE: 182, emphasis added), and, as quoted, that 'rational conduct on the basis of the idea of the calling' is 'one of the fundamental elements of the spirit of modern capitalism, and not only of that but of all modern culture'; also, in 'Science as a Vocation' an 'inner devotion to the task' is accorded to the artist as well as the scientist (SV: 137). Further, the places where he discusses the aesthetic sphere, the *Intermediary Reflection* and *Economy and Society*, are not texts that discuss vocation in modernity; so, perhaps, a sense of vocation might be added to Weber's account here.

If art is considered in terms of Weberian vocation, then certain tensions become apparent. Hard, routinised, rational labour is often included in the artist's own sense of what the calling demands; but, on Weber's analysis, the extra dimension that is needed to gain the meaning for the task within the aesthetic value-sphere must include the sense of salvation against routinisation, the rational spheres and, in part, the very labour that the Protestant tradition of the calling demands. It might then be imagined that a tense relationship between the two sides of the calling will be seen to arise in any notion of 'art as a vocation'. However, if this routine of mundane labour is just a means to the salvation afforded by the realisation of aesthetic values then such conflict is manifestly dissipated, as long as the rationalised routines *beyond* the aesthetic value-sphere are still clearly identifiable as those 'skeletal hands' that irrational experience must escape. Indeed, the internal structure of meaning for the aesthetic value-sphere – at least in terms of the relation between the means of labour and the end of salvation – takes on a shape reminiscent of the originating Protestant model of religious meaning.

The more general point that arises from these brief, speculative remarks on art and vocation is that the vocational sense of meaning can be expanded beyond Weber's own examples, whilst still employing Weber's own terms of analysis. To find one's vocation in the modern world is part of the polytheistic vision of meaning for Weber, where different vocations can be likened to the warring gods of antiquity. Each vocation, like each of the ancient gods, will have its own internal histories of how it has been formed and how it should be followed; and Weber's accounts of science and politics provide the tools of analysis that enable an understanding of just how these other vocations do function as meaning in modernity. Conditions will vary from vocation to vocation, from god to god, but at some fundamental level all vocational meaning must succumb to the logic of paradox. So to 'set to work to meet the demands of the day' in any vocation – as Weber recommends you should do – will take strength, as with science and politics, to meet the paradoxes that fatefully await.

If vocational meaning can be seen as prescribed by Weber through his theory of the value-spheres, we can now turn to consider his prescriptions for 'human relations' in modernity.

The Advocacy of Brotherliness[5]

With the analysis provided in previous chapters a sufficient understanding of 'brotherliness' can be pieced together to enable a discussion of Weber's

---

5   It should be noted that some recent translations of the Vocation lectures have rendered '*Brüderlichkeit*' as: 'fraternal act' and 'fraternal relations' (Dreijmanis, 2008: 51; Weber, 2004: 30); 'neighbourly contacts' (Weber, 2004: 93); and, the more common but less drastic mistranslation, 'brotherhood' (in the Peter Lassman and Irving Velody version of 'Science as a Vocation' reprinted in Whimster, 2004: 286–7). But sometimes 'brotherliness' is in fact retained (Dreijmanis, 2008: 206). Other aspects of these newer translations make some improvements on the standard Gerth and Mills wording, but this particular determination is to be regretted. What then happens to all the other uses of '*Brüderlichkeit*' scattered throughout Weber's works, especially with the *Intermediary Reflection* where it is a central concept? Are all these other uses to be retranslated with this weakened if more accessible terminology, which really loses the basic religious connotation that is manifestly being stressed by Weber? It is also clear from these examples that the term is being inconsistently translated; with Whimster (2004), for example, maintaining 'brotherliness' in his reworking of the *Intermediary Reflection*. So some basic conflict is apparent which should be resolved in terms of Weber's overall theory and use of the term. However, to be fair to these translators, the fact that these problems have arisen is indicative of the way the dominant interpretive tradition has overlooked 'brotherliness' as an important category in Weber's sociology of religion.

prescriptions for the ethic of brotherliness outlined in 'Politics as a Vocation' and 'Science as a Vocation'. In essence, Weber's empirical works indicate that an *ethic* of brotherliness can only prosper in personal relations where the suffering of the other can be directly appreciated. Whereas it once did have a tenuous and tension-filled existence in the medieval, traditionalistic ethics of vocation, this is now impossible in the vocational life of modernity because of the unyielding domination of impersonality. However, brotherliness is still a determining presence in modernity and should, Weber tells us in the Vocation lectures, be followed.

Politics as a Vocation

'Politics as a Vocation' includes quite a lengthy excursion on the religious attempts to meet the problem of a supposedly omnipotent God's creation of 'an irrational world of undeserved suffering …' (PV: 122); that is, the problem of theodicy. How Christianity tried to deal with politics – a contract 'with diabolical powers' – is given in a series of examples which all recall Weber's religious writings as we have discussed in some of the previous chapters. This list includes the uneasy compromises of the Church (PV: 124), the Protestant legitimation of the violence of the state (PV: 124) and the acosmic form of universal love (PV: 126). Weber's aim here is to stress the tension and conflict between politics and religion, especially when love is still the central ethic in any religious answer given to the problem of theodicy (PV: 126). For Weber, the ultimate ends of such religions cannot be pursued responsibly in the modern vocation of politics, chiefly because the tasks of politics 'can only be solved by violence' (PV: 126).

Undoubtedly, Weber's purpose in this lecture is to illustrate the qualities necessary for entering the vocation of politics, and this cannot include the caritative, religious solutions to the problem of suffering in any ideal sense.[6] The point for our present argument is that this problem of love and suffering, which can be fully understood by reference back to Weber's religious works, is brought back at the very end of the lecture, within two pages of the religion/politics discussion. Yet it is re-engaged in terms that had not previously been used in this particular lecture, and so it might appear that this late, brief reference is disengaged from the almost immediately preceding summary of the theodicy problem. An acquaintance with how the meaning of suffering and love is dealt with elsewhere by Weber, however, shows otherwise. After listing the ways in which those who thought of themselves as politicians will not have 'measured up to the world as it really is …' (as quoted, PV: 128), Weber concludes:

---

6 As discussed, the ideal of brotherliness might well form part of the motivation of the 'cause' in a political vocation, but the compromises will necessarily be so heavy that such a practical engagement must be judged harshly from the perspective of the 'genuine' ethic of brotherly love.

Objectively and actually, they have not experienced the vocation for politics in its deepest meaning, which they thought they had. *They would have done better in simply cultivating plain brotherliness in personal relations.* And for the rest – they should have gone soberly about their daily work. (PV: 128, emphasis added)[7]

Importantly, Weber's reference to brotherliness and personal relations here is prescriptive. We have seen what this might amount to in the foregoing accounts of brotherliness. It is in personal relations that the brotherly ethic of care, of concern with the suffering of the other, can be maintained, although there is continuous tension with the logic of impersonality. Brotherliness is advocated here by Weber seemingly as part of the Christian, indeed Catholic, origins of Western modernity. 'Personal relations' have always been the site of this ethic, but are here clearly contrasted to the sphere of politics which must, on the whole, be dominated by the impersonal.[8]

It is tempting to explain what the personal means here as the *private*,[9] as opposed to the *public* life of politics. This would be a mistake, it can be argued, for two reasons. Firstly, Weber does not talk in terms of the public/private divide in his writings, or only to a minor extent (ES: 356); rather, as we have seen, his understanding encompasses the impersonality of the spheres of modernity, as opposed to the different way the 'public' orders of the world (like the economy and political sphere) in the past have been structured and legitimated. 'Personal', at least in one important sense, refers back to how the pre-modern West, and other societies like Confucian China, constituted relations between people throughout society. The personal was part of the public life of these societies, but has been overtaken by the impersonal structures of the more modern forms of the social.

Secondly, the ethic of brotherliness, as demonstrated above, is universal, on the cusp of the impersonal, and comes from neighbourly community care and the great problem of theodicy. It is *not* based in natural family bonds. On the contrary, brotherliness arose in direct opposition to 'natural relations and to the matrimonial community' (IR: 329). The essential constitution of brotherliness is what Weber had indirectly been discussing in his excursion on religious ethics in 'Politics as a Vocation' just before he actually used the term itself at the end of the lecture. This brotherly universal love is obviously not the usual stuff of the private. It is not family love, if this has maternal particularity as the main model; and it is certainly

---

7 '... *sie haben den Beruf zur Politik, den sie für sich in sich glaubten, objektiv und tatsächlich im innerlichsten Sinn nicht gehabt. Sie hätten besser getan, die Brüderlichkeit schlicht und einfach von Mensch zu Mensch zu pflegen und im übrigen rein sachlich an ihres Tages Arbeit zu wirken*' (PB: 251).

8 Again, there are extra dimensions to 'Politics as a Vocation', where it is argued that politicians, as opposed to the bureaucracy, must and should be personal. But it is not ethical.

9 As, for example, Bellah (1999) does.

not erotic or romantic love. It is a religiously formed universal love engendered by the brutal fact of suffering.[10]

'Cultivating plain brotherliness in personal relations' means trying to maintain this traditional Christian ethic outside religion; and pursuing this value in human relations that have not been consumed into the necessary but unethical realms of impersonal modernity; or are not dominated by other, 'private' values or loves. Weber does not specify what this might mean, so some speculative projections might be allowed here. It can be suggested that Weber is advocating a manner of treating people whenever the demands of the value-spheres will allow it. The 'personal' as the site of this universal ethic should be cultivated when possible. This means always being aware of the limits of impersonality; or knowing when the ethics of the personal can begin. Perhaps this would be with strangers, or neighbours of course, but also with others within the vocational sphere when the values of that sphere allow (which might indeed be rare). Again, it has to be stressed, the overwhelming emphasis in 'Politics as a Vocation' is on the heroic strength needed for the vocation of politics, but it would be odd for Weber to have abandoned the ethic which he had discussed so much in other important works, even when these works have shown the essential antagonism between the impersonal spheres of the modern and brotherliness.

If this is the nature of 'plain brotherliness in personal relations' the quotation is still unclear because it is not certain who is supposed to be able to follow this imperative. Weber says '*they* would have been better in simply cultivating ...', with 'they' here seemingly referring to those would-be politicians who did not measure up to the world as it really is. Without a real vocation for politics brotherly love should be cultivated, and 'for the rest',[11] or apart from that, the daily sober routines of work – without vocational meaning – should be followed. The implications of this brief statement are twofold. Firstly, brotherliness is something that everyone can and should follow. However, secondly, it would seem that those who are able to be engaged in the calling of politics might only be 'cultivating plain brotherliness' to a diminished extent, if at all, since Weber would appear to be saying that it becomes a much more viable option, or easier to do, once it has been accepted that vocational meaning has been extinguished.

We have seen why it is the case that brotherliness will be so hard to follow in the presence of vocational meaning: these twin poles of meaning stand in a paradoxical relation to each other. As emphasised in the *Intermediary Reflection*,

---

10 Of course, there are personal relationships that are ethical and loving but are not examples of brotherliness. As stated, Weber mentions the case of married life where, if there is a great deal of luck, the couple can grow old together in love (IR: 350). This might be labelled the 'private', but this aside in the *Intermediary Reflection* does not directly mention brotherliness and does not comfortably fit into his previous descriptions of the nature of brotherly love.

11 Gerth and Mills's translation of '*und im übrigen*' as 'for the rest ...' is somewhat misleading, and is better put as 'apart from that' or 'in other respects'.

the value-spheres stand in opposition to brotherliness, so that to be *vocationally* engaged in one of the value-spheres is to be following a course of meaning and values with such 'passion and perspective' (PV: 128) that it is likely that the ethical conduct of brotherly love will be lessened even more than usual. Indeed, brotherliness and a concern for the personal might well be considered a restriction on the ability to complete the vocational task. Heroic strength is needed to carry out the vocation in modernity, but still greater strength is needed to fulfil what modernity has to offer in terms of vocation *and* brotherliness.

Science as a Vocation

'Science as a Vocation' reiterates and partially clarifies this account, but, again, only with a few brief remarks. 'Brotherliness' is mentioned twice directly and once indirectly in some famous passages at the end of the lecture.

Firstly, 'brotherliness' is present in the following context. After stressing how religious belief and science are now irreconcilable in terms of the 'sacrifice of the intellect' (SV: 154), and the dismissal as 'humbug' the activities of some modern intellectuals who dabble and play with 'sacred images from all over the world' to produce a surrogate mysticism, Weber then states:

> It is, however, no humbug but rather something very sincere and genuine if some of the youth groups who during recent years have quietly grown together give their community the interpretation of a religious, cosmic or mystical relation, although occasionally perhaps such an interpretation rests on a misunderstanding of the self. True as it is that every act of genuine *brotherliness* may be linked with the awareness that it contributes something imperishable to the super-personal realm, it seems to me dubious whether the dignity of purely human and communal relations is enhanced by these religious interpretations. But this is no longer our theme.
>
> The fate of our times is characterised by rationalisation and intellectualisation and, above all, by the 'disenchantment of the world'. Precisely the ultimate and most sublime values have retreated from public life either into the transcendental realm of the mystic life or into the *brotherliness* of direct and human relations. It is not accidental ... that today only within the smallest and intimate circles, in personal human situations, in *pianissimo*, that something is pulsating that corresponds to the prophetic *pneuma* which in former times swept through the great communities like a firebrand, welding them together. (SV: 155, emphasis added for 'brotherliness')[12]

---

12 '*Durchaus kein Schwindel, sondern etwas sehr Ernstes und Wahrhaftes, aber vielleicht zuweilen sich selbst in seinem Sinn Mißdeutendes ist es dagegen, wenn manche jener Jugendgemeinschaften, die in der Stille in den letzten Jahren gewachsen sind, ihrer eigenen menschlichen Gemeinschaftsbeziehung die Deutung einer religiösen, kosmischen*

Secondly, the indirect reference to brotherliness is present at the very end of the lecture, when Weber makes the comment (which began this discussion) about meeting 'the "demands of the day" in *human* relations' (SV: 156, emphasis added), as well as in vocational duty.

Within these first passages we find rare praise for a certain religious communalism, where brotherliness seems to be the chosen ethic. However, for Weber it is still based on misunderstanding and cannot enhance the morality of suffering. If the wider writings of Weber on this area are again employed, this would seem to mean that the historical conditions cannot allow religion the role of 'enhancing' ethics as of course they once did. But the fact that this ethic is being enacted, however mistakenly, draws a rare compliment from Weber. He then says that this is not 'our theme', but in fact is soon drawn back to the problem, as he then moves on to make the famous statement about rationalisation and disenchantment. The point for him on this occasion, however, concerns 'ultimate and sublime values' which cannot exist in the public spheres but only in mystical life or in the 'brotherliness of direct and human relations' (*'in die Brüderlichkeit unmittelbarer Beziehungen der Einzelnen zueinander'*). Again, the *Intermediary Reflection* and other works have made the meaning here clear. The public life of previous eras, as witnessed in the organic social ethics of Medieval Christianity, could contain the religious ethic, albeit in strained circumstances; the increasing forces of impersonality of modernity, however, have denied a public place for this meaning and these values. Now all that is possible is brotherliness being extended out into its mystical form; or, (and this is new and associated with 'Politics as a Vocation') brotherliness can survive in modernity in direct, human relations. Here is a place for the meaning of these ultimate values. Such meaning must be referring back to the Christian tradition of suffering – brotherliness is expressly made the point of reference. Weber then expands on this briefly, by emphasising how it is in 'personal, human relations', '*Mensch zu Mensch*', that a remnant of the old religious ethos and cosmological understanding is still present. In this last sentence there is certainly the possible interpretation that the modern *pianissimo*

---

oder mystischen Beziehung geben. So wahr es ist, daß jeder Akt echter Brüderlichkeit sich mit dem Wissen darum zu verknüpfen vermag, daß dadurch einem überpersönlichen Reich etwas hinzugefügt wird, was unverlierbar bleibt, so zweifelhaft scheint mir, ob die Würde rein menschlicher Gemeinschaftsbeziehungen durch jene religiösen Deutungen gesteigert wird. – Indessen, das gehört nicht mehr hierher. –

Es ist das Schicksal unserer Zeit, mit der ihr eigenen Rationalisierung und Intellektualisierung, vor allem: Entzauberung der Welt, daß gerade die letzten und sublimsten Werte zurückgetreten sind aus der Oeffentlichkeit, entweder in das hinterweltliche Reich mystischen Lebens oder in die Brüderlichkeit unmittelbarer Beziehungen der Einzelnen zueinander. Es ist weder zufällig, daß unsere höchste Kunst eine intime und keine monumentale ist, noch daß heute nur innerhalb der kleinsten Gemeinschaftskreise, von Mensch zu Mensch, im pianissimo, jenes Etwas pulsiert, das dem entspricht, was früher als prophetisches Pneuma in stürmischem Feuer durch die großen Gemeinden ging und sie zusammenschweißte' (WB: 109–10).

content of the personal might be greater than the brotherly ethic. However, the context is one in which it has just been stated that the 'most sublime and ultimate values' are now reduced to brotherly personal relations; and, in this case, the standard English translation can lead the reader slightly astray. The introduction of the term 'intimate' to make sense of '*innerhalb der kleinsten Gemeinschaftskreise*', is suggestive of a more romantic, private love than brotherliness and is doubtfully present in the original. Further, the translation of '*Mensch zu Mensch*', as 'personal human relations' loses some of the punch of the direct, unmediated feeling apparent in the German. This phrase, '*Mensch zu Mensch*', is also the one we have seen used in *Economy and Society* to describe the personal relationships which might allow the 'virtue of charity' (even in the case of complete enslavement), as opposed to the depersonalisation of the capitalist economy (as quoted in ES: 585; WG: 378); and these are the words used in 'Politics as a Vocation' to indicate the site of the advocated brotherliness at the end of the lecture, as discussed above (*die Brüderlichkeit ... von Mensch zu Mensch*).[13] So we might assume that this is also the meaning of the phrase in 'Science as a Vocation'.

In sum, these short sentences indicate what Weber regards as the most valuable ethics historically available and where they can still be sought.

With the indirect reference, when Weber states that the demands of the day have to be met in human (*menschlich*) relations, as well as vocationally, this interpretation is strengthened. Most of the lecture (as in 'Politics as a Vocation') had been devoted to what the vocational task entailed, but what is this 'human' dimension? It might be suggested that its meaning had in fact just been provided in 'Science as a Vocation' as the ultimate, sublime values of brotherliness in *Mensch zu Mensch* relations; *and* this must also refer back to 'Politics as a Vocation' and 'cultivating brotherliness' in personal relations. Weber has told us the content of meeting the human demands of the day in some of the last statements of his lecture on the political vocation. Moreover, in 'Science as a Vocation' he has plainly

---

13 They also appear in the 1905 and 1920 publications of *The Protestant Ethic and the Spirit of Capitalism* in a confirming footnote related to the Calvinist version of brotherliness: 'The Christian who took the proof of his state of grace seriously acted in the service of God's ends, and these could only be impersonal. Every purely emotional, that is not rationally motivated, *personal* relation of *man to man* [*persönliche Beziehung von Mensch zu Mensch*] easily fell in the Puritan, as in every ascetic ethic, under the suspicion of idolatry of the flesh' (PE: 225n, emphasis added). However, it should be noted, and as this quotation suggests, the phrase does not necessarily have to include the brotherly ethic in its meaning. Two further occurrences of the phrase help our understanding here. In the *Intermediary Reflection* it is used to indicate the intensely personal aspect of the relation of love exhibited in the erotic value-sphere: '... the erotic relation seems to offer the unsurpassable peak of the fulfilment of the request for love in the direct fusion of the souls of one to the other' (*Mensch zu Mensch*) (IR: 347). And, as a point of contrast, *The Religion of China* makes use of this term to show the personal, but 'cool' side of Confucianism: '... this cool temperature [*kühle Temperierung*] of inter-human relations [*der Beziehung von Mensch zu Mensch*] is truly Confucian' (China: 168).

stated, as opposed to the ambiguities of 'Politics as a Vocation', that there are human *and* vocational demands to be met. Individual toughness, then, is needed in human relations as well as in the vocational life, and it should be part of the demanding task for the few who can make the hard vocational choice. If we bring the concluding statements of 'Politics as a Vocation' and 'Science as a Vocation' together, each lecture can help explain the other in this way.

It follows that the two Vocation lectures – in some highly abbreviated comments – offer an extraordinary prescription on meaning and morality. The Christian tradition of love and suffering is advocated by Weber as an ethic of brotherliness, now uprooted from its religious setting, and available only in direct, personal relations that lie beyond the dominant impersonal logics of the value-spheres of modernity. Endangered and difficult to cultivate, all should try to follow such maxims in these circumstances. However, it is now even clearer how hard it is for those who have also taken up the vocational task, so that, for Weber, it does take real heroism and strength to 'meet the "demands of the day" in human relations as well as in our vocation'.[14]

Paradox and the Advocacy of Brotherliness

The brotherly ethic witnessed in the Vocation lectures might be developed through further consideration of the different forms of brotherliness outlined in the previous chapters, particularly the ideal-typical, genuine form of brotherly love.

As we have seen, in the *Intermediary Reflection* it is especially clear that Weber is using the 'pure' type of brotherliness as the standard by which to judge the historical exemplifications of this religious ethic; all the historical forms will fail to measure up to the ideal in different ways, and modernity is extremely hostile to

---

14 Although the present argument has set out to be based on Weber's empirical writings and not his personal life, two reported, biographical comments might also aid in our understanding the importance of the Christian tradition for Weber. In Hans Staudinger's memoirs, Weber was asked the question: 'What is your supreme value?' Weber replied that he does not have one and saw how he lived in the following way: 'Imagine that hanging from the ceiling of my study there are violins, pipes, and drums, clarinets and harps. Now this instrument plays, now that. The violin plays, that is my religious value. Then I hear harps and clarinets and I sense my artistic value. Then it is the turn of the trumpets and that is my value of freedom. With the sound of pipes and drums I feel the value of the fatherland. The trombone stirs the values of community, solidarity. There are sometimes dissonances ...' (Hennis 1988: 166). And Marianne Weber wrote of her husband: 'He never lost his profound reverence for the gospel of brotherhood [*Brüderlichkeit*], and he accepted its demands relating to personal life ... [But] for him, the God of the Gospels did not have any claim to exclusive dominion over the soul. He had to share them with other 'gods', particularly the demands of the fatherland and of scientific truth' (Marianne Weber, 1975: 90). These ad hominem reflections at least give a measure of concurrence between Weber's own beliefs and his writings as recounted above. They perhaps help to direct attention to the way his religiously derived, ethical position is worked into his writings.

this religious ethic, with every value-sphere pursuing meaning in direct opposition to brotherliness. In fact the brotherly ideal cannot gain empirical reality. However, the ideal form is what Weber uses as part of his religious perspective on modernity, and it is this ideal that is still extant in the modern world, both for Weber to employ in his own analysis and as the source of guilt that besets all contemporary culture. It might be deduced that the brotherliness that the Vocation lectures are advocating must also be this 'genuine' model of empirical impossibility.

It follows that to advocate this ethic of brotherliness entails not just that it will be largely excluded from vocational life (as the *Intermediary Reflection* argues, and which is hinted at in 'Politics as a Vocation'), but that its minor but telling role in the 'personal' areas of modernity must be one where the ideal again is unable to find empirical expression, except in the most compromised terms. The brotherly ideal should be pursued in personal relations, says Weber; but that unqualified love, with its universal, personal, uncompromising appreciation of suffering, will necessarily be highly diminished whenever it can find some kind of empirical realisation. The forces of modern rationalisation work against it, and the fact that it is only in small spaces within the modern world that it might be enacted shows how the ethic cannot be lived in a way that even approximates the ideal. Some final words from the *Intermediary Reflection* make this point in terms of those figures from religion who might be said to have come closest to having followed an uncompromised ethic of brotherly love:

> And, in the midst of a culture that is rationally organised for a vocational workaday life, there is hardly any room for the cultivation of acosmic brotherliness, unless it is among strata who are economically carefree. Under the technical and social conditions of rational culture, an imitation of the life of Buddha, Jesus, or Francis seems condemned to failure for purely external reasons. (IR: 357)

That the *ideal* of brotherliness is sought but is so very difficult to realise in modernity, indicates how paradox is again the logic on display – meaning is pursued and lost, to varying degrees, in that very pursuit.

It might be added that the overall guilt of modernity is in fact increased, beyond its existence in the culture of the modern world, in so far as the ideal cannot be gained with any practical application of the brotherly ethic within the realms of the personal. Brotherliness is taken up because it is what primarily constitutes the Western response to suffering; but the paradox at work – where so little can be achieved, and so much of the ideal lost, in any actual practice of the ethic – sustains both the pure form of love as the measure of goodness and, also, the guilt that ensues when this absolute standard cannot be met.

The Secondary Literature

But how does this interpretation sit with those secondary accounts where an attempt has been made to exhibit Weber's position on ethical conduct in modernity? Although there are numerous secondary studies which do try to provide an insight into Weber's moral vision of modernity, most will ignore the brotherliness aspect, usually concentrating on the ethics of responsibility/ultimate ends debate (originating particularly in 'Politics as a Vocation'), and/or on the meaning of the heroic personality (Brubaker, 1984; Roth and Schluchter, 1979; Schluchter, 1996; Turner and Factor, 1984). The general pattern in which these interpretations operate has already been mentioned: Weber's ideas are understood through external academic debates, and/or through the use of the ideas of other thinkers, particularly Nietzsche. As we have discussed, the Nietzschean perspective has necessarily been particularly hostile to the recognition of a Christian morality of brotherly love in Weber. Crucially, the overall understanding of Weber in terms of meaning is, almost always, absent.

If this is the general trend in the secondary literature, let us see how it is played out in more detail when the last moments of the Vocation texts are included. If the final prescriptions do in fact come to be examined, the interpretations usually choose simply to ignore the extra-vocational words, even to the extent of editing quotations to overlook this aspect of Weber's ideas. For example, Turner and Factor, who had carefully placed Weber within the political and intellectual context of the early- to mid-twentieth century, discuss the exhortations of 'Science as a Vocation' in the following way:

> The final non-illusory choices for the intellectual turn out to be limited to three: to return to the old churches, to 'tarry for new prophets', or to meet the 'demands of the day' *in a vocation*. (Turner and Factor, 1984: 156, emphasis added)

The full expression of the last and decisive possibility, to meet the demands of the day in *human* as well as vocational terms is simply, and without explanation, truncated to exclude the human dimension.

When, on those rare occasions, the specific ethical terms at the end of 'Science as a Vocation' are actually engaged (the 'brotherliness' reference in 'Politics as a Vocation' is almost never discussed) the interpretations are varied. Brubaker, with a clear emphasis on the Nietzschean heroic 'Personality', does mention 'the brotherliness of direct and personal human relations', but considers that the adoption of such an ethic would be part of a return to the ever-open arms of the church and the consequent rejection of the rigours of the vocation of science (Brubaker, 1984: 106). Like Factor and Turner, the human aspect of meeting the demands of the day is ignored. Mitzman does consider this human dimension and says that it consists of 'the private cultivation in personal relationships of a quasi-mystical "pneuma"' (Mitzman, 1971: 230). A religious content is to be called upon by the scientist alongside her vocation (as against going back to the Church) but the ethic of brotherliness (previously given in quotation by Mitzman) is ignored. On the other hand, Bologh assumes Weber had followed Freud in believing that the world was loveless (Bologh, 1990: 193) and that Weber had completely rejected brotherly love as stifling. Bologh cites the 'Science as a Vocation' quotation that the 'ultimate and most sublime values have retreated from public life ...', and interprets these values as those that achieve 'greatness for the nation through political and military exploits and decisive heroic action' (Bologh, 1990: 193). Such values have retreated because of the German defeat in WWI and, in consequence, the men were forced back to the inferior level of everyday vocations and the human as substitute for the lost greatness of public life. 'Human' here is taken to be the home, as in 'doing one's duty at home and at work'. This is the meaning of meeting the demands of the day (Bologh, 1990: 194). The religious context is not included at all by Bologh.

Of these interpretations, Mitzman comes closest to the mark; Weber is arguing that something from the religious past ought to fill the human or personal dimension in modernity, but Mitzman does not recognise what that religious content is.

Ethics and Meaning

Difficult questions arise as to what sort of ethics Weber is actually advocating, and on what basis his prescriptions can be made. The easiest way to try to address these issues, initially, is to say what he is *not* doing. Weber's vast sociological studies of religion indicate that the kind of brotherliness which is still extant in the West is not a universal human ethic, either anthropologically or psychologically. A 'neighbourly ethic' might be commonly found but it is the specific combination of factors that develop within particular religions that is all-important for Weber. It is also not an ethic or value which Weber is advocating as an answer derived only from rational argument; Weber is not rationally concluding that brotherliness is the best ethic to follow over other possibilities. There is not, then, a philosophical argument for brotherliness.

If this is what it is not, what can we say that it is? Simply, as we have witnessed, it is ethics as meaning in a meaningless world. The brotherly ethic that Weber prescribes was cast in the religious formation of the West, and it is now part of our historical fate. It is an imperative that arises from the problem of theodicy – of unjust suffering in the world – which is still part of our cultural makeup, but shorn of its greater religious meaning; and it has become the standard of goodness in the modern world. Weber seems to consider that brotherliness is the common, everyday assumption of what goodness is in modernity (similar to the way vocational meaning is part of the modern worldview). That brotherliness has this status can, of course, be questioned but, *prima facie*, it would indeed seem to be the case that, at least in the modern West, the best individual who can be ideally imagined is one who dedicates themselves to the personal care of the suffering of others, without discrimination. Again, Weber's sociology of religion argues that this ideal is not universal – it is the fate of the West.

Culturally, brotherliness is part of what we are in an ideal form. To advocate brotherliness, then, is to direct our human interests in meaning to what this meaning has in fact become. Isolated now from the cosmic worldview in which it was formed, brotherliness is all that religious meaning can still provide on how to act in the face of suffering.

Although still troubling, something like this position would appear to be the basis for Weber's advocacy of the ethic of brotherly love. This might be clarified further, however, when a seeming contradiction within Weber's argumentation in 'Science as a Vocation' is investigated.

Contradiction, Greek Terms and the Iron Cage

Contradiction, Subjective Choice and Relativist Values

To argue that Weber is actually advocating the vocational life and an ethic of brotherliness would seem to put Weber himself into a serious state of contradiction. 'Science as a Vocation', in particular, is where Weber opposes the idea that there can be rational arguments for the advocacy of any ultimate value position in an intellectual setting (e.g., SV: 147). He argues that intellectual reason can only give clarity on the consistency of means and ends and, perhaps, show how certain practical stands are derived from one ultimate value and not another (SV: 151–2); but this is all that science can do in terms of ultimate meaning, including the sense of vocation:

> This proposition, which I present here, always takes its point of departure from the one fundamental fact, that so long as life remains immanent and is interpreted in its own terms, it knows only of an unceasing struggle of these gods with one another. Or speaking directly, the ultimately possible attitudes toward life are irreconcilable, and hence their struggle can never be brought to a final conclusion. Thus it is necessary to make a decisive choice. Whether, under such conditions, science is a worthwhile 'vocation' for somebody, and whether science itself has an objectively valuable 'vocation' are again value judgments about which nothing can be said in the lecture-room. (SV: 152)

This is in keeping with the overarching argument in 'Science as a Vocation' on the meaninglessness of modern intellectual reason – answers to Tolstoy's ultimate questions must lie outside science.

On the basis of this Humean argument on reason and values in 'Science as a Vocation', Weber's overall position is most commonly read in terms of a basic subjectivist or, perhaps, existentialist view of each person having to make ultimate value decisions for themselves,[15] with reason a possible guide but now disqualified as the final arbiter. The various values or ultimate positions, it follows, are regarded in relativist or, perhaps, nihilist terms, so that no one position can rationally be judged as right or superior. Therefore, on the basis of the theories of modernity exhibited in 'Science as a Vocation', Weber cannot be advocating some particular ethical path to follow.

On one level this standard interpretation is undoubtedly valid but, again, it cannot be the whole story. Two points can be made to show the limitations of the usual subjectivist/relativist position and, at the same time, try to provide an explanation for the apparent contradiction within Weber's argument in 'Science as a Vocation'.

Firstly, as we have seen, in 'Science as a Vocation' Weber is arguing for disenchanted meaninglessness *and* for the meaning of the vocation of science and brotherliness – this is the message about the nature of intellectual reason that he wants to impart to his audience of aspiring social scientists. A complex pattern of paradoxes was shown to be a possible way of understanding such meaning within meaninglessness. This layered concept of meaning can help us understand how Weber can both forbid intellectual prescriptions of ultimate value beliefs and advocate the vocational life and the ethic of brotherliness. Science/ intellectual reason cannot answer Tolstoy's questions on ultimate metaphysics; nor can it argue that science itself is worthwhile or that brotherliness is the best or correct way of living an ethical life. However, from the perspective of his sociology of religion, what Weber *can* argue is that one should take up a vocation and follow brotherliness since here is where meaning can still be found within the disenchanted senselessness of modern life. It is our historical fate that: firstly, the vocation can generate some measure of meaning for mundane labour; and, secondly, that an ethical response to suffering – Christian brotherliness – is part of the makeup of the culture (as we have just discussed) and selfhood (see below) of modernity. These concepts of vocation and brotherly love that arise in Weber's immense theory are not just relativistic values that lie beyond rational judgement, but points of meaning that have been created or have been sustained from the religious past, and it is on this basis that Weber can offer his limited answer to the question of 'what shall we do?'

---

15 A stress on subjective choice and decision in these final moments of 'Science as a Vocation' can be seen, for example, in Turner and Factor (1984: 42) and Lassman and Velody (1989: 204); Brubaker (1984) regards it as a non-resolvable existentialist struggle for the individual in a Nietzschean setting; and Owen and Strong (2004: xxxiiiff) carry on the Nietzsche theme and cast the end of this lecture as a final acceptance of fate. Scaff puts the final prescriptions of Weber in terms of 'self-creation' and the play between aesthetic subjectivity and the rationalised material (Scaff, 1991: 240) – but the vocational meaning is absent. Again, the general pattern is one of modern values and concepts of subjectivity interwoven with external theorists and intellectual settings.

Secondly, Weber questions the nature of the subject who is making these final decisions. From the sociology of religion perspective, Weber does not see the modern world in terms of Enlightenment subjectivity; rather, in terms of meaning, we are caught in inescapable conditions that are derived largely from the religious history of the West. Our ultimate values are not just a matter of subjective choice by free individuals but framed within cultural determinants that Weber has tried to lay out for us in a wide set of texts. On this basis Weber will in fact provide a curious view of the modern self that will allow him to both deny and maintain prescriptions of meaning.

The Daemon and other Greek Terms

The key term here is the 'daemon'[16] given in the very last line of 'Science as a Vocation':

> This, however, is plain and simple, if each finds and obeys the daemon who holds the threads of his very life. (SV: 156)[17]

Why does Weber use this term, with its reference back to Greece and Socrates[18] in particular, and how might this link up with other Greek ideas like 'polytheism' and 'fate' that Weber also employs in his account of the modern world?

Three points might initially be made to make sense of the term 'daemon'. Firstly, this individualised, internal addition of the daemon upsets the model of the interior subject as the maker of free choices. This disruptive element is difficult to describe in modern terms but might be said to work in the following two ways:

---

16   Most commentators on 'Science as a Vocation' tend to ignore the daemon, or it is just absorbed by assumption into some notion of modern subjectivity. Scaff does try to understand the 'daemon' directly, but he does so by taking it out of the context of the end of 'Science as a Vocation' and linking it back to Goethe, with the resultant, very useful definition being one of fate and the law of destiny as the 'preformed essence of individuality' (Scaff, 1991:69). It should also be noted here that it is likely that its use as the inspiration, or genius, for a vocational life was once widely understood. Although just one example, it is there in Shelley's hugely popular *Frankenstein* (Shelley, 2012: 21).

17   '*Die aber ist schlicht und einfach, wenn jeder den Dämon findet und ihm gehorcht, der* seines *Lebens Fäden hält*'. (WB: 111) The translation here is slightly modified from Gerth and Mills's, in line with other current renditions of this phrase. The use of 'fibres' by Gerth and Mills instead of 'threads' or 'strings' has been, one suspects, a particular source of mystification over the years.

18   In *Economy and Society*, Weber makes the Socratic link explicit: 'Socrates' "genius" (*daimonion*) reacted only to concrete situations, and then only to discourage and admonish. For Socrates, this was the limit of his ethical and strongly utilitarian rationalism, which corresponded to the position of magical divination for Confucius. For this reason, Socrates' genius cannot be compared at all to the "conscience" of a genuine religious ethic; much less can it be regarded as the instrument of prophecy' (ES: 446).

it is an external force that now resides as part of each internal self; and, since it 'holds the threads of [your] very life', it is this force that is ultimately determinate of the most important sense of what the self is, so that one has to find it and obey it in order to fulfil oneself. Secondly, the use of this Greek point of reference allows Weber to make a comparison between the Greeks and us in terms of how the new age of reason is still beholden to older forms of meaning. Weber, it might be postulated, is aiming to reproduce the shock that the modern reader feels when first being told, perhaps in *The Apology*, of Socrates' dependence on his inner oracle or daemon. As the great philosopher of reason and truth was guided by some semi-divine being, so the modern self, in the age of disenchanted science, also possesses a kind of daemon that binds it to past meanings. And, thirdly, the meaning that the modern daemon holds comes only minimally from classical antiquity and is derived chiefly from the Christian religious history in which modern senselessness is set. Socrates' daemon is linked back to the enchanted cosmos of Homer, but it must be from the Christian worldview that the modern 'genius' gains its power. The two Christian elements that constitute the daemon, as this bearer of older meaning, are: the Protestant vocation, and Catholic brotherliness.

As others have noted, it is the Protestant vocation that the modern daemon most plainly represents. In 'Politics as a Vocation' two references make this explicit: the politician has to have a 'passionate devotion to a "cause", to the god or demon [Gott oder Dämon] who is its overlord' (PV: 115); and 'The genius or demon [Der Genius, oder Dämon] of politics lives in an inner tension with the God of love' (PV: 126).[19] Onto these statements it can be added that vocation must surely also be the content of the daemon stated in the last line of 'Science as a Vocation'. The modern self then, in terms of meaning, is constituted by the Protestant legacy, with the fact of capitalism guaranteeing the ongoing presence of this condition.

In addition to the calling, brotherliness might be added to this continuation of religious meaning into the very nature of the modern self. Although not as explicitly clear, it can be inferred from the concluding statements in 'Science as a Vocation' that the daemon carries this meaning of suffering along with vocation – the Protestant means to salvation.

The assumption by Weber would seem to be that each modern self has its own daemon. In terms of the calling, the particular vocational task will vary of course, but some sense of vocation is there, it would seem, for every individual to find. However, just because a calling is found and followed does not mean that the vocation will be fulfilled. If sufficient strength and/or understanding are lacking the deed will not be done. In 'Politics as a Vocation', it will be remembered, Weber makes an appreciation of the paradoxes of the political value-sphere constitutive of the very definition of 'vocation'. In the case of brotherliness there would seem to be more of an unchanging daemonic content, as opposed to the varieties of

---

19 The context here is of the necessity of violence for any vocation of politics, as discussed above.

vocation on offer; but difficulties in practically fulfilling this aspect of the daemon are, like the vocation, substantial – as we have seen Weber argue in detail.

The use of the term 'daemon', as a way of comparing the Greek condition with our own, is made clearer when it is set beside other Greek reference points in Weber's works. In 'Science as a Vocation', as we have witnessed, Weber puts the modern condition of competing values in terms of disenchanted, warring gods and polytheism. Such terminology gives considerable weight to the idea that the content of the value-sphere structure is indeed concerned with meaning. Again, the Greek terms are chosen because they can carry with them the ancient worldview of moving from the enchanted cosmos into reason and the more human meaning of the polis; while content is given to this Greek form predominantly from the tradition of Western Christianity. This polytheism might be seen as the external social structure of meaning, as compared to the internal structure of the self with its daemonic character. Both reflect each other to conjure up the sense of how past meaning is being carried into the present, as was the case with the ancient Greeks, who honoured and performed the rituals to the gods even when they argued against the very existence of such divinities.

Along with the daemon and the gods, the modern condition is frequently referred to as our 'fate' by Weber. 'Fate' has one fairly common connotation of how ordinary things come to pass, but the choice of such a term by Weber in the conclusions to some of his most important treatises[20] must also be referring back to Greek fate and is made in order to challenge standard views of historical determinism.

Weber distinguishes between two kinds of fate in those warrior cultures best exemplified by the Greeks:[21]

> The irrationality of 'fate' [*die Irrationalität des 'Schicksals'*] and, under certain conditions, the idea of a vague and deterministically conceived 'destiny' [*'Verhängnisses'*] (the Homeric *Moira*) has stood above and behind the divinities and demons [*Göttern und Dämonen*] who were conceived of as passionate and strong heroes, measuring out assistance and hostility, glory and booty, or death to the human heroes. (IEEWR: 283)

---

20 To recall the most important of these references: 'But fate [*Verhängnis*] decreed that the cloak should become an iron cage'. (PE: 181); 'The fate of our times is characterised by rationalisation and intellectualisation and, above all, by the "disenchantment of the world"' (SV: 155; *Schicksal* is used throughout SV); 'To the person who cannot bear the fate of the times like a man …' (SV: 155); 'Fate, and certainly not science, holds sway over these gods and their struggles …' (SV: 148). Also see other references to fate or destiny in 'Science as a Vocation': three times on scientific 'fulfilment' (SV: 137–8); also in reference to specialisation and the 'fate of his soul' (SV: 135); and to 'those who tarried for more than two millennia' (SV: 159).

21 '… the Hellenic man of culture was and remained primarily ephebe and hoplite' (China: 122; also ES: 473; GEH: 328ff).

How can these twin meanings of Greek fate be transferred into the modern worldview? Firstly, the sense of a vague, enchanted 'destiny' that is apparent with the prophecies concerning, for example, Oedipus and the death of Achilles, might be assumed to be necessarily excluded in a modern context, since such prophecy depended on the long lost cosmos of Greek understanding.[22] However, although it has a far more joyful ending than the tragic Greek examples, Weber would seem to allow at least one small place for such fate within the inner cosmos of the erotic value-sphere:

> No consummated erotic communion will know itself to be founded in any way other than through a mysterious *destination* for one another: *fate* [*Schicksal*], in this highest sense of the word. (IR: 348, Weber's emphasis)[23]

Secondly, it is the overarching irrationality of Greek fate that constitutes the content of Weber's usual use of 'fate' in his theories of modernity. Following the quote given above, fate lies beyond the power of the Greek gods/divinities and daemons, who are limited in their power and in fact provide little in terms of meeting ideal interests (which are more obviously met by the Greek concept of the citizen-warrior). Similarly, today, irrational fate is the broad fact of existence in which are found the circumscribed gods and daemons of modern meaning, such as the different vocations and, in a slightly different way, the ethic of brotherly love. These are the conditions which constitute 'the demands of the day'. There is no basic pattern of meaning for the modern self to find or make; there are only the

---

22 Perhaps some vague sense of destiny might be experienced, for example, with the sense of vocation; but this has now been relegated in status from its originating place in the divine order of Calvinist predestination to the level of the disenchanted, warring gods, where irrational fate is determinant (SV: 148).

23 On the German terminology for 'fate' used by Weber, Baehr will stress how *Verhängnis*, which is used at the end of *The Protestant Ethic and the Spirit of Capitalism*, has the connotations in German of foreboding and even doom, while *Schicksal*, which is used just about everywhere else by Weber, is more flexible in its German usage (Baehr, 2008: 56). This contrast does capture the gloomier conclusions of *The Protestant Ethic and the Spirit of Capitalism* as compared to the Vocation lectures (see below). However, Weber would seem to want to maintain a distinction derived from the Greek view of fate. From these two quotations (see also China: 207), it might be discerned that the fate (*Verhängnis*) of the 'iron cage' at the end of *The Protestant Ethic and the Spirit of Capitalism* is not really of the kind meant by the Greek *moira* (*Verhängnis*), but is more aptly part of the overarching irrationality of fate (*Schicksal*) that includes, for example, the fate of disenchantment. And in the case of the fate of the lovers, the Greek *Verhängnis* would seem to be more apt than the term (*Schicksal*) that is used by Weber (although, the sense of tragedy is clearly not apparent in this case). So, there is a *Greek* distinction that should be preserved, but it is not clearly sustained in Weber's use of the German terms for fate. Perhaps this inconsistency is merely a result of the fact that the Greek meaning cannot be reflected in the German terms, which are divided along the lines Baehr describes.

given historical circumstances, such as disenchantment and capitalism, that have to be accepted and within which human action has to proceed.[24]

The Greek and modern worldviews are linked in terms of fate by Weber not just because of this common layered sense of a limited meaning (the polytheistic gods and daemons) set within an overarching state of uncontrollable circumstance, but also because Weber will advocate that the modern self should follow the Greek imperatives for action in the face of this comparable fate of meaning. A strength is needed which recalls the power of the heroes and citizen-warriors of antiquity – the times are befitting of a 'human heroism which has always proudly refused to believe in a benevolent providence' (China: 207). To be able to follow the modern, disenchanted gods and individualised daemons of vocation and brotherliness, as part of an accepted fate of overall meaninglessness, is a mark of such heroic strength for Weber. And, perhaps, this Greek dimension of hero and fate might help our understanding of what exactly has been demanded of 'the person who cannot bear the fate of the times like a man'.

In these ways Weber uses the Greek worldview in order to reveal to us the irrational fate of modern, disenchanted meaninglessness, and the meanings – the gods and daemons – that lie within. Certainly it has to be recognised that, without the polis/warrior meaning of the ancient world, modern meaning/meaninglessness must be differentiated from the Greek perspective, but Weber wants the overall structure of both worldviews to be maintained together in order for the problem of meaning not to be lost amidst the growing forces of rationalisation. Indeed, it might be argued that Weber's insistent use of the Greek terminology of daemon, polytheism and fate is a strategy to show, and try to circumvent, the limits of intellectualised, Western reason itself. Without such words of ancient meaning – tied together with Christian concepts – modern meaninglessness would simply equate with a secularised absence of meaning.[25]

In the end, from the viewpoint of Weber's theory of meaning, both the subjectivist/relativist interpretation of Weber, and also the associated, seeming contradiction that appears to come into play with any attempt to show prescriptive elements in Weber, are able to be met and explained. This explanation can be achieved, we have seen, through a concentration on the final terms of 'Science as a Vocation'.

The Iron Cage

If the last moments of 'Science as a Vocation' might be given some measure of understanding in this way, how does this compare with the (in)famous ending of

---

24 A clarifying contrast might be made here between the extremes of the Calvinist worldview of predestination, with its assumption of a rational destination for all, and the 'belief in the irrational power of "fate"' (IR: 359).

25 It has to be said again that, even with the presence of these concepts from worldviews of the past, the dominant traditions of Weberian scholarship have tended to favour just such a definition of disenchanted modernity.

The Protestant Ethic and the Spirit of Capitalism? A lengthy quote is needed to remind us of the specific context of the 'iron cage'.[26]

> The Puritan wanted to work in a calling; we are forced to do so. For when asceticism was carried out of monastic cells into everyday life, and began to dominate worldly morality, it did its part in building the tremendous cosmos of the modern economic order. This order is now bound to the technical and economic conditions of machine production which to-day determine the lives of all the individuals who are born into this mechanism, not only those directly concerned with economic acquisition, with irresistible force. Perhaps it will so determine them until the last ton of fossilized coal is burnt. In Baxter's view the care for external goods should only lie on the shoulders of the 'saint like a light cloak, which can be thrown aside at any moment'. But fate decreed that the cloak should become an iron cage. (PE: 181)

The 'iron cage' can be taken as the general condition of rationalised modernity; or as a more specific concern with materialism ('external goods'); or, and this is the view towards which the current argument leans, it is referring to vocation (which 'we are forced to' follow) and the 'spirit' of capitalism – the dominant theme of this most well-known of Weber's texts. On this basis, vocation is tied to the 'irresistible force' of the 'mechanism' of capitalism so that, as we have seen, whatever meaning that is available is almost completely limited to mundane labour itself, even for those whose work extends beyond the 'acquisition' of the economic value-sphere; while for the workers who must endure the brutal routinisation of capitalist, manual labour the imposed vocation will simply inflict soul-destroying senselessness. Weber, then, is not prescribing any course of action here, and the oft-noted tone of gloomy pessimism is apparent, if what finally results is:

> ... mechanized petrification, embellished with a sort of convulsive self-importance. For of the last stage of this cultural development, it might well be truly said: 'Specialists without spirit, sensualists without heart; this nullity imagines that it has attained a level of civilisation never before achieved'. (PE: 182)

A significant contrast can therefore be found between the fate of vocation in the economic value-sphere as described at the end of *The Protestant Ethic and the Spirit of Capitalism* and the fate of the calling in the Vocation lectures, especially as it is told at the end of 'Science as a Vocation'. Capitalist culture preserves the Protestant legacy of rationalised work, but this bare, begrudging meaning of the vocation – the spirit of capitalism – can be added to, as we have seen, by various deeds and tasks which are borne by the daemon of the modern self. There is no escape from the condition of the calling derived from Calvinism, where the task

---

26 See Baehr (2001) for discussion of Parsons' translation here.

set by God has been drained away to such an extent that only labour itself is left, or left as the primary source of meaning. However, what has been argued here is that the Protestant legacy has also given us the sense of a divinely-given task to which such worldly work must be devoted; and the Christian tradition more broadly – especially as exemplified in forms of Catholicism – has also been the source of our fate with the continuation into modernity of the inescapable ethical judgement of brotherliness. Weber can recommend the pursuit of these values on the basis of his overarching theory of the fate of modern meaning/meaninglessness, with this theory incorporating the forbidding conclusions to *The Protestant Ethic and the Spirit of Capitalism*.

But how are we to understand this overall situation of the possibilities of meaning within meaninglessness in terms of the metaphor of the 'iron cage'? This translation of '*Stahlhartes Gehäuse*' does capture the hard unchanging nature of capitalism that is apparent here at the end of *The Protestant Ethic and the Spirit of Capitalism*, and serves as a strong contrast to any Marxist ideas of fundamental economic change. It is also useful in capturing the more extended Weberian view of modernity where impersonal, instrumental reason and bureaucracy are deemed to be fatefully determinant. However, it has the added result of making it difficult to align this work with other writings by Weber, especially those where meaning is the focus. The problem is: if we do add the extra dimensions of vocation that Weber assumes in the Vocation lectures should we then consider that we are still in the iron cage, although the conditions of Calvinist labour and the economic value-sphere have therefore been deemed to be insufficient to account for modern meaning? Or, have we left the cage because of such additions to vocational meaning even though the economic conditions and culture of capitalism described at the end of *The Protestant Ethic and the Spirit of Capitalism* still necessarily prevail? The Parsons translation makes this difficult to resolve, and perhaps the difficulty only lies in the use of the concept of the prison or cage.[27] As an alternative, if '*Stahlhartes Gehäuse*' is translated as something like 'steely housing' or 'shell as hard as steel' then this allows for a way that the condition of capitalist labour might be considered as something that cannot be just thrown off – unlike Baxter's cloak; but it also allows the possibility that other courses of meaning can be advocated and followed, even though this 'shell' is still attached or inhabited.

---

27 The 'iron cage', it should also be noted, serves as both a confirmation and determinant of an Enlightenment reading of Weber, where the fate of such imprisonment sets up the scenario of imagining some form of escape by the modern subject from this deprivation of liberty. The doubtful use of the term 'iron cage' has set the scene as one that is concerned with individual freedom and the forces that Weber has ranged against this prime value in the secularised worldview of Enlightenment and capitalism – such an *American* translation, it might be said (for more on this point, see Baehr, 2001: 155–6).

Conclusion

Weber does provide an answer to Tolstoy's problem of 'What shall we do and how shall we live'. This answer is stated most emphatically when 'Science as a Vocation' concludes with the lines we have been examining:

> We shall set to work and meet the 'demands of the day', in human relations as well as in our vocation. This, however, is plain and simple, if each finds and obeys the daemon who holds the threads of his very life.

Let us conclude by summarising what now might be said about these famous last words.

Initially it has to be recognised that Weber is addressing us as seekers of meaning. The 'very life', whose 'threads' each daemon holds, is this deep human need for meaning – we must try to meet our ideal interests. Then, in order to make sense of the more specific content of these two sentences, we are helped by Weber's complex theory of meaning and modernity which has been pieced together in the preceding chapters. On this basis, we are able to understand how the senselessness of disenchanted modernity might be mitigated, as far as it can be, in the areas of work and personal/human relations, if vocation and brotherliness – these traces of meaning sustained from our religious history – are pursued. At the level of the self it can be imagined that there presides a 'daemon' who is the bearer of these religious remnants, and it is in this way that the daemon can be thought of as ultimately controlling the fate of our very lives. Therefore, Weber prescribes that the daemon should be found and obeyed.

This might well seem a relatively minor result in terms of modern values of self-creation and freedom (and its opposite 'the iron cage'). Such judgements tend to assume the perspective of a secularised world, where Weber is the great theorist of how the structures of impersonal, rationalised meaninglessness actually work. However, if the perspective of the sociology of religion is adopted, then these conclusions might be regarded as having some weight, concerned as they are with ideal interests. It has to be admitted, however, that the first perspective will inevitably prevail over the second. As Weber himself, in a somewhat different context, said:

> The modern man is in general, even with the best will, unable to give religious ideas a significance for culture and national character which they deserve. (PE: 183)[28]

---

28 The context is one of direct opposition to a crude Marxist materialism. The quote famously goes on to say: 'But it is, of course, not my aim to substitute for a one-sided materialistic an equally one-sided spiritualistic causal interpretation of culture and of history' (PE: 185). Such Marxism might have faded, but the appreciation of religious ideas *within* modern culture might still be considered to be, at the very least, problematic.

If the elements of Weber's prescriptive position are understandable in this way, some final, brief comments can still be made on how Weber's theory might advantage further investigation into the way meaning works in modernity. This is the theme of the final chapter.

Chapter 9
Applications

Introduction

The reconstruction of Weber's theory of meaning and modernity has now been completed. This chapter is designed to present some auxiliary arguments on how this theory might be applied in two contemporary empirical examples: the question of re-enchantment in modernity; and some elements of the development of meaning and modernity in Australia. These topics are far too large to be fully examined here so that it needs to be emphasised that the following points are merely suggestive and speculative, and are only being put forward tentatively in order to test some possible implications of Weber's understanding of meaning.

W1.0 and W2.0

In order to pursue these examples, and for the sake of theoretical convenience, two broad interpretative perspectives might be employed. They can be designated as W1.0 and W2.0.

The dominant view of Weber, with its oceans of use and interpretation, is W1.0. This is that deterministic cold world, where capitalism is our fate and the economic labour once chosen by the Puritans is now forced upon us. Here the term 'iron cage' can be appropriately applied, and this grim depiction of capitalism can be extended out to cover 'modernity' more fully in terms of disenchantment, instrumental reason, rationalisation, impersonality, bureaucracy and meaninglessness. Further, such understanding can be tied to the interpretation of Weber as an 'Enlightenment' thinker in the sense that his theory is considered to be one concerned with a secularised modernity cut off from the religious, pre-Enlightenment orders of the world.

This standard view of Weber's theory of the modern world – W1.0 – is incomplete, as we have seen, because meaning itself is missing. It is to be hoped that there is now a greater appreciation of Weber's arguments concerning the meaning that exists within this seemingly barren meaninglessness, and how this can be discerned even in 1904/05 when the 'spirit' evoked in the very title of *The Protestant Ethic and the Spirit of Capitalism* fairly clearly exhibits the theme of the decline of vocational meaning to the current state of compulsion and mere sport. Such decline does *not* indicate that meaning has therefore disappeared; and, even in this text, the whisper of the leitmotif of brotherliness can be heard, already playing around the dominant argument on vocation and worldly work.

Here are the elements that we have seen can be elaborated into Weber's theory of meaning: W2.0.

Note that these two general perspectives are not discrete. W2.0 assumes most of the theoretical framework of W1.0 as part of its own position (as we have witnessed many times). Also, although W2.0 must be seen as emerging from and, at times, critical of W1.0, it is not a replacement for it – the way modernity works without consideration of meaning has been and will be the major way that Weber is used. But when W1.0 does inevitably stray into the realm of meaning in its incorporation of ideas like 'vocation' and 'value-sphere' then there must be conflict between these broad interpretative standpoints. As an example, it has been shown how the prescriptions of the Vocation lectures would seem to demand an attempt to make sense of Weber's understanding of 'vocation' and 'brotherliness' in terms of meaning and modernity, so that W2.0 would seem to be the more fitting theoretical framework in this instance.

Re-Enchantment

An increasingly common perception has arisen that Weber's understanding of the fate of disenchantment in modernity is, fairly obviously, mistaken. What will be proposed here is that when we apply the W1.0 and W2.0 templates it can be observed that a certain line of interpretation becomes more favoured from within the W1.0 perspective – an escape from disenchantment seems almost obvious; but, from the standpoint of W2.0, such an alleged escape might in fact be explained in Weberian terms.

There is then a host of claims that forms of enchantment and re-enchantment can be identified as arising in modern times and, in fact, arising within the very structures of senseless modernity. Such cases are seen as a clear rebuttal of the famous definition given by Weber in 'Science as a Vocation': 'The fate of our times is characterised by rationalisation and intellectualisation and, above all, by the "disenchantment of the world"' (SV: 155). If such claims are true then modern meaninglessness is not as impregnable as we have been assuming and some sense of enchanted meaning is not only possible but common in the very heart of the rationalised world.

Two groups of alleged re-enchantment need to be distinguished from each other.

Firstly, there are new forms of religion and spirituality that seem to abound in the modern social order and such enchanted views of the world would appear to run counter to the rationalised meaninglessness of Weber's theory of modernity (e.g., Jenkins, 2000; Lee and Ackerman, 2002). Importantly 'disenchantment' from this perspective is understood to include the notion that there will be a decline in magic and an increase in secularisation in modernity, so that the identification of these novel religious enchantments would seem to be a refutation of Weber's thesis.

Such an argument clearly has some cogency if Weber is understood in terms of the W1.0 model but it becomes, perhaps, less convincing when the W2.0 template starts to be employed.

In W2.0 the secularisation thesis is put into doubt for a number of interconnected reasons. Ideal interests are constantly at work even in meaningless modernity and it is not only unsurprising but in keeping with Weber's theory of meaning and modernity for new forms of enchanted belief to arise. However, any such belief must be sidelined into the irrational realm of religion, whatever *subjective*, emotional importance such ideas might hold. The result is that these religious/ spiritual forms do not affect the basic value-sphere structure of modernity which remains encased in disenchantment.

These points can be filled out in the following manner. The irrational realm, into which religion has been pushed, can change and be refilled, but is not of sociological interest to *Weber's* theory of meaning. And it should also be recalled that Weber himself, especially in 'Science as a Vocation', provides a list of ways that religious/spiritual beliefs constitute a continuing, not diminishing fact of modernity. So as we have seen, and has so often been noted, in this lecture Weber speaks of the attraction that new kinds of belief will hold, particularly for youth, in this era of disenchanted science. He also famously considers the constantly available option of going back to the church, whose doors are always open – and there is, at times, a touch of sympathy for those who, in the face of the fate of disenchanted meaninglessness, take either of these paths into the irrational realm. However in addition and without sympathy on Weber's part there are also the surrogate belief constructions and attempts to bridge the science/religion divide that will tempt intellectuals to act, as we have already discussed, like big children. All these alternatives would seem to indicate that increasing secularisation is not part of Weber's theory of meaning; on the contrary, an increase in the variety and quantity of religious belief can in fact be considered as entirely consistent with the ongoing disenchantment of the modern world in terms of the value-sphere structure of modernity.[1]

In this first group of re-enchantments in modernity the concept of 'enchantment' is apt in the sense that a meaningful, perhaps magical, cosmos of religion is being invoked, and this is precisely why such beliefs will necessarily be separated from the rationalised structures of the modern world. However, the second group of re-enchantments is claimed to be part of the very structures of modern life and is not making direct reference to religion or spiritual beliefs. The argument on offer here is that even if Weber does give a creditable theory of rationalised modernity this theory is inadequate to account for developments that have largely occurred

---

1 It should also be remembered that there were many new religious and spiritual belief systems that were present in Weber's time and soon after, but most have now been almost entirely forgotten; and, it might be assumed, a similar fate awaits much of the current wave of novel, enchanted attractions.

since his time in areas of irrational pleasure like cinema, eating and sport.[2] And a major aspect of this post-Weber view revolves around the way Weber's economic understanding is restricted to labour and production but does not, and indeed cannot, include the advertising/shopping dimensions of consumption (e.g., Campbell, 1989; Ritzer, 1999). These various irrational sites of the modern and post-modern[3] are designated as spaces where magic and enchantment have been recreated, so that it is on this basis, for example, that the shopping mall can be labelled a 'cathedral of consumption' (Ritzer, 1999).

Again W1.0 seems highly amenable to this sort of theorisation and provides the content for the definition of 'disenchantment' used in these arguments for re-enchantment in modernity. But what happens when W2.0 is applied?

Firstly, in terms of this theory of meaning and from the perspective of Weber's sociology of religion, the idea of 'enchantment' at work here seems questionable. Unlike the first grouping of modern re-enchantments there is no direct link to religion or magic in the sense of the supernatural or a meaningful cosmos. The disenchanted, scientific, rational order of W1.0 is in fact accepted, so that 'enchanted' here comes to be understood as the emotional states that develop in contrast to the routinisation of the rationalised value-spheres and which might indeed be described as 'magical' by those who are experiencing these pleasures. In terms of the value-sphere theory of modernity this bears a strong resemblance to the religiosity of the erotic sphere and the overall salvation from the mock death of rationalised routine that constitutes the framework of meaning for the irrational spheres of Weber's account. In other words, the logic of paradox is at work in

---

2   Jenkins (2000) and Ritzer (1999) provide substantial, overlapping lists of these new post-Weber enchantments. On this link between sport and meaning in modernity see Drefyus and Kelly (2011a). It is worth noting that Dreyfus and Kelly advocate and use the (somewhat theoretically undeveloped) concept of 'whooshing up' to capture the state of irrational pleasure that is possible in these modern arenas, and propose a return to a kind of Homeric polytheism to try to escape the nihilism of modern senselessness. In this instance Weber is a shadowy presence but is not referenced directly. See also Bennett (2001) and Saler (2012). Both Bennett and Saler give a standard W1.0 version of Weber and disenchantment which allows their own respective versions of re-enchantment to open up – Saler's in terms of fictionalised fantasy novels from the late nineteenth century until Tolkien.

3   To take up, briefly, just one postmodern theorist, Bauman does seem to intend that his 'liquid' postmodern forms be understood as examples of a '"re-enchanted"' world (Bauman, 1993: 33; also quoted in Ritzer, 1999) and certainly Bauman does consistently target Weber as one of the old theorists of modernity who needs to be rejected, with instrumental rationality taken as the defining characteristic of Weber's outmoded theory (Bauman, 2000: 4, 59–60, 113). Bauman, then, firmly sustains the W1.0 understanding of Weber as a position to be argued against in his contrast between the old modernity and his new postmodern strains (see Gane (2012) for an account and critique of Bauman's position on Weber; also Gane (2002) for a comparison of Weber and other postmodern theorists in terms of meaning).

such cases to create a form of meaning within meaninglessness – it is enchantment within disenchantment.

Secondly, the theory of meaning contained in W2.0 – the value-sphere structure – might be able to be recalibrated to account more fully for these 're-enchantments' of late modernity and post-modernity. What needs to be recalled is that the irrational spheres are not fixed – they are part of a polytheism which, as in ancient Athens, allows for the inclusion of new deities. So the cinema, sport, other aspects of popular culture and, especially, advertising/consumption (with the shopping mall as representative), might be added to art and the erotic as irrational value-spheres because they are formed under Weber's very logic of meaning: they are salvations from rationalised routine and manage to create their own inner cosmos of values into which one can enter and experience the psychological pleasure, even ecstasy, of meaning.

The inclusion of capitalist consumption might seem problematic since it is undoubtedly part of the economy and so, it might be assumed, cannot be counted in distinction from the economic value-sphere. But as Ritzer stresses, it is the very contrast between the 'enchantments' of consumption and the grim labour of capitalist production (which informs Weber's Protestant understanding of the economic value-sphere) that is important. In this sense it might be possible to understand the consumption side of capitalism as creating an inner cosmos of salvation[4] either within the value-sphere of the economy or separate from it – such detail is unimportant. The point is that once the theory of meaning behind the value-spheres is recognised, and it is remembered that the value-spheres are polytheistic, then these kinds of additions are possible in some sort of configuration (although the way the internal values of these new irrational spheres have been intellectually developed and are internally structured would still need to be theorised).

One other instance of how this process might be seen to be at work is with sport. The irrational passion that is expressed within a very clear cosmos of internal meaning (constituted, for example, by the rules of the game, the winning of competitions and the spaces of contest, especially the modern sports arena) allows a sense of salvation from the world of W1.0. Words like 'magic' are commonly used, and the results mean everything within the arena and virtually nothing outside of it, where disenchanted rationalisation remains intact and dominant. Also, the possibility that the integrity of this internal cosmos can be compromised by the rationalised spheres – especially the economy – is well known. In short, sport would seem to be able to be added to the pantheon of value-spheres in its quite transparent exhibition of the logic of meaning.

It might perhaps be possible that all of the numerous examples from this second group of claims that the world has been re-enchanted could be placed under the logic of meaning within meaninglessness. There has been no return of magic and enchantment in terms of an explanation of suffering, nor as part of a

---

4 It might be added that the shopping mall provides a quite physical and rather obvious example of an inner cosmos of meaning at work.

new cosmic meaning; and disenchanted modernity, as Weber described it, is not only unscathed but actually reinforced by such claims. In fact, as with art and the erotic, such irrational salvations depend on this meaningless, rationalised order for their very meaning.

To conclude, it is certainly understandable from the perspective of W1.0 how Weber's essential conjectures on disenchantment might be regarded as having been refuted; however, from the perspective of W2.0 these new kinds of 're-enchantment' might themselves be able to be *partly* explained by Weber's theory of disenchanted modernity. And, as a final telling note, every one of these instances of re-enchantment, as with all the value-spheres, is apparently inimical to brotherliness – Weber's understanding of the fate of modern guilt, at least in terms of this debate, would still seem to be applicable.

Elements of Meaning in Australian Modernity[5]

W2.0 – Weber's theory of meaning and modernity – can be taken as an ideal-type in the double sense of being both a rationally articulated theory with which empirical examples can be compared, as well as an historical factor itself which, in contrast to ideal-typical brotherliness, gains part of its historical force through the very fact of its rationalised form. That is, the empirical example should be gauged not just in terms of how far it actually resembles the ideal-type, but also in terms of how far the forces of rationalisation have been successful in transforming the historical reality into the ideal-type. Both of these factors might be seen to be at work in the empirical example of Australian modernity[6] to be touched on here: a certain significant difference to the ideal-type of W2.0 can be identified; but it is also the case that this anomaly would seem to have been largely ironed out under the seemingly unstoppable increase in the scale and influence of the ideal-typical model of modernity in Weber's theory.

An initial general observation can be made that until about the 1960s W2.0 did not quite match the Australian example in at least two interlinked areas: disenchantment and brotherliness. Let us briefly examine each of these topics and see what might be gained through an application of Weber's theory of meaning and modernity to this particular historical/cultural formation.

---

5 All that is possible here is to sketch in some speculative ideas that will try to show how Weber's theory of meaning might have some explanatory traction. This being the case, and because they would be so numerous, references to these ideas will not be given. The brief arguments to follow are merely suggestions for how Weber's theory might be developed when applied to specific cultural formations.

6 It is assumed that all national cultures will have their own specific historical structure of meaning that might be compared to W2.0. Whether there is anything to be theoretically gained by such a project is, of course, an open question.

Firstly, the disenchantment of the world was strangely incomplete for the non-indigenous population of Australia. Certainly the natural world was to a large degree seen in terms of the European vision of economic labour, scientific knowledge and aesthetic values, but from the experiences of explorers, writers and workers in the most hostile areas of the continent arose a perception of Australian nature as a seemingly anti-human blank – where human meaning was virtually impossible. In this understanding of the harsh interior, enchanted elements of meaning had not been present and there was no clear process of disenchantment to a world that would allow the modern self to thrive.

This anomalous Australian experience allows us to reflect back on Weber's theory and perhaps see more clearly how disenchantment works, i.e., certain assumptions of the European experience can be more easily discerned through this comparative analysis. Disenchantment, then, entails both that the world once had enchanted meaning, but also that the process of demagicalisation will open up the world for the pursuit of the values and paradoxical meaning of the value-spheres of modernity. Disenchantment in this dual sense was what was seemingly absent in this particular European experience of Australian nature. So it was that the successful presence of economic labour, scientific knowledge, aesthetic sensibility, and even the legitimacy of the state was put into considerable doubt in this part of Australia. With Western values unlikely to be attained, the likely outcome of human engagement with this most difficult area of the Australian environment came to be understood in terms of suffering and even death.[7]

If we assume the W2.0 view of meaning for the European in Australia faced with these confronting conditions then, since the paradoxical meanings of the value-spheres were not readily sustainable and partly[8] based on the threat of suffering in this unforgiving landscape, a form of brotherliness can be recognised as coming into being – this was the ethic of Australian 'mateship'. Although stripped of its explicitly religious meaning, mateship clearly drew on the Christian ethic for its basic content and, at least in the myths of its origins, this variant of brotherly love arose in the harsh outback as an absolute ethic of care for the suffering of any other – this was the measure by which all humans were to be judged. A consequence of this viewpoint was, as we have seen in the foregoing discussion of brotherliness, that the achievements of the value-spheres would come to be judged as fundamentally unethical; or, in other words, success in the spheres of the economy, politics, science and art was viewed with due scepticism from the perspective of the mateship ethic.[9] But it should also be noted that, as

---

7 Death here is not part of some kind of meaningful belief in salvation, but just the last meaningless stage of human suffering.

8 Also, it is often noted that European immigration and transport to Australia necessarily favoured the lower classes who, as Weber emphasises, will usually have more of an ideal interest in suffering rather than in the life/death/salvation nexus.

9 This is the so-called 'tall poppy syndrome', which would itself be increasingly condemned the more the structures of modernity hardened in Australia.

with every empirical example of brotherliness, mateship would fail to replicate the ideal-type of brotherly love and in this case what is most usually mentioned is the way the *universal* dimension of the ideal form was so heavily qualified by race and gender; that is, mateship centred around white males.

Arguably then there are these dual, inter-related factors that are anomalous to the ideal-type of meaning and modernity presented by Weber in W2.0, yet the terms of this theory might still be seen to allow us some partial explanation of these elements of the Australian example. But what happened to this anomaly as modernity progressed in Australia? Essentially, mateship faded as a kind of brotherliness[10] and one of its preconditions – the view of nature as immune to enchantment/disenchantment – was, it would seem, completely lost.

Initially it should be noted that, as perhaps with all developing cases of modernity, there was a seemingly inexorable rise of the intellectual and aesthetic spheres – after the 1960s in the case of Australia. As a result the value-sphere structure came to more closely approximate the ideal-type than when the disenchantment/brotherliness anomaly was at its height. The stronger presence of the highest cultural values of modernity would in itself work against the less intellectualised worldview of mateship.[11] However, a more specific cause (among many) for the decline in this aspect of Australian meaning might be pinpointed – the greater appreciation of Aboriginal culture.

There are numerous reasons for the increased recognition of the indigenous worldview in the dominating European culture,[12] but Weber's theory might allow us to understand this shift in terms of meaning and modernity. Basically, the whole of the Australian landscape would come to be unproblematically appreciated in terms of Western enchantment/disenchantment once it was understood to be subject to Aboriginal belief in an enchanted cosmos. In this new worldview the self of European sensibilities could experience the interior as a spiritual site of ancient human meaning, with the old fears of an inhuman land of suffering dispelled; and then, after this journey into the cosmos of enchantment is over there could be a return to the disenchanted value-spheres of Australian modernity. Australia is given its very own history of enchantment/disenchantment and the

---

10 It is still a presence, but now perhaps more bound to national sympathies associated with war, and restricted more to the neighbourly ethic of helping those in need. Certainly the fire/drought/flood view of the Australian landscape maintains a perception of the harshness of nature, but nature is not now beyond the meaning of disenchantment (as discussed immediately below).

11 That is, as the balance between W2.0 and the mateship/brotherliness critique tipped in favour of Weber's ideal typical conception of meaning and modernity, the more the pattern of valorisations embedded in the value-spheres could be affirmed without qualification.

12 Arguably the most important of these causes was the, now well-documented, political and legal struggle that was pursued beneath the guiding Enlightenment values of equality and freedom. The question being put here is: how might our understanding of this historical change be aided by the addition of the perspective of meaning?

anomalous empty spaces where all human meaning seemed absent are now filled with culture. Ideal interests within modernity can therefore be seen to be met in this reinforcing pattern of meaning and meaninglessness: a variant of belief that belongs to the irrational realm has been opened up, the paradoxical meaning of the value-spheres is no longer in doubt and the overall disenchantment of the world is affirmed. So, bearing the anomalous state of meaning in Australia in mind, the more that Aboriginal culture became part of the European worldview, the more the European subject felt at home in Australia – the structure of Western disenchanted meaning was in fact aided by the recognition of the importance of indigenous enchanted meaning.[13] In other words, the inclusion of Aboriginal culture was a key factor in the establishment of a fully-fledged Australian variant of W2.0; or, in terms of the logic of paradox, the pursuit of indigenous, traditional meaning can be understood as an integral part of the fateful meaninglessness of Western modernity in its Australian guise.

In this way, Weber's theory of meaning might aid our understanding of a specific manifestation of modernity. Through the employment of Weber's categories of Western meaning a significant variation to the ideal-type of W2.0 could be identified in Australia; and it was also the case that the historical strength of this ideal-type would ensure that it would prevail over the anomalous Australian construction of modernity, although this outcome was partly achieved via the extraordinary use of a traditional enchanted belief-system.

Conclusion

In the introductory chapter the dilemma was put that if there was something new to be found in Weber's theory of meaning then it could not be assumed that this new understanding would also have the undoubted explanatory power of the Weberian

---

13 It is in the sphere of art that a great deal of this recognition has taken place, with Aboriginal art – especially paintings associated with traditional ties to the land – famously soaring in importance from the 1970s. A detailed argument cannot be pursued here, but the point can be made that when viewed through the lens of W2.0 it might be recognised how, although the aesthetic values of the inner cosmos of salvation are enhanced by this new art, two other jarring sets of values are also in play. Firstly, two sites of irrational salvation – the inner cosmos of art and a traditional cosmos of enchanted belief – are combined together here in a relationship of both great appeal in terms of meaning but also one of great and necessary tension. That is, the purely aesthetic values of taste, form, and the creative subject must, on one level, be opposed to the authenticity of traditional belief, so that to enter into the irrational realm of the enchanted cosmos entails, to some degree, that the irrational cosmos of aesthetic modernity be left. Secondly the suffering of the indigenous population in the past and present will bring forth the guilt of the ethic of brotherliness that must stand in utter, irreconcilable opposition to the appreciation and promotion of Aboriginal culture as part of the value-sphere of art (despite the many attempts at uniting these fatefully divergent poles of Western meaning).

formulations of old. In the last two chapters an attempt has been made to test the worthiness of W2.0. In terms of the prescriptions made by Weber himself, the argument is on surer ground than in this last chapter where the proposals are much more exploratory and should really be regarded as an addendum to the detailed consideration of Weber's actual writings. However, even if these current arguments are found wanting, it may well be that others will be able to find some use for this particular theory of meaning and modernity.

Bibliography

Baehr, P. (2001) 'The "Iron Cage" and the "Shell as Hard as Steel": Parsons, Weber and the *Stahlhartes Gehäuse* Metaphor in The Protestant Ethic and the Spirit of Capitalism', *History and Theory*, 40(2): 153–69.
——. (2008) *Caesarism, Charisma and Fate: Historical Sources and Modern Resonances in the Work of Max Weber*, New Brunswick, NJ: Transaction.
Baehr, P. and Wells, G. (2002) 'Introduction', in Weber, M., *The Protestant Ethic and the 'Spirit' of Capitalism and Other Writings*, New York: Penguin.
Baert, P. (1991) 'Unintended Consequences: A Typology and Examples', *International Sociology*, 6(2): 201–10.
Barbalet, J. (2008) *Weber, Passion and Profits: The Protestant Ethic and the Spirit of Capitalism in Context*, New York: Cambridge University Press.
Bauman, Z. (1993) *Postmodern Ethics*, Oxford: Blackwell.
——. (2000) *Liquid Modernity*, Cambridge: Polity.
Bellah, R. (1967) 'Civil Religion in America', *Daedalus*, 96(1): 1–21.
——. (1970) *Beyond Belief*, New York: Harper and Row.
——. (1975) *The Broken Covenant*, New York: Seabury.
——. (1999) 'Max Weber and World-Denying Love: A Look at the Historical Sociology of Religion', *Journal of the American Academy of Religion*, 67(2): 277–304.
Bendix, R. (1977) *Max Weber: An Intellectual Portrait*, Berkeley: University of California Press.
Bennett, J. (2001) *The Enchantment of Modern Life: Attachments, Crossings and Ethics*, Princeton: Princeton University Press.
Berger, P. (1967) *The Sacred Canopy*, New York: Doubleday.
Bologh, R. (1990) *Love or Greatness: Max Weber and Masculine Thinking – A Feminist Inquiry*, London: Unwin Hyman.
Boudon, P. (1982) *The Unintended Consequences of Social Action*, New York: St Martin's Press.
——. (1990) 'The Two Facets of the Unintended Consequences Paradigm', in Clark, J., Modgil, C. and Modgil, S. (eds), *Robert K. Merton: Consensus and Controversy*, London: Falmer.
Brubaker, R. (1984) *The Limits of Rationality: An Essay on the Social and Moral Thought of Max Weber*, London: Allen and Unwin.
Campbell, C. (1989) *The Romantic Ethic and the Spirit of Consumerism*, Oxford: Blackwell.
Chalcraft, D. (2008) 'Why Hermeneutics, the Text(s) and the Biography of the Work Matter in Max Weber Studies', in Chalcraft, D., Howell, F., Lopez

Menendez, M. and Vera, H. (eds), *Max Weber Matters: Interweaving Past and Present*, Farnham: Ashgate.

Cherkaoui, M. (2007) *Good Intentions: Max Weber and the Paradox of Unintended Consequences*, Oxford: Bardwell Press.

Danto, A. (2010a) 'Sitting with Marina', *The New York Times*, 23 May.

———. (2010b) 'On Art, Action and Meaning', *The New York Times*, 3 June.

Dietz, H. (2004) 'Unbeabsichtigte Folgen – Hauptbegriff der Soziologie oder verzichtbares Konzept?' ('Unintended Consequences – A Fundamental Concept of Sociology or an Inessential Idea?'), *Zeitschrift für Soziologie*, 33(1): 48.

Dreijmanis, J. (ed.) (2008) *Max Weber's Complete Writings on Academic and Political Vocations*, (translation: Wells, G.), New York: Algora.

Dreyfus, H. and Kelly, S. (2011a) *All Things Shining: Reading the Western Classics to Find Meaning in a Secular Age*, New York: Free Press.

———. (2011b) 'Saving the Sacred from the Axial Revolution', *Inquiry*, 54(2): 195–203.

Gane, N. (2002) *Max Weber and Postmodern Theory: Rationalisation versus Re-enchantment*, London: Palgrave.

———. (2012) *Max Weber and Contemporary Capitalism*, London: Palgrave Macmillan.

Gerth, H. and Mills, C. (1948) 'Introduction: the Man and his Work', in Gerth, H. and Mills, C. (eds), *From Max Weber*, London: RKP.

Giddens, A. (1992) 'Introduction' in Weber, M., *The Protestant Ethic and the Spirit of Capitalism*, London: Routledge.

Goldman, H. (1992) *Politics, Death and the Devil: Self and Power in Max Weber and Thomas Mann*, Berkeley, CA: University of California Press.

Guttandin, F. (1998) '*Paradoxe Umbrüche*' in Guttandin, F., *Einführung in die 'Protestantische Ethik' Max Webers*, Opladen/Wiesbaden: Westdeutscher Verlag GmbH.

Habermas, J. (1984) *The Theory of Communicative Action*, Vol. 1, London: Heinemann.

———. (2007) *The Dialectics of Secularization: On Reason and Religion*, (with Ratzinger, J.), San Francisco: Ignatius Press.

———. (2008) *Between Naturalism and Religion*, Cambridge: Polity.

———. (2010) *An Awareness of What is Missing: Faith and Reason in a Post-secular Age*, Cambridge: Polity.

Hennis, W. (1988) *Max Weber: Essays in Reconstruction*, London: Allen and Unwin.

Jenkins, R. (2000) 'Disenchantment, Enchantment and Re-Enchantment: Max Weber at the Millennium', *Max Weber Studies*, 1: 11–32.

Keynes, J.M. (1963) 'Economic Possibilities for our Grandchildren', in Keynes, J.M., *Essays in Persuasion*, New York: Norton.

Kontos, A. (1994) 'The World Disenchanted and the Return of Gods and Demons', in Horowitz, A. and Maley, T. (eds), *The Barbarism of Reason*, Toronto: University of Toronto Press.

Lassman, P. and Velody, I. (1989) 'Max Weber on Science, Disenchantment and the Search for Meaning', in Lassman, P. and Velody, I. (eds), *Max Weber's 'Science as a Vocation'*, London: Unwin Hyman.
Lee, R. and Ackerman, S. (2002) *The Challenge of Religion after Modernity*, Aldershot: Ashgate.
Löwith, K. (1982) *Max Weber and Karl Marx*, London: Allen and Unwin.
Luckmann, T. (1967) *The Invisible Religion*, New York: Macmillan.
McIntosh, D. (1983) 'Max Weber as a Critical Theorist', *Theory and Society*, 12(1): 69–109.
Merton, R.K. (1936) 'Unanticipated Consequences of Purposive Action', *American Sociological Review*, 1(6): 894–904.
———. (1968) *Social Theory and Social Structure*, New York: Free Press.
———. (1970) *Science, Technology and Society in Seventeenth Century England*, New York: Harper and Row.
Mitzman, A. (1969) *The Iron Cage*, New York: The Universal Library.
Mommsen, W. (1985) *Max Weber and German Politics: 1890–1920*, Chicago: University of Chicago Press.
———. (1992) *The Political and Social Theory of Max Weber*, Cambridge: Polity Press.
Mommsen, W. and Osterhammel, J. (eds) (1987) *Max Weber and his Contemporaries*, London: Unwin Hyman.
Nelson, B. (1969) *The Idea of Usury: From Tribal Brotherhood to Universal Otherhood*, Chicago: University of Chicago Press.
———. (1976) 'On Orient and Occident in Max Weber', *Social Research*, 42: 114–29.
Owen, D. and Strong, T. (2004) 'Introduction', in Weber, M., *The Vocation Lectures*, Indianapolis: Hackett.
Pudsey, J. (1996) *The Limits of Reflexivity: A Weberian Critique of the Work of Pierre Bourdieu*, PhD Dissertation, University of Western Sydney.
Ritzer, G. (1999) *Enchanting a Disenchanted World: Revolutionising the Means of Consumption*, Thousand Oaks, CA: Pine Forge Press.
Saler, M. (2012) *As If: Modern Enchantment and the Literary Prehistory of Virtual Reality*, Oxford: Oxford University Press.
Sayers, D. (1990) *Capitalism and Modernity: An Excursus on Marx and Weber*, London: Routledge.
Scaff, L. (1991) *Fleeing the Iron Cage*, Berkeley: University of California Press.
———. (2000) 'Weber on the Cultural Situation of the Modern Age', in Turner, S. (ed.), *The Cambridge Companion to Weber*, Cambridge: Cambridge University Press.
Schluchter, W. (1979a) 'The Paradox of Rationalisation: On the Relation of Ethics and World', in Roth, G. and Schluchter, W., *Max Weber's Vision of History: Ethics and Methods*, Berkeley, CA: University of California Press.

———. (1979b) 'Value-neutrality and the Ethic of Responsibility', in Roth, G. and Schluchter, W., *Max Weber's Vision of History: Ethics and Methods*, Berkeley, CA: University of California Press.

———. (1981) *The Rise of Western Rationalism*, Berkeley, CA: University of California Press.

———. (1996) *Paradoxes of Modernity: Culture and Conduct in the Theory of Max Weber*, Stanford: Stanford University Press.

Schroeder, R. (1992) *Max Weber and the Sociology of Culture*, London: Sage.

———. (1995) 'Disenchantment and its Discontents: Weberian Perspectives on Science and Technology', *Sociological Review*, 43(2): 227–50.

Seabrook, J. (1988) *The Leisure Society*, Oxford: Blackwell.

Seidman, S. (1983) 'Modernity, Meaning and Cultural Pessimism in Max Weber', *Sociological Analysis*, 44(4): 267–78.

———. (1985) 'Modernity and the Problem of Meaning: The Durkheimian Tradition', *Sociological Analysis*, Vol. 46, 2: 109–30.

Shelley, M. (2012) *Frankenstein*, New York: Norton.

Sica, A. (2004) *Max Weber: A Comprehensive Bibliography*, New Jersey: Transaction.

Stauth, G. (1992) 'Nietzsche, Weber and the Affirmative Sociology of Culture', *European Journal of Sociology*, 33: 219–50.

Taylor, C. (2007) *A Secular Age*, Cambridge, MA: Harvard University Press.

———. (2011) 'Recovering the Sacred', *Inquiry*, 54: 2.

Tenbruck, F. (1980) 'The Problem of Thematic Unity in the Works of Max Weber', *British Journal of Sociology*, 31(3): 316–51.

Turner, B. (1993) *Max Weber: From History to Modernity*, London: Routledge.

———. (1996) *For Weber: Essays on the Sociology of Fate*, second edition, London: Sage.

Turner, C. (1992) *Modernity and Politics in the Work of Max Weber*, London: Routledge.

Turner, S. and Factor, R. (1984) *Max Weber and the Dispute over Reason and Value: A Study in Philosophy, Ethics and Politics*, London: RKP.

Vernon, R. (1979) 'Unintended Consequences', *Political Theory*, 7: 35–73.

Warren, M. (1994) 'Nietzsche and Weber', in Horowitz, A. and Maley, T. (eds), *The Barbarism of Reason*, Toronto: University of Toronto Press.

Weber, Marianne (1975) *Max Weber: A Biography*, New York: John Wiley & Sons.

Weber, Max (1920) 'Einleitung', in Weber, M., *Gesammelte Aufsätze zur Religionssoziologie* Vol. 1, Tübingen: J.C.B. Mohr (Paul Siebeck).

———. (1920) 'Die Protestantische Ethik und der Geist des Kapitalismus', in Weber, M., *Gesammelte Aufsätze zur Religionssoziologie*, Vol. 1, Tübingen: J.C.B. Mohr (Paul Siebeck).

———. (1920) 'Zwischenbetrachtung', in Weber, M., *Gesammelte Aufsätze zur Religionssoziologie*, Vol. 1, Tübingen: J.C.B. Mohr (Paul Siebeck).

———. (1948) 'Politics as a Vocation', in Gerth, H. and Mills, C. (eds), *From Max Weber*, London: RKP.

———. (1948) 'The Protestant Sects and the Spirit of Capitalism', in Gerth, H. and Mills, C. (eds), *From Max Weber*, London: RKP.

———. (1948) 'Religious Rejections of the World and their Directions', in Gerth, H. and Mills, C. (eds), *From Max Weber*, London: RKP. [Referred to throughout as *Intermediary Reflection*.]

———. (1948) 'Science as a Vocation', in Gerth, H. and Mills, C. (eds), *From Max Weber*, London: RKP.

———. (1948) 'The Social Psychology of the World Religions', in Gerth, H. and Mills, C. (eds), *From Max Weber*, London: RKP. [Referred to throughout as *Introduction to the Economic Ethic of the World Religions*.]

———. (1949) *The Methodology of the Social Sciences*, Glencoe, IL: Free Press.

———. (1950) *General Economic History*, Glencoe, IL: Free Press.

———. (1951) *The Religion of China: Confucianism and Taoism*, Glencoe, IL: Free Press.

———. (1952) *Ancient Judaism*, New York: Free Press.

———. (1958) *The Religion of India: The Sociology of Hinduism and Buddhism*, New York: The Free Press.

———. (1958) *The Protestant Ethic and the Spirit of Capitalism*, New York: Charles Scribner's Sons.

———. (1958) 'Author's Introduction', in Weber, M., *The Protestant Ethic and the Spirit of Capitalism*, New York: Charles Scribner's Sons.

———. (1978) *Economy and Society*, Berkeley, CA: University of California Press.

———. (1988) *The Agrarian Sociology of Ancient Civilisations*, London: Verso.

———. (1992) 'Wissenschaft als Beruf', in Weber, M., *Wissenschaft als Beruf, Politik als Beruf, Max Weber-Gesamtausgabe*, MWG I/17, Tübingen: J.C.B. Mohr [Paul Siebeck].

———. (1992) 'Politik als Beruf', in Weber, M., *Wissenschaft als Beruf, Politik als Beruf*, MWG I/17, Tübingen: J.C.B. Mohr (Paul Siebeck).

———. (1996) *Die Wirtschaftsethik der Weltreligionen: Hinduismus und Buddhismus*, MWG I/19, Tübingen: J.C.B. Mohr (Paul Siebeck).

———. (2001) *Wirtschaft und Gesellschaft: Religiöse Gemeinschaften*, MWG I/22, Tübingen: J.C.B. Mohr (Paul Siebeck).

———. (2004) *The Vocation Lectures*, (translation: Livingstone, R.), Indianapolis: Hackett.

Whimster, S. (ed.) (2004) *The Essential Weber: A Reader*, London: Routledge.

Whimster, S. (2007) *Understanding Weber*, Abingdon: Routledge.

Wilson, B. (1976) *Contemporary Transformations of Religion*, New York: Oxford University Press.

Index

administrators, vocation 67
aesthetic value-sphere 82–5
    brotherliness, exclusion of 124–5
    erotic value-sphere, contrast 130–31
    form 125
        vs content 83
    impersonality 126
    judgements of taste 83
    and salvation 124
    subjectivity 83
    vocation 149
art
    and fulfillment 84
    paradox of cultural values 84
    religion, distinction 82–3, 83–4
    as value-sphere 81
    and vocation 149–50
asceticism, and vocation 41, 43
Australia
    brotherliness (mateship) 179–80
    meaning and modernity 178–81

Bellah, Robert 3, 96
Bologh, R. 96, 160
brotherliness (brotherly love) 10, 19, 26, 37, 91, 95–117, 154–5
    advocacy of 150–54
        paradox 157–8
    aesthetic value-sphere, exclusion from 124–5
    Australia (mateship) 179–80
    and capitalism 121
    charismatic communistic 100, 101–2, 114–15
    commentaries on 95–9
    economic value-sphere 120–22
    erotic value-sphere, antagonism 129, 130
    and the Essenes 114
    ethic of 10, 95, 160, 161
    acosmism 108, 114, 133
    charismatic communism 114
    and economic value-sphere 26
    and erotic value-sphere 127–32
    and guilt 143–4, 181
    ideal-type 100–103
    non-religious setting 157
    personal 126
    presence in modernity 120
    universality 28, 152
    and vocation 161, 162
as goodness 160
ideal-type 100–103
and impersonality 119
intellectual/scientific value-sphere 134
and Luther 112–13
meanings 150fn5
medieval Christian 100, 111–14
    cosmic nature of 111
    personal dimension 112
and modernity 119, 138
mystic 100, 108–11
    acosmism 108, 109–10
    Buddhism 108–9
    impersonality of 108
    withdrawal from the world 110
and paradox of meaning 95, 139–43
and personal relations 152–3, 155–6
in political value-sphere 122–4, 141–2
Puritan 29, 100, 104–7
    impersonality of 105–6
Schluchter on 96
and suffering 28, 95, 141
and theodicy 103, 160
typology 100, 116
value-spheres 103, 119, 120–38, 139
    and guilt 137–8
in war 122, 141fn21
Buddhism
    and hierarchy 21–2

mystic brotherliness 108–9
    impersonality 109
bureaucracy
    dangers of 72–3
    in the modern state 71–2
    in political value-sphere 71
    and Western religious rationalisation 72

calling *see* vocation
Calvinism 26, 30
    and problem of evil 29
capitalism
    and brotherliness 121
    and disenchantment 31fn13, 31–2, 33, 50–51
    economic compulsion of 47–8
    and Protestant ethic thesis 16, 24–5, 106, 121
        paradox 17, 18, 19, 23–4
    and religion, disconnect 46
    vocation in 47, 48
charisma
    and paradox 18–19
        in political value-sphere 70
    routinisation 21, 22, 70
Cherkaoui, Mohamed 16, 19
the concept, Weber on 31
consumption, and the shopping mall 176, 177
cultural values
    endlessness of 85
    intellectual/scientific value-sphere 134–6
    of mind and taste 84
    paradox of, and art 84
culture, Weber on 7

daemon
    meanings 163–4
    and the self 164
death
    meaning of 28, 31
    meaninglessness of 28, 38, 63
    and suffering 8fn16
    Tolstoy on 1, 62
disenchantment 31–2, 31fn13, 33, 87, 178
    and capitalism 50–51
    meaning of 179

non-indigenous Australian population 179
and re-enchantment 174
and science 59

economic value-sphere 42–53
    brotherliness in 120–22
    capitalism as 53
    and ends 43–4
    and ethic of brotherliness 26
    meaning within meaninglessness 47
    paradox of meaning 44–5
    vocation, as sport in 46, 48, 49, 53, 55
erotic value-sphere 81, 85–90
    aesthetic value-sphere, contrast 130–31
    brotherliness
        antagonism 129, 130
        ethic of 127–32
    and love of mystic salvation 129–30
    meaning, sustainability of 86
    meaning within meaninglessness 86, 130–31, 139
    and natural life 127–8, 130
    and religion 88–9, 128–9, 130
    and suffering 129
    value of natural/nature 86–8
Essenes, and brotherliness 114
evil, problem of, and Calvinism 29

fate
    irrationality of 166–7
    twin meanings of 165–6
form, and aesthetic value-sphere 125
Franklin, Benjamin 42, 52
    maxims 43, 45
    Weber on 45

gods, belief in, in Ancient Greece 50
goodness, brotherliness as 160
guilt, brotherliness
    ethic of 143–4, 181
    value-spheres 137–8
Guttandin, Friedhelm 16, 18–19

Habermas, Jürgen 4, 16

ideal interests, 11fn21, 37, 52, 58, 139
    vs material interests 9
    and religion 9

impersonality
    aesthetic value-sphere 126
    and brotherliness 119
    intellectual/scientific value-sphere 133–4, 136
intellectual/scientific value-sphere 56–65, 132–6
    assumption of meaning 62
    brotherliness 134
    cultural values 134–6
    impersonality 133–4, 136
iron cage metaphor 168–9, 173
    and meaning within meaninglessness 169

Jesus Christ, as magician 110
Judaism, paradox of 27fn12

labour, lack of meaning in 48–9
Lassman, P., and Velody, I. 16
life-conduct, Tolstoy on 7, 28, 147
    Weber's answer 170–71
Luther, Martin 41
    and brotherliness 112–13

meaning
    and paradox 15, 23, 47, 91
    of science 58
    search for 26
    and subjectivity 138–9
meaning and modernity 1–2, 3, 5, 8, 9, 11, 120, 139–44, 170
    applications 173–81
    Australia 178–81
    elements 6–7
    standard view 173
meaning within meaninglessness 9, 48, 90, 120, 144
    economic value-sphere 47
    erotic value-sphere 86, 130–31, 139
    and iron cage metaphor 169
    paradox as 74–5
    politics as 66, 68, 141
    and re-enchantment 177–8
    and value-spheres 37–8, 91
    and vocation 52, 65, 77
meaninglessness
    of death 28, 38, 63
    meaning within 9
    in modernity 5, 64, 77
medicine, presuppositions 60–61
Merton, Robert 16–17
Mitzman, A. 159
modernity
    Australian, meaning in 178–81
    and brotherliness 119, 138
    meaning, formation of kinds of 36
    meaninglessness in 5, 64, 77
    and the political value-sphere 66
    power in 69
    theory 2
    and value-spheres 42
    see also meaning and modernity

Nietzsche, Friedrich
    Genealogy of Morals 98
    influences on Weber 97–8
    resentment thesis, Weber's critique 98–9

paradox 10
    of asceticism 20
    and charisma 18–19
    etymology 15
    of Judaism 27fn12
    and meaning 15, 23, 47, 91
    as meaning within meaninglessness 74–5
    and Protestant ethic thesis 17, 18, 19, 23–4
    of Puritanism 26–7
    and religion 20–22, 30, 33
    value-spheres 74
    Weber's use of 15–19
personal relations, and brotherliness 152–3
Plato
    Republic 57
    The Apology 164
political value-sphere 65–74
    brotherliness in 122–4, 141–2
    and modernity 66
    paradoxes 68–9, 73, 74
        bureaucracy 71
        charisma/routinisation 70
        necessities of state 65–6, 69–70
        party machineries 70–71

and religion 66
and violence 69–70
see also politics
politicians
and 'cause', paradox of 68
and faith 68
motivations 67
and the state 67
politics
ethics of responsibility 73
ethics of ultimate ends 73
as meaning within meaninglessness 66, 68, 141
as vocation 66, 67–8, 69, 73–4, 141, 151–4
polytheism, value-spheres as 50, 82
power, in modernity 69
predestination 29, 30, 32–3, 41
Protestant ethic thesis
and capitalism 16, 24–5, 106, 121
and paradox 17, 18, 19, 23–4
Protestantism, and problem of theodicy 29
Puritanism
and brotherliness 29, 100, 104–7
paradox of 26–7

rationalisation
and irrational assumptions 36–7
Protestant 37
re-enchantment 174–8
and disenchantment 174
and meaning within meaninglessness 177–8
and new religious forms 174
reason, Platonic view 78
religion
art, distinction 82–3, 83–4
and capitalism, disconnect 46
and elimination of magic 32
and the erotic value-sphere 88–9, 128–9
and paradox 20–22, 30, 33
and the political value-sphere 66
and resentment 98–9
and vocation, disconnect 46–7
religions, charismatic origins 22
Ritzer, G. 176, 177

salvation 25, 108
and aesthetic value-sphere 124
quest for 7, 57
and sport 177
and vocation 57
Schluchter, Wolfgang 16
on brotherliness 96
science
and disenchantment 59
and faith 65
intellectualism, escape from 79
meaning of 58
meaningless of, Tolstoy on 58
presuppositions 59–60
results, temporary nature of 58
as vocation 154–62
vocation for 56–7, 59, 64, 154–61
limitations 58
secularisation 3, 175
in modernity 174
the self, and daemon 164
shopping mall, and consumption 176, 177
sport, and salvation 177
state, and politicians 67
subjectivity, and meaning 138–9
suffering
and brotherliness 28, 95, 141
and the erotic value-sphere 129
and God's will 29
problem of 28, 102
see also theodicy

Taylor, Charles 4
theodicy
problem of 8, 10, 26, 37, 95, 106–7, 151
and brotherliness 103, 160
and Protestantism 29
see also suffering
Tolstoy, Leo
on death 1, 62
on life-conduct 7, 28, 147
Weber's answer 170–71
on meaningless of science 58
Turner, Bryan 98fn5
For Weber 16
Turner, Charles 5fn13
Turner, S., and Factor R. 159

value-spheres
    and art 81
    brotherliness 103, 119, 120–38, 139
        and guilt 137–8
    competing 91
    differences between 55
    irrational 79, 90, 126, 139–40
    and meaning 35
    and meaning within meaninglessness
        37–8, 91
    model 5, 6
    and modernity 42
    paradox 74
    as polytheism 50, 82, 91
    rationalised 77–8
    theory 35, 77
    see also aesthetic value-sphere;
        economic value-sphere; erotic
        value sphere; intellectual/scientific
        value-sphere; political value-sphere
vocation (calling) 37, 39–42
    administrators 67
    advocacy 147–50
    aesthetic value-sphere 149
    and art 149–50
    and asceticism 41, 43
    in capitalism 47, 48
    coerciveness of 51–2, 53
    and ethic of brotherliness 161, 162
    for the glory of God 39, 41, 42
    as God-given task 39, 40, 42
    Lutheran 111, 112
    and meaning within meaninglessness
        52, 65, 77
    non-religious form 52
    politics as 66, 67–8, 69, 73–4, 141, 151–4
    and religion, disconnect 46–7
    and salvation 57
    for science 56–7, 59, 64

science as 154–62
    as sport, in economic value-sphere 46,
        48, 49, 53, 55
    and wealth acquisition 42

war, brotherliness in 122, 141fn21
wealth acquisition, and vocation 42
Weber, Marianne 157fn14
Weber, Max
    on the concept 31
    on culture 7
    on Franklin 45
    interpretations of 2–5
        mining metaphor 3, 5
    Nietzsche
        influences 97–8
        resentment thesis, critique 98–9
    secondary literature on 2, 159–60
    works
        Economy and Society 5, 38, 80, 82
        General Economic History 23
        Intermediary Reflection 6, 7, 10,
            26, 28, 29, 38, 42, 79, 80, 82,
            85, 95, 100, 128, 139–40
        *Introduction to the Economic Ethic
            of the World Religions* 7, 36,
            61–2, 100
        'Politics as a Vocation' 38, 55, 66,
            73, 148, 151, 164
        *The Protestant Ethic and the Spirit
            of Capitalism* 6, 10, 21, 24, 25,
            38, 39, 42, 43–4, 46, 122, 140,
            149, 168–9
        'Science as a Vocation' 1, 10, 31,
            38, 55, 56, 61, 64–5, 75, 78,
            127, 148, 161–2, 165, 175
Wesley, John 41
    on paradox of Puritan asceticism 20–21